D1232889

Lily, Duchess of Marlborough

Lily,
Duchess of Marlborough
(1854–1909)

ॐ

A Portrait with Husbands

Sally E. Svenson

© 2012 Sally E. Svenson
All Rights Reserved.

Book design by Liz Trovato, liz@liztrovato.com

No part of this publication may be reproduced, stored in a retrieval system, or
transmitted, in any form or by any means, electronic, mechanical, photocopying,
recording, or otherwise, without the written permission of the author.

First published by Dog Ear Publishing
4010 W. 86th Street, Ste H
Indianapolis, IN 46268
www.dogearpublishing.net

ISBN: 978-1-4575-0776-2

This paper is acid free.
Printed in the United States of America

"If I had a daughter or a sister, I should teach her adaptability, and that learned I should have no further anxiety for her future. . . . Let her please, not men alone, but people, and the race is hers."

—Lily, Duchess of Marlborough, 1890
Elizabethtown (NY) Post, 18 Dec 1890

As always, to Charlie, Alicia, and Tait

TABLE OF CONTENTS

Preface and Acknowledgments

American-born Lily, Duchess of Marlborough, came to my attention several years ago in the course of writing about church architecture in the Adirondack region of upstate New York. An historical account of St. Mary's Episcopal Church in the town of Lake Luzerne suggested that she might have provided the funds with which to build a chapel added to the church in 1893, a possibility that seemed to me more than a little fanciful. It required, however, only superficial research to learn that there *had* been a connection between Lily and Lake Luzerne (although she had nothing to do with the financing of the chapel). The same research led me to discover that what little had been written about Lily, as well as about two of her three husbands, was not accurate, and for some reason I thought her story needed to be retold. From such beginnings, I suspect, are many biographical undertakings born.

It became obvious that one of the reasons Lily has received scant attention in the many histories of England's Churchill family in the late nineteenth century is because she left behind a negligible personal record. This was hardly unusual. The world of the English aristocracy in which she eventually moved subscribed to the principle that it "hide its life," and Lily was remarkably successful in doing so. She was, however, a subject of interest to the writers of social columns in newspapers and popular magazines, particularly in the years 1886 to 1900. In the absence of more traditional source material, I have had to rely on this kind of reportage.

A journalist who wished to succeed in the field of "society journalism," wrote Lucie Armstrong in an 1890 article on the subject, required a specialized writing skill: "what is called the society touch, an indefinable lightness, an airy way of putting things without which she can never attain any degree of success." I have endeavored to make a virtue of necessity in quoting material that retains the flippant spirit of such coverage. This approach cannot offset the fact that Lily appears as little more than a cardboard character in her own biography, but does, I hope, add period flavor to her history. It has been a pleasure to examine her life in terms of social customs that are now so out of style.

There are many organizations and individuals to thank for their roles in providing the material and guidance that made this book possible. Key institutions in New York City include the New York Society Library (of which Lily and her first husband were members) and the New York Public Library. The rich newspaper collection of the British Library was also of inestimable value, as was the Churchill Archives Centre, Churchill College, Cambridge, where Katharine Thomson and Dr. Lynsey Robertson were helpful in providing translations of a few difficult-to-decipher phrases in the letters of Churchill family members and friends.

Other public and private organizations and their staff members and volunteers provided details that enriched Lily's story. Among these were Agnew's Gallery, London, UK (Venetia Harlow); Brookside Museum and Saratoga County Historical Society, Ballston Spa, NY; Sterling and Francine Clark Art Institute Library, Williamstown, MA (Karen Bucky); College of Physicians of Philadelphia Library, Philadelphia; Cooper-Hewitt National Design Museum, New York; The Cooper Union Library, New York (Carol Solomon); Corcoran Gallery of Art, Washington, DC (Marisa Burgoin); Dorking Museum and Heritage Centre, Dorking, Surrey, UK (Mary Turner and Yvonne Durell); Emma Willard School, Troy, NY (Nancy Iannucci); Frick Reference Library, New York; Georgetown University Library Special Collections Research Center, Washington, DC; Greenbrier Resort, White Sulphur Springs, WV (Robert Conte); Keeneland Association, Lexington, KY (Phyllis Rogers); Special Collections Library, University of Kentucky, Lexington (Gordon E. Hogg, Jim Birchfield, and Rob Aken); Metropolitan Opera Association, New York (John Pennino); National Academy Museum and School of Fine Arts, New York (Mark Mitchell); New York City Bar Association Library, New York; New-York Historical Society, New York; New York State Library, Albany; Newport Historical Society, Newport, RI (Bert Lippincott III); Northport Historical Society, Northport, NY; Oakwood Cemetery, Troy, NY (Terry Page); Oxford Central Library, Oxfordshire, UK (Louise Trevelyan); Rensselaer County Historical Society, Troy, NY; Royal Archives and Royal Photograph Collection, Windsor Castle, Windsor, UK; Science and Engineering Library,

Stony Brook University, Stony Brook, NY (Aimée deChambeau, Kristen Nyitray, and F. Jason Torre) Troy Public Library, Troy, NY; and the Historical Society of Washington, DC.

Many individuals also provided assistance and support, among them Lady Sarah Aspinall; Peter Atkinson and Judith Wermuth-Atkinson; Jeri Bapasola; Lord John Hubert de la Poer Beresford; Beatrice Evens, Lake Luzerne, NY, Town Historian; Rebecca Hamel; the late Louis Gordon Hamersley, Jr. and his sons, Gordon and Nicholas Hamersley; Lord Frederick Howe; Anne Jordan; Elisabeth Kehoe; Janet Letteron; Sir John Leslie; Ruth O'Hare; Mary Van Rennselaer Cruger Pendl; Elsa Prigozy, Howard Renshaw, Christian Sonne; Kathy Vockery; and Peter Watts. I thank them all.

My grateful thanks to the Masters and Fellows of Churchill College, Cambridge, for permission to quote from letters in the Churchill Archives; Her Majesty Queen Elizabeth II for permission to quote from letters in the Royal Archives at Windsor Castle; Tarka King for permission to quote from the published and unpublished work of his grandfather, Sir Shane Leslie; the Dorking Museum and Heritage Centre, Surrey, for permission to quote from an unpublished manuscript in its collection by Dorothy Langdon; the Brookside Museum and Saratoga County Historical Society for permission to quote from the autobiography of Becky Jones; the Joseph Downs Collection of Manuscripts and Printed Ephemera, Winterthur Library, for permission to quote from the diary of Eva Purdy Thomson; and the Harry Ransom Center at the University of Texas at Austin for permission to quote from a letter in its collection. Quotations from the published work and letters of Winston Churchill are reproduced with the permission of Curtis Brown London, on behalf of the Estate of Sir Winston Churchill, Copyright © Winston S. Churchill. If I have unwittingly omitted to secure any necessary permissions, I would appreciate hearing from copyright holders so that I can rectify the errors.

—SALLY E. SVENSON

Prologue

"The glass sweeps the tiers," observed the New York Herald of a November 1887 performance at the Metropolitan Opera House, "and rests upon the place where Mrs. Louis Hamersley generally sits to chat pleasantly through some heavy German opera. She is not present—for her 'The Trompeter' has had no charm."[1]

Lily Price Hamersley missed the New York premiere of Viktor Nessler's Trompeter for what she considered a valid reason. Less than three weeks earlier she had met an attractive man who was leaving the country in three days time, and who knew when, or if, she would see him again. Opera was her passion, but it was worth foregoing an evening's performance if she could spend more time in getting to understand her new acquaintance better and to assess his apparent interest.

Thirty-three-year-old Lily Price Hamersley was one of the wealthiest and most beautiful women in New York City. But the four years since the unexpected death of her husband had been a period of personal torment. His socially powerful family loathed her, and it was proving difficult for her to make her way as a widow in the city's elite milieu that had been her home during her marriage. Despite the awkwardness of her position, conjecture about her romantic life was a staple of society gossip; less than a month earlier, a newspaper had reported that she would soon wed again. But such rumors had circulated before, and Lily had so far shown herself to be conspicuously free from serious attachments. Indeed, her most frequent companion in the prominent box she occupied at the opera was another young woman—one who, like her, had arrived in New York as an outsider, married into society, and lost her place when she lost her husband— although, in the companion's case, the loss had been due to divorce and not to death.

The focus of Lily's attention was George Charles Spencer-Churchill, the eighth Duke of Marlborough, who had arrived from England for an extended visit more than two months earlier. Marlborough held one of the most elevated titles in Britain, but he was a social pariah at home and had been dogged by derogatory journalistic attention since his arrival in New York. Everyone who followed society news was aware of his scandalous history, and public opinion painted him as a most unsavory character.

Some of Lily's acquaintances would have been puzzled by her interest in the duke. They knew her as a cautious, conservative woman of impeccable background, certainly not as a "tuft-hunter"—one of those toadying arrivistes who sought to curry favor with the English nobility in order to enhance their own status. They had shunned the titled tourist, and assumed that Lily shared their attitude. But Lily had met him—and found him charming.

Lily was well aware that her looks and money made her a sought-after trophy in the marriage market. The Duke of Marlborough recognized his star status too, and knew that, despite his tarnished reputation, his position in the English peerage made him a desirable matrimonial catch in the United States for affluent American families with daughters and social aspirations. Indeed, it was rumored that the duke had come to the United States for the purpose of making a financially advantageous match. The offensive press treatment he suffered after his arrival little deterred motivated sponsors, and a number of wealthy girls had been thrown at him during the past months. But they were young, shallow, and, presumably, inexperienced. The duke had taken no real interest in any of them and was about to go home empty-handed.

The duke was perhaps as surprised to discover Lily at the close of his American tour as she was to discover him. Here was a mature but rich and comely woman whom he understood to have suffered a generous dose of demeaning publicity herself. Yet she seemed to have risen above her circumstances without bitterness and with grace and humor. Perhaps this was the bride he had been looking for?

Lily had a great deal to think about as she weighed the possible outcome of Marlborough's sudden attentiveness. She believed she understood what he was after: a marriage of convenience that would provide him with access to the money he needed and seemed unable to raise otherwise. But what did she want? She had means, hard earned at that, but they had brought her little in the way of happiness or social recognition. Did her future lie in New York, often hostile to her now, or might she do better for herself on the other side of the Atlantic? She had no social entrée of her own in England, but would marriage to a social outcast with a lofty title enhance or weaken her position? And what about the duke himself? He presented himself as an amiable man, but she recognized that there were valid reasons for his reputation. Could she, and did she want to, handle—even try to tame—him?

While the British upper class discounted love as a motivation for marriage, its American counterpart, more elastic in its membership, allowed wider latitude to the sentimental feelings of the parties involved. But Lily, whose family had given her little *direction or support when it came to choosing a husband, had not shown herself overly romantic in her first choice. Now she had an opportunity to take an even greater leap of faith. Was she ambitious and self-assertive enough to do so?*

The answer, as proclaimed in the title of this book, was that she was. Lily married the Duke of Marlborough, and in doing so, became a celebrity. She was one of the first women in the United States to attract notice of the sort that film stars and popular singers enjoy today. The public on both sides of the Atlantic recognized her name, followed her comings and goings, and had opinions about her.

The improbable aspect of Lily's story was that it happened at all. It was bold for a girl of her conventional upbringing to orchestrate a life so different from what was expected for her. Yet Lily did so, during a period in which, observed feminist scholar Linda Wagner-Martin, "the narrative of women's lives remains a marriage plot."[2] She did so, moreover, within the framework of that narrative. Her future would be beset by sorrow and defeat as well as by triumph.

CHAPTER I

Family Background, Childhood, and Youth

ఎ.

Eliza Warren Price was born in Troy, New York, on 10 June 1854. Named for her maternal grandmother, she was called "Lillie" from childhood, later streamlined in spelling to the shorter "Lily." Her father, Cicero Price, hailed from Lancaster, Kentucky, deep in the rolling Bluegrass Country and the county seat of present-day Garrard County. This region served as the setting for Harriet Beecher Stowe's novel, *Uncle Tom's Cabin*, often called the kindling wood of the Civil War, and was the site of the war's first Union recruiting station south of the Ohio River. Carrie Nation, the colorful temperance figure of the late nineteenth and early twentieth centuries, was a native of Garrard County.

Cicero's father, William Price, relocated to Kentucky from Virginia in 1781 as the head of a contingent of soldiers escorting a large party known as the "Traveling Church." This group made its way to Kentucky through the Cumberland Gap in what was the largest mass movement to date of settlers into the opening region. In 1804 William married Lucy Jennings, the daughter of a Lancaster pioneer who had taken up the four hundred Kentucky acres he received as "land script" in payment for army service during the Revolutionary War. Cicero was born on 1 December of the following year, and in time four younger brothers and a sister joined the family on the Price farm carved out of his father-in-law's wilderness allotment.[1] The crop yield from its arable soil, like that of other farms in the region, was likely to have been a mix of tobacco, grain, hemp, and corn.

One of Cicero's brothers, Jennings, became a physician and prominent local politician; he was twice president of the Garrard County Deposit Bank. Another physician brother, Johnson, was a one-time candidate for the national Congress from Kentucky, served as a captain in the Mexican War, and eventually relocated to California. Napoleon Bonaparte Price, the youngest brother, managed the family farm, which descended to successive generations of the Price family.[2]

Twenty-year-old Cicero left behind the land-locked rural countryside of his birth in 1826, joined the United States Navy as a midshipman, and went to sea. The naval branch of the armed services then comprised an active force of fewer than two dozen warships and pursued a narrowly defined mission: to advance American commerce through combating piracy, policing smuggling, and showing an American presence in ports around the world. Its busiest area of operations in the mid-1820s was the Caribbean, where an estimated 3,000 pirate attacks against merchant ships took place between 1815 and 1823. As seaborne commerce expanded, so did the navy's responsibilities, and by the 1850s the service had taken on a vital role in supporting the increasingly powerful American maritime empire. Naval voyages of scientific and geographic exploration provided the kind of precise information necessary to open new markets for American trade, and the service's far-flung presence in Latin America and overseas gave protection to merchant ships and created the environment of respect necessary for the conduct of diplomatic and commercial negotiations. By 1860 the navy had established a reputation as the aristocratic arm of the American military establishment.[3] Price spent more than half of the forty-one years following his enlistment on the world's oceans, serving in both the Atlantic and Pacific naval squadrons and accomplishing, while doing so, a complete tour of the world. His assignments took him to the West Indies, Brazil, the Mediterranean, and Africa.[4]

Price, "a tall, striking looking man, reserved in manner and a thorough aristocrat,"[5] met his future wife, Elizabeth Homer Paine, while serving ordnance duty in Washington, D. C., during the early 1850s. Elizabeth could not have come from a more disparate background than that of her husband-to-be. Born in 1828, she was twenty-three years younger than Cicero and descended from two leading families

Cicero Price in naval uniform, 1860s
COURTESY OF HOWARD RENSHAW

of Troy, New York, a city on the east bank of the Hudson River some 150 miles north of New York City. Troy was a bustling urban center at the time of Elizabeth's birth and growing rapidly, doubling its population in the decade between 1820 and 1830 thanks to its happy location as the terminal of both the Erie and Champlain canals. It was one of the wealthiest municipalities in the nation at mid-century and reached a peak population of 61,000 in 1890.[6]

Elizabeth's mother, Eliza Warren, descended from a founding resident of Troy who arrived by sloop from Connecticut with his family in 1798, the year in which the settlement was legally constituted a village. The Warrens flourished, opening a store that sold groceries, dry goods, and hardware, and investing their profits in real estate. Elizabeth's grandfather served as mayor of the city from 1820 to 1828, an office that would be held by members of two succeeding generations of the expanding family. Warrens were presidents of Troy

Elizabeth Price, Luzerne, early 1900s
COURTESY OF PETER WATTS

banks and other business institutions, and according to an 1880 local history, "these different trusts they have discharged with credit to themselves and advantage to the stockholders."[7] They were a family to be reckoned with in Troy, and Lily would proudly retain Warren as her middle name throughout life.

Elizabeth's father, John Paine, was the son of another early Troy resident, a graduate of Schenectady's Union College, and a lawyer. He was an organizer of the Bank of Troy and became its cashier (manager) in 1837, a position he held until his death in 1852. He and his wife were the parents of three children: Elizabeth and two younger brothers, Esaias and John. The brothers became Troy businessmen and were involved in the start-up of a number of ventures in the growing city with, among others, their Warren cousins: the Troy Malleable Iron Company, the Incorporated Gas-Light Company of Troy, the Rensselaer and Saratoga Railroad Company, and the Troy Steamboat Company.[8] While the family name was well known in Troy, it did not carry quite as much civic weight as did Warren.

The Washington milieu in which Elizabeth Paine and Cicero Price met represented a third, totally other environment from those of Lancaster, Kentucky, and Troy, New York. The national capital was then a shabby, sprawling town with a peculiar blend of settled residential and transient society. It took its southern flavor from the local elite: descendants of the planter families who had migrated in from neighboring Maryland and Virginia, the two states that contributed the land for the new federal district in 1790. Elizabeth's maternal aunt Phebe Warren Tayloe, with whom she was staying when she met Cicero, was at the apex of that elite as the second wife of Benjamin Ogle Tayloe, a widower with six children whose first wife had been a Troy girl and a close friend of Phebe's.

Ogle, as Phebe's husband was called, was a son of John Tayloe III, a 1798 transplant to Washington who had been one of the most affluent landowners in Virginia and was "undoubtedly the wealthiest citizen of Washington in the first quarter of a century of its history."[9] An ardent horseman, John had been the acknowledged leader of American horseracing in his day, built the first racecourse in Washington (providing a venue for "the one fascinating social amusement of the capital"),[10] and served as president of the Jockey Club that operated it. His son, educated at Exeter Academy and Harvard University, was attached to the American Legation in Paris in 1818 and by mid-century was a "conspicuous personality" in Washington.[11] "Remaining steadfastly in private life, against many solicitations to accept office," Tayloe "nevertheless exerted a powerful influence in national affairs, and was the intimate and trusted friend of half a dozen presidents."[12] Like his father before him, he pursued an array of business interests and bred and raced his own stable of horses. He was the author of *The History of the American Turf from Eighty Years Since*, a seminal work on early horseracing in America, and wrote regularly for sporting periodicals.[13]

Elizabeth Paine's aunt Phebe, "a woman of fine taste and broad views," ranked in the conspicuous top echelon of "hostesses renowned for their beauty and wit and vivacity [who] vied with each other in evolving novel social relaxations."[14] She had no children of her own but was attached to her stepchildren and close to her niece

Elizabeth. There were multiple ties between the Tayloes and Phebe's Troy relations: one of Ogle's daughters was married to the younger of Elizabeth's two brothers, John Paine; another was the wife of a Warren cousin.

English author Anthony Trollope visited Washington in the winter of 1860–61 but was not taken with the capital city, calling it "the most ungainly and most unsatisfactory" of all the places he knew. He was, however, impressed by Lafayette Square, the site of the Tayloe home, located directly across from the White House in what he described as "certainly the most attractive part of the city."[15] Trollope was a frequent guest of the Tayloes during his stay and, writing later to his hostess, observed, "I spent more hours in your house than in any other in Washington, and certainly felt myself more at home there."[16] The front windows of the thirty-room Tayloe mansion, which still stands, commanded a beautiful view across the White House grounds. Covered porches at the rear looked out on a sizeable garden set with trim box hedges and an unusually large stable and carriage house. The interior of the residence was locally famous as "a museum of things rare and beautiful":[17] paintings, bronze and marble statuettes, Sèvres porcelain, and furniture of historical importance. This home not only provided the backdrop for the courtship of Elizabeth Paine and Cicero Price, but would also serve as the setting for much of the childhood, adolescence, and young adulthood of their daughter Lily.

Lieutenant Price's name first appeared in Elizabeth Paine's family correspondence in March 1852 when Stephen Warren, a cousin of Elizabeth's who often visited Washington, wrote of Cicero to his brother, "When you become acquainted with him you will find him very agreeable."[18] The following March, Stephen's mother reported to her son from Troy that she had seen Miss Paine at church, that she was "looking very well and appeared very happy," and that "she allows her engagement. I have told her all the nice things you say about Mr. Price."[19] The couple married in Troy a month later, on 19 April 1853. They settled in Washington, where Price remained on naval duty and where Stephen Warren dined at their home in 1855.[20]

Elizabeth traveled north to Troy in 1854 to be close to her

mother in anticipation of the birth of Lily, her first child. For the next fifteen years she and her husband divided their time between Troy and Washington. This was a practical arrangement that kept the couple close to the naval nerve center in Washington, while ensuring Elizabeth of family companionship and support during her husband's long sea voyages. Two more daughters were born in Troy: Cora Elizabeth in 1857, and Lucy Jennings in 1858.

Thanks to Elizabeth's family connections, the Prices were quickly absorbed into Troy's cliquish social elite. Money was not a determining factor in assigning status, but the pair was very comfortably settled. The 1860 federal census, which recorded them as Troy residents, credited the Prices with a combined estate valued at $58,000; ten years later their joint worth was estimated to be $80,000. Census records indicate that the Price household included four female servants during this period, among them two women—one of Irish and one of Canadian birth—who were with the family in both 1860 and 1870.[21]

The commencement of the Civil War fragmented the life of the Price family, as it did those of so many others on both sides of the national rift. Elizabeth, despite having married Cicero with the expectation of long periods of separation from him as he pursued his naval career, could hardly have anticipated the spate of disquieting war years between 1861 and 1865 when her husband was mostly absent from home and she was left to raise the couple's three young daughters alone. Price served during the first year of the war as commanding officer of the steamer *U. S. S. Huntsville*, a ship posted to the Gulf Blockading Squadron as part of the increasingly effective effort to cut the Confederacy off from the foreign—predominantly British—commerce on which it relied for essential goods. In March 1862 the *Huntsville* was reported to have arrived in New York, under Price's command, carrying enemy seamen as well as some 200 bales of cotton and 247 bales of tobacco taken in the capture of Confederate vessels.[22]

Price's next assignment took him to the other side of the world. Promoted to captain in July 1862, he was given charge of the schooner *U. S. S. Jamestown* in September and sent to defend American interests in the East Indies and along the coast of China.[23] He served in the region for three years, returning to the United States in October 1865. His removal from the conflict at home may have been, in some ways, a relief. For, although Price's allegiance to the Union cause was unquestioned, his home state of Kentucky was divided in its loyalties, his brother Jennings was a slaveholder, and he had relatives serving with the Confederate forces. Price was unlikely to face them in battle on the distant side of the Pacific Ocean.

Elizabeth's uncle Ogle Tayloe was southern in his loyalties through inclination as well as background. With Lincoln's arrival in Washington, his hometown became an uncongenial place for him and for other members of its old elite, many of whom left the city at the outbreak of war. Tayloe stayed on and adopted a neutral stance during the conflict; he did, after all, have a northern wife and children living in the North (although one son served with the southern forces from Alabama). He may also have shared the attitude of a relative, Elizabeth Lomax, who, like him, had a son in the Confederate army and who spent part of the war in Washington. "I should leave with great reluctance," she confided to her diary, "as war news is authentic and reaches me quicker than elsewhere."[24] Ogle's wife no longer welcomed guests in the lavish style of former years, but "ordered summer dress for her rooms" to protect the expensive fabric on her chairs and sofas and went into social hibernation. "When the world was righted and her friends returned," announced Phebe, "her red silk upholstery would be uncovered and she would receive once again."[25] She pointedly snubbed the wartime president, proclaiming proudly that she had not crossed the threshold of the White House since his predecessor, James Buchanan, left office.[26]

During Captain Price's absence, his wife and children were frequently in residence at Ogle and Phebe Tayloe's Washington home. It was more than the Tayloes' hospitality that kept Elizabeth Price in Washington during the war years. Her married life had begun there, and she had friends and a respected social position in Washington naval circles. Like Mrs. Lomax, she no doubt appreciated her proximity to reliable news pertaining to military operations and war movements, and welcomed opportunities to share fears and concerns with other wives in the same situation as herself. Her native Troy was at a distance from the day-to-day life of the war; by choosing to stay in the capital city with her children, Elizabeth remained at the conflict's pulsating center.

National events transformed the once sleepy southern town of Washington. Its strategic location and political importance meant the continual threat of Confederate attack, and the city in wartime took on the appearance of a combined armed camp and military hospital. The population escalated from 75,000 to 120,000 over the course of five years,[27] and as residents with Confederate sympathies left town they were replaced by a curious and chaotic mix of men from the North, Midwest, and West. The encroaching culture was profoundly shocking to members of the old aristocracy who remained in the capital.

For children, life in Washington during the war brought moments of exhilaration as well as episodes of terror. One well-bred little girl close to Lily in age remembered

> the soldiers and the brass buttons and all the trappings of war—and the bands, too. The bands most of all, for they were constantly marching down the streets, playing "Yankee Doodle," and "Marching Through Georgia." . . . It was a great show for us. Then some days, not soldiers, but ambulances would go by, sometimes with the wounded, and sometimes with three or four coffins piled on each other, and then— then we were silent—and frightened.[28]

Lily, who was six years old when the war began, was ten when it ended.

Virginia Clay, the wife of an Alabama senator who left Washington with her husband before the start of the war, was back in the city from November 1865 until April 1866. In writing of her several visits to the Tayloes during this early post-war period, she mentioned young Lily Price, who smiled down at her "from her coign of vantage at the top of the stairway of the Tayloe residence." She was then, Mrs. Clay wrote, "a fairy-like little slip of a schoolgirl, who, in the intervals between Fridays and Mondays, was permitted to have a peep at the gay gatherings in her aunt's home."[29] This, the earliest known historical reference to Lily, situates the eldest Price daughter in Washington at the immediate close of the Civil War. It also identifies her as a young scholar.

That an eleven-year-old child, particularly a female child, would have been going to school at this time can hardly be assumed. It was only in 1852 that Massachusetts passed the first compulsory school law in the nation, making school attendance by children between the ages of eight and fourteen mandatory for at least twelve weeks each year.[30] Racial issues dividing Washington, which had a large black population, meant that spotty attention was given to local education at mid-century, and only 29 percent of white children of school age were enrolled in its public schools in 1860, compared to 78 percent in some northern states. In 1870, less than 50 percent of all white children in Washington went to any school at all, and of those who did, half went to private schools—including elementary programs for young children as well as forty-two men's academies and young ladies' seminaries dotted about Washington and neighboring Georgetown.[31] Lily was educated at a private school, although at which of the many then operating in Washington is unknown.

How to educate women was hotly debated in the United States throughout the nineteenth century. Those concerned with maintaining the "natural" separation of men's and women's spheres were opposed to a single method of instruction for both sexes. "To preserve throughout the distinction made by God is the highest and the first of all canons of education," intoned one male thinker as late as 1883. "For a woman taken out of place and trained among men, and as a man, is not an object which men can admire or love." Yes, it was agreed that a woman should receive some sort of schooling, but one suited to "her own sphere and her own place . . . a training which will qualify her to make her own home, to keep it pure and sweet, to rule and govern it prudently, to make it in the eyes of men the most attractive scene, the abode of goodness, beauty and truth."[32] Such an education, needless to say, was to emphasize the mastery of domestic and social skills over intellectual content.

Despite the resistance of both sexes to the idea of academic instruction for women, there had been considerable evolution in thinking about women's education by 1850. One of the most important early experiments took place in Elizabeth Price's hometown with the founding in 1821 of the Troy Female Seminary, later renamed the Emma Willard School in honor of its founder. Elizabeth's aunt Phebe Tayloe had been a pupil of Mrs. Willard's even before the establishment of the seminary, attending a school run by her in Waterford, New York, in 1820. Phebe's father, Esaias Warren, served as a founding trustee of the seminary and Phebe was one of its earliest enrollees; her niece Elizabeth followed in her footsteps as a student from 1836 to 1838.[33]

The Troy seminary was the first women's school in the nation to offer a curriculum that included rigorous academic subjects heretofore available only to men: mathematics, science, modern languages, Latin, history, philosophy, geography, and literature. The school's success was due to Mrs. Willard's ability to merge the conventional ideology of the patriarchal family and its stress on woman's passive domestic role "with a subversive attention to women's intellectual development." It is "only in retrospect," noted a late twentieth century analyst, "that the school can be seen to have been an important source of feminism and the incubator of a new style of female personality."[34]

The quality of Lily's Washington education can be measured to some degree by her success as an enrolled day student at the Troy seminary for a single term in the fall of 1866. It is likely that she was in Troy because her mother wanted to be on hand to care for her own mother, then sixty-five years old and in failing health. The seminary was flourishing, despite displacements caused by the war, and its enrollment of 238 girls included boarders from as far away as Selma, Alabama; San Antonio, Texas; and San Francisco, California.[35] A classmate of Lily's later offered a brief sketch of her long-ago acquaintance as she remembered her from that time. "She was slender," she recalled, "and wore her light hair straight back from her face. It was held there by a round comb, and was cut off short behind. It seems to me now that she almost always wore a dress of red, green and blue plaid." Lily, she said, had "a quiet little dignity of her own. . . . Her manners were always ladylike and she spoke in a sweet voice. . . . She was just like the rest of us then; only more timid than some, more ladylike than others."[36]

Twelve-year-old Lily, according to school records, studied arithmetic, reading and spelling, writing, composition, chronology (history), and French.[37] While at the seminary, she took a New York State Regents' examination required of state students to measure scholastic achievement. "Some of the questions," noted her former schoolmate, "would have baffled older and wiser heads than ours. Walking down the street together afterward, talking it over, [Lily] expressed the greatest concern for fear she would not pass. When we all had our certificates she was the most delighted."[38] Lily's grandmother died in late December and Lily and her mother presumably returned to Washington; Lily was not registered at the seminary for the spring semester. Her enrollment at her mother and great aunt's old school during the few months she was in Troy suggests not only that education held high status in the Price family, but also confirmed the extended Warren family's confidence in Mrs. Willard's precepts about women's ability to reason independently.

Captain Price was promoted to the rank of commodore in late 1866 and celebrated his sixty-second birthday on 1 December 1867. Having reached mandatory naval retirement age, he was placed on the retired list on 2 December.[39] The Prices stayed on in Washington. Their continued residence in the city was facilitated by the 1866 departure of Ogle and Phebe Tayloe for an extended tour of Europe, during which they invited Phebe's niece and her family to make their Lafayette Square residence their home. This the Prices did so convincingly that the Price name became linked in the public mind with the Tayloe mansion—the *Philadelphia Inquirer* reporting in 1897 that "formerly" the residence "was known as the Price house, where Commodore Price lived and entertained lavishly for many years."[40]

Washington was not the same town after 1865 that it had been before the war, and the social scene continued to evolve. Northern, midwestern, and western industrialists, many of whom had made new fortunes out of the war, set the tone, displacing the old southern elite that had lost numbers, fortune, and reputation as a result of the conflict.[41] The recent arrivals introduced an era of conspicuous show, labeled the "Gilded Age" by Mark Twain and Charles Dudley Warner in their 1873 novel of that title. According to the two authors, the city's "Middle Ground"—its respectable "official" society whose menfolk held positions in the executive and legislative branches of government—was "the best aristocracy of the three" castes that dominated the city.[42] The old elite, cumulatively nicknamed "the Antiques," distanced itself from official society as well as from the vulgar newcomers, or "Parvenus," by affecting outdated fashions and modes of transport and seldom attending public functions.[43] Thirty-one members of this refined social remnant founded the Association of the Oldest Inhabitants of the District of Columbia in 1865. The organization pursued a two-fold mission: "to keep alive the reminiscences of the [city's] past," and "to lend its aid in every way to its prosperity and improvement in good order, right government, and social intercourse."[44] Ogle Tayloe, who as a resident of the city since 1801 claimed to be its very oldest inhabitant, served as the organization's first president before his departure for Europe.[45]

Tayloe died in Rome in February 1868, and his wife returned to Washington. Her repossession of her home, as well as Elizabeth Price's inheritance of the old Paine family residence in Troy after her mother's death, led the retired naval officer and his family to relocate permanently in 1869 to Troy and the house where all three Price girls had been born. Lily's sisters, twelve-year-old Cora and eleven-year-old Lucy, were enrolled in their turn in the Troy Female Seminary, entering in the fall of 1869 and graduating together in June 1872. Fifteen-year-old Lily stayed on in Washington to complete her education and serve as companion to her widowed great aunt when school was in session. "Washington society," noted the *Washington Post* in 1885, had known Lily "since her girlhood, which was passed here. She was always much liked by her school friends, who have a kindly memory of her frank and unaffected ways."[46]

The Price family settled effortlessly into Troy life. "In our community," it was later recalled, Cicero Price "solicited no notoriety and he courted retirement." Known as "fond of his home and his books," he was something of a scholar in his later years—a devoted fan of Thomas Carlyle, the Scottish historian, essayist, and satirist whose struggles to reconcile Calvinist values with loss of faith in organized religion reverberated with many Victorian intellectuals. Price was described as "comfortably well off, but was not considered to be a man of wealth." "Decidedly unpretentious" in manner, he was "a very genial, but yet a conservative man, who always lived within his means." His firsthand knowledge of the world made him "a good conversationalist, well informed and very entertaining," and he "had many intimate friends" in his adopted city.[47] Elizabeth Price, a tall, energetic woman, was considered, like her husband, to be without show. She devoted herself to her family and was an active member of St. Paul's Episcopal Church in Troy,[48] where Lily was confirmed, as were her sisters. The Prices' affluence and high social standing were tempered by their modest lifestyle and their disinclination for ostentatious display.

The family made short summer visits to fashionable watering places, among them Long Branch, New Jersey, and Saratoga, New York, some twenty-five miles north of Troy, where Lily was later recalled as a famous croquet player and a belle in her circle.[49] Another preferred holiday destination was the lakeside village of Luzerne (now Lake Luzerne) in the nearby foothills of the Adirondack Mountains. There, Commodore Price was to be seen in July 1873 riding in a carriage behind flag- and banner-waving Sunday School children and Sons and Daughters of Temperance as he represented the navy in a parade celebrating the consecration of the town's new cemetery.[50]

It came as a surprise, no doubt, to Elizabeth and Cicero to discover in 1870 that at the ages of forty-two and sixty-four they were once again to become parents. Their son, William, was born in August of that year. To his parents' sorrow, "Willie" was not a normal child, and at the age of seven he was placed in the Private Institution for the Education of Feeble-Minded Youth in Barre, Massachusetts. Established in 1848, the Elm Hill School, as it was later called, was widely respected as the first facility dedicated to the education and development of mentally disabled children, and the first, too, to emphasize individualized attention in a small, family-plan or "cottage" setting.[51] It "long remained," noted a late twentieth century medical historian, "an attractive alternative for wealthy parents who did not wish their children placed in a public institution."[52] Willie's twenty-year-old cousin, Estelle Tayloe Paine (child of his uncle John Paine and his late wife, a daughter of Ogle Tayloe), joined him as a resident at the school in 1888. On the basis of the Stanford-Binet intelligence test, formulated in the early twentieth century, it was determined that Willie had as an adult the mental capacity of a five-year-old, and his cousin Estelle that of a ten-year-old.[53]

The distinction between mental retardation and mental illness was blurred in the 1870s, as was the connection between heredity and both types of disorder. Physicians were fascinated by what appeared to be "the continuity of disabilities over generations," and were in general agreement that "a disabled child was the result of the poor 'genetic environment' of the parent compounded by the poor home environment into which the child is born." There was, moreover, a common belief that "degeneracy among generations could take on markedly different forms—a drunk in one generation, a prostitute in another, and an idiot in yet another."[54] This amalgamation of accepted truths explains the peculiar juxtaposition of facts relating to Willie's history that were recorded in the Elm Hill School's register upon the boy's arrival. His "case study" summarized his "abnormal heredity" as follows: "mother and maternal grandmother endowed with passionate wills uncontrolled, and of hyper nervous organization. Two maternal uncles [one of them Estelle's father] inebriates wasting their property in consequence."[55]

This account provides a rare insight into Lily's family situation, and suggests that there may have been a certain amount of mental distress in the Price home and in those of Lily's maternal uncles in the 1870s. It also implies that Lily's mother could be a difficult woman to live with. Some of her anguish at the time of Willie's commitment would certainly have been due to the recent loss of her middle daughter, Cora. For in the spring of 1875 the family traveled north to the Adirondack town of Luzerne for a reason wholly other than summer relaxation. Luzerne was advertised as beneficial to sufferers from pulmonary complaints, and it was said that "children and others who have been brought here almost at the point of death, have recovered, and shortly put on the full blush of vigorous health."[56] Cora had tuberculosis, the little-understood disease that carried off so many young victims, and the Prices hoped that Luzerne's healthy environment would bring their daughter some respite from its symptoms. Cora died there in May at the age of eighteen.

Both Troy and Washington later claimed Lily as "a belle and beauty,"[57] and she spent her young adult years shuttling between her parents' Troy home and that of her great aunt in Washington. It is unknown to what degree she was involved in the playing out of the family tragedies of that period, but it is certain that her parents would have been too preoccupied to worry much about her future or to devote themselves to the tasks of launching her into society and finding her a suitable husband. Mrs. Price does not seem, in any case, to have been the type to undertake the kind of social adventurism in the marriage market practiced by the ambitious mothers portrayed in Edith Wharton's novels detailing elite society of this period. Given her family's status in both Troy and Washington, social opportunities would have come Lily's way. It was expected that she would make the most of them.

In Troy, at least, Lily was given a great deal of personal freedom, as girls in smaller cities were not generally subject to the kind of strict chaperonage insisted upon in large eastern metropolises. A New York hotel bellboy later remembered having encountered Lily when she was in her late teens or early twenties. He was driving a Troy ice-cream wagon then, and described "a sort of lawn party" at a military arsenal across the river from Troy at which Lily was one of the guests. "The luncheon and the sports over," he recalled, "Miss Price came to me and said: 'Mr. Lucas, It is a long way to the horse cars. Would you mind driving me to Troy? 'Certainly I'll do it,' I replied, and Miss Price jumped into the wagon. As we neared her house she remarked: 'I suppose some people would find fault with my riding in an ice-cream wagon, but I don't care, do you?'"[58] Lily's disarming question, as well as her comfort level in hitching a ride with a wagon driver in the first place, enhances the general opinion of her as a down-to-earth and self-sufficient young woman.

It was while living in Washington with her great aunt that Lily met Lucy Madison Worthington, a young woman who became a lasting friend and is likely to have served as something of a life model for Lily during the next several years. Born in Kentucky in 1852, Lucy's middle name celebrated her distinguished ancestral roots as a relative of President James Madison. She arrived in Washington in late 1871 with her maternal aunt Puss Bower to assist in discharging the Washington social obligations of General William Belknap, President Ulysses Grant's Secretary of War and the recently widowed husband of Puss's sister. Lucy made her debut as a hostess at Belknap's New Year's Day reception in 1872,[59] where she immediately captivated members of the press with her good looks and intelligence. She became a fixture at Washington's official entertainments, serving as a frequent hostess at General Belknap's gatherings and attending other parties escorted by him or by her aunt Puss (for both of whom she unwittingly acted as a foil, as the pair reached an understanding early on and married in December 1873). Lucy was singled out at President Grant's second inaugural ball for her lovely dress of "blue silk, trimmed with Valenciennes lace, ornaments pearls and diamonds."[60] This was one of the earliest of what would be hundreds of newspaper descriptions of Lucy's attire over the ensuing decades—now in Washington and later in New York City and Newport, Rhode Island.

How and where did Lily and Lucy make one another's acquaintance? It is unlikely to have been in official society, where Lucy moved, as Lily's name never appeared in the paper in connection with its chronicled doings, and members of the residential aristocracy in which Lily's aunt Phebe was a fixture assiduously avoided press attention. But Lucy's Kentucky birth and family associations would have guaranteed her entrée into Mrs. Tayloe's social milieu, and it is probable that the two girls met at the kind of tame event considered suitable entertainment for the younger generation of the city's upper class. Given Lily's girlish timidity, a trait that led a one-time acquaintance to believe it impossible that Lily could ever take a conspicuous role in society,[61] her world can only have expanded upon meeting the more worldly Lucy. She had neither a costly wardrobe nor a sponsor with the energy of Lucy's aunt Puss, but the girls' intimacy and its Washington genesis were frequently mentioned by journalists in later years.

Lucy married Henry Clews, a New York stockbroker and banker, in 1874, and moved from Washington into the social elite of New York. She was lucky, it transpired, to have left her Washington connections behind her. Congress's discovery that Belknap had accepted bribes—having been encouraged to do so by Lucy's two maternal aunts—led to his 1876 resignation, an effort to impeach him, and his departure from public life. Lucy conveniently forgot her early social triumph in Washington and her role in the household of the one-time Secretary of War.

Lucy made an enviable marriage, but her friend Lily was still several years away from following in her footsteps. She continued to move back and forth between Troy and her aunt Phebe's Washington home throughout the 1870s, and made a visit to Europe as Mrs. Tayloe's companion in 1876.[62] She also met the man she would marry: Louis Carré Hamersley.

CHAPTER 2

Louis Carré Hamersley

ℒℴ

ouis Carré Hamersley was the scion of a more than well-to-do
New York family. His paternal great-great-grandfather, William
Hamersley, was a direct descendant of Sir Hugh Hamersley, lord
mayor of London in the 1620s, and served as an officer in the British
navy during the 1701–14 War of the Spanish Succession. William
arrived in New York City around 1716, entered commerce, and
married the daughter of one of the city's early Dutch families. His
second son, Andrew, prospered as an importer and accumulator of
city real estate. (A stretch of Manhattan's present West Houston
Street was originally named Hamersley Street in recognition of his
land holdings in that vicinity.) The Revolutionary War significantly
diminished Andrew's capital, but an estate inherited from a maternal
uncle in the West Indies, Louis Carré, augmented the family treasury
for the next generation. Andrew's third son, Lewis Carré Hamersley,
born about 1767 and named in honor of his benevolent relation,
continued the family tradition as both merchant and amasser of real
estate—an occupational pairing that underlay most early New York
City fortunes. He also played a role in the development of local banks
and other financial institutions.[1]

Andrew Gordon Hamersley, father of Lily's husband-to-be, was
born in 1805 to Lewis Carré Hamersley and his wife, Elizabeth
Finney of Accomack County, Virginia. A sister, Harriet, and a
younger brother, John William, completed the family. Gordon, as
he was called, was "a man of extended knowledge, great cultivation,
delightful manner, and entertaining in conversation."[2] He and his

brother were "dashing young men, having traveled extensively, and in their day were considered two of the chief beaux of the city." Gordon attended Columbia University as a member of the class of 1826 but did not graduate. He was attached to the American Legation at the Court of the Tuileries during the period 1829–32, and was known abroad as "a graceful, easy dancer, and a great favorite at the Court balls and other entertainments. He lived much in Paris, met many distinguished people, and fully enjoyed and appreciated the refined life and culture of the light-hearted city on the Seine."[3]

Returning to New York, Gordon wed Sarah Jones Mason, a young woman noted for her striking beauty and great personal charms, in 1838. Louis Carré, their only child, was born in 1840, and Sarah died eight years later. Gordon never remarried but lived simply and quietly, devoting himself to his real estate and investment interests and to the rearing of his son.[4]

The marriage of Gordon, who possessed inherited wealth, and Sarah created the foundation for a substantial fortune. Sarah's father, John Mason, had been another of those city merchants who did well in New York's formative years. His name first appeared in a 1796 city directory as partner in a dry goods store, and by 1813 his financial and social position were such that he was a leading organizer in the effort to finance the unsubscribed portion of a $16 million loan authorized by Congress to meet expenses related, in part, to the War of 1812. Mason and members of his extended family, which included an assortment of Joneses as well as Masons, served as directors and shareholders of what became the Chemical Bank; by 1831 Mason was its president. Much of his wealth was invested in real estate, including a large undeveloped holding in what is today the heart of fashionable Manhattan—a parcel that included most of the land from Fifty-fourth to Sixty-third streets between Fifth and Park avenues. At Mason's 1839 death his estate was estimated to be $800,000, making his one of the half-dozen greatest American fortunes of his day.[5]

John Mason had eight children, and three of his sons-in-law, including Gordon Hamersley, were closely connected with the Chemical Bank as directors and large shareholders. Mason left the bulk of his wealth to them and their families, suggesting a partiality that led to a protracted lawsuit over disposition of his estate. The contest was initiated by two of Mason's children—a son who married a young actress and a daughter who, like her brother, wed against her father's wishes; both were left nothing but $2,500 annuities under the original terms of their father's will.[6] The litigation over the Mason inheritance dragged on until 1854, when the charge of "undue influence" was indirectly upheld in court and a more equitable division made of the property. In the final settlement, Gordon Hamersley, who was one of Mason's executors, received downtown buildings and lots as well as the uptown blocks between Sixtieth and Sixty-first streets, all of which had increased dramatically in value during the long-drawn-out court case.[7] Louis, as his mother's heir-at-law, was directly assigned fifteen lots fronting on Fifth Avenue and the adjoining block of Fifty-fifth Street.[8]

Just where and how Louis passed his childhood remains obscure. The best information, surprisingly, comes down to us from Rebecca (Becky) Jones, the Hamersley housekeeper for nearly forty years, who dictated a short autobiography sometime before her death in 1905. Becky, born in 1822 of Welsh and Dutch descent in upstate New York, moved with her parents and siblings to Ballston Spa in Saratoga County around 1841 and went into domestic service among the New York City families who passed part or all of their summers in what was then a fashionable health resort. There she met Gordon and Sarah Hamersley, and with their family she spent the rest of her working life. Her employers, according to Becky in the clumsy phraseology and spelling of the scribe who took down her account, spent many years in Europe during the 1840s and 1850s. She "stayed with them, went to Paris, France, several times. Mr. & Mrs. Hamersleys borded at a hotel and the onily son, a small boy, went to school. And I was his and hers housekeeper. For 3 years he atended the military acadimy school and graduated and recieved medals several from several grades."[9]

Still accompanied by Becky, the family returned to the United States,

> was here for several years & then took a voyage to London, from London to Germany, the city of Maden-Maden, from their to America. Several years here again, then to London,

this is the last voyage. We also had our household goods shiped before we voyaged from London. They were lost in the heavy storms, never to be found. We came sometime after but it was a severe voyage. We thought we all would be lost but fortunate enoughf we landed all safe. That stoped all of our voyages, never went again.[10]

For some reason the death of Louis's mother did not enter into Becky's narrative. Nor did she mention the year Louis spent as a student at Christ Church College, Oxford, before his return to the United States.

It is unlikely to have been a rough sea voyage that put an end to the family's travels, but it is true that in September 1860 "Gordon Hamersley, son and servant" arrived in New York on the steamship *Adriatic* from Southampton and settled down, more or less for good. Louis was twenty years old. He did not serve in the Civil War. In 1863 he was awarded a diploma by the New York Law School (part of New York University), and was shortly thereafter admitted to practice law in New York State.[11] Despite his qualification to do so, he never pursued a legal career.

Father and son moved in with Gordon's widowed mother and went about their business, working from home and calling upon bankers, lawyers, and agents as necessary to assist in the general management of their assets, particularly the buying, selling, and rental of real estate. They occupied themselves, noted Gordon's lawyer brother, John, "the same as we all do, rent our houses, collect our rents and pay our taxes." Earnings were invested in more real estate, bonds, mortgages, and "solid" securities: the stocks of banks, insurance companies, and railroads. Gordon dominated the father/son partnership, and according to John Hamersley, his nephew had no specific occupation except taking care of his property and being constantly in attendance on his father. His uncle John wasn't sure what else Louis did, but conjectured that he followed "the ordinary occupation of a young man; he used to go to college, and he used to drive out in the park, and he used to go to Europe."[12]

Gordon and his son were inseparable and their celebrated intimacy was commented upon within the family and in the press. "They hardly ever went upon the street, to the club, the opera, or theatre, or church, except in each other's company," it was noted. "Their remarkable display of mutual affection was the wonder and remark of all who knew them and the cause of many sarcastic remarks."[13] One observer went so far as to compare the two to *Dombey and Son*—a reference to Charles Dickens's novel of that name and its plot line centered in a father's excessive focus on his young son as the successor to his firm and carrier of the family name.[14]

To Louis, the explanation for his relationship with his father was simple. "Especially I remember," he was later quoted as saying, "that I have no mother, and that my father has taken a mother's part in time past for me as well as a father's. I consider it to be my duty to sacrifice myself to my father and always be with him."[15]

Gordon suffered from vertigo during the last fifteen years of his life, and Louis, who was unwilling that he should have an attendant, chose to fill that role himself, always making his arm available for his father to lean on. He also took it upon himself to intermediate in conversation for Gordon, who was by now nearly completely deaf. As a business associate explained, "I generally told Mr. Louis what I would like to have communicated to his father, and he would do it; I could not speak loud enough to make the old gentleman hear me." For a once gregarious man such as Gordon, who in his younger years had a reputation as a gifted raconteur, this inability to interact socially must have been painful. "He had to proceed by guesswork a good deal," observed a lifetime friend. Yet, he continued, Louis and old acquaintances tried to ease Gordon's isolation. At table with one or two companions, "Louis always sat next to him, and from habit he could make it easier and plainer; he could hear better what Louis said, and Louis would call in his ear to give him the cue." Louis appeared to be perfectly content with his restricted life. He was, his uncle John later recalled, "a very good son."[16]

The Hamersleys, like other well-heeled descendants of New York's early merchants, belonged to the city's oldest and most stable social elite, collectively referred to as "the Knickerbocker set" in honor of the short breeches worn by early Dutch settlers. Its members, according to novelist Edith Wharton (born Edith Jones and herself affiliated with the Mason/Jones clan), were "not exceptional." They were "mostly cut on the same convenient and unobtrusive pattern; but they were often exceedingly 'nice.'"[17] The Knickerbockers were looked up to socially and could, it was said, "come forward and exercise their power" whenever they chose, but were more likely to participate in society in a quiet and inconspicuous manner, "like to gods to sit upon Olympus."[18] The Hamersleys socialized quietly within their extended family circle—mostly at dinner parties, where conversation consisted of amiable chat about "small parochial concerns": property, food, wine, sport, travel, and mild culture.[19] At lunchtime father and son could be spotted at the Union Club, New York's most prestigious private club, of which Gordon had been a founding member. They owned a forty-acre farm in Westchester County north of New York City and paid short visits in summer to resort destinations popular with other comfortably settled Northerners during the summer months. Like their social peers, they were staunch Protestants and close-fisted when it came to money. Louis had no interest in the role of man-about-town, and his name rarely appeared in the spare social columns of New York City newspapers before his marriage to Lily.

What might a young woman have seen in Louis Hamersley? He was perhaps a little too closely tied to his father, and he was certainly not handsome: short and round-shouldered with an oddly shaped-head—described as "very prominent . . . long and large in front and behind, with some depression along the side."[20] His personality, however, was pleasant. He was characterized as mild and gentle, intelligent and quiet in his manners, "appreciative . . . apparently fond of a joke, rather humorous." According to a Hamersley cousin's husband, his close friend of many years had a lovely disposition. Noting that he himself was called bad-tempered, he explained that "if Louis had been as quick-tempered as I am, we should not have been such good friends; he was forgiving." Retiring in his private relationships, in business dealings Louis was considered a shrewd, sharp businessman, "very capable in making a bargain, hard and very close."[21] While he may not have been a man of good looks, fire, or wide-ranging interests, Louis, with his patrician background, his wealth, and his commendable if modest personal qualities, was excellent husband material.

CHAPTER 3

Courtship and Marriage I

ﬆ

M ost of those who knew them believed that Lily Price and
Louis Hamersley were introduced to one another at Phebe
Tayloe's Washington home in the early 1870s. Louis's uncle John
Hamersley remembered first meeting Lily at about the same time at
White Sulphur Springs, West Virginia.[1] This fashionable watering
place, known as "the White," had roots in the late 1700s as an untidy
collection of log cabins and tents surrounding a spring of restorative
mineral water, and grew in the course of the following decades to
include a hotel for 700 guests as well as privately owned cottages that
lodged another 1,200 or 1,400 patrons. The resort was famous for its
sulphur-laced waters and for its languorous sociability—a holdover
from the antebellum years when it was dominated by the free and easy
ways of "the Southern element." It was celebrated, too, for its belles,
beautiful young single women "full of life and joy, with their sweeping
trains, round arms, smiles, blushes, and curls—natural or borrowed,"[2]
who came each season to amuse themselves, and with luck, to find a
husband.

Lily was later described as a White Sulphur Springs belle, and
reportedly owed much of her vogue to the patronage of wealthy
Washingtonian William Wilson Corcoran, a respected, longtime
cottage owner at the resort who "was in the habit of surrounding
himself in the Summer at the springs with beautiful girls."[3] Corcoran
had a reputation for giving impecunious, would-be belles a helping
hand, but this would hardly have been his motive in championing the
interests of Lily, whom he had known since she was a child. Born in
Georgetown in 1798, Corcoran had been a longtime Lafayette Square,

Washington, neighbor and intimate friend of the Ogle Tayloes. An immensely rich banker, he retired from business in the 1850s and devoted himself to good living and good works. Among his many gifts to his native city were the Corcoran Gallery of Art, one of the earliest public art museums in the United States, and the Louise Home, a living facility erected in 1879 and named in honor of his deceased wife and daughter for the support of "destitute, but refined and educated, gentlewomen." Phebe Tayloe was the first president of the all-female board of directors that maintained the home,[4] and Corcoran's role as Lily's sponsor at the White was a natural extension of his connection with Mrs. Tayloe and her family.

Louis was thirty-two years old in mid-1872, approximately the time at which he and Lily met, making him fourteen years older than his future bride, then eighteen. The age difference would have meant little to Lily; it was certainly narrower than the twenty-three years that separated her parents. The two had a number of things in common: conservative upbringings, for one thing, in circles that were not far apart in terms of conveyed prestige; the Episcopal religion, for another, a faith that found most of its adherents among comfortably placed families such as those to which Lily and Louis belonged. They shared a temperateness of personality too, a trait that was remarked upon by acquaintances of both. Louis was more mature than men of Lily's own age, and more experienced. He had once been engaged to a New Yorker, a member of the Knickerbocker set like himself, but it had come to nothing and it was said that the girl had thrown him over.[5] Lily no doubt looked up to and found much to admire in her sympathetic and socially connected older suitor.

There was also, of course, Louis's undeniable access to money, and Lily would have been well aware of its power to lift her to the pinnacle of society. As she watched the new life of her transplanted Washington companion Lucy Worthington Clews take root in the rich soil of New York's elite, she might easily have dreamed of following a similar path. She saw that Lucy had immediate social status as the wife of Clews—an amiable, financially successful Englishman six years older than Louis. According to Clews family lore, Lucy and Henry's alliance was, on Lucy's part at least, a "business proposition."[6] Lily may have been aware of her friend's motives in marrying Clews and found them as reasonable a basis as any for taking a husband. What was wrong with marrying for money and position where there was also respect and affection? Lily had several years in which to consider her options.

It was Lily, according to Becky Jones, who took the lead in advancing the relationship. "She came to New York time and time again," later recalled Becky, "and made calls after calls and she proposed to the young gent." Becky considered herself responsible for the final approval given by Gordon Hamersley to his son's marriage. "I said to the old gentleman I thought it would be all right so his father consented to his weding," she reported. Becky characterized Lily as a "poor honest girl" (although, in regard to her poverty, she added, "she soon forgott it after the weding").[7] Thanks to the combined efforts of Lily on her own behalf, of Becky Jones and, no doubt, of others, Lily became Mrs. Louis C. Hamersley in a simple wedding ceremony at her parents' residence in Troy on 5 November 1879. Lily was twenty-five years old; Louis was thirty-nine. Lily's great aunt Phebe gave two elegant Washington receptions in honor of the newlyweds shortly after their marriage.[8]

The New York City home at 257 Fifth Avenue to which Louis brought Lily as a bride was his father's. It was, in fact, the same stately row house between Twenty-eighth and Twenty-ninth streets into which Gordon and his son had settled after their return from Europe in 1860. Elizabeth Hamersley, Gordon's mother, had purchased the house that year and on her death it passed by inheritance to Gordon. His brother, John, and his family lived in an identical row house next door in a domestic arrangement that was commonplace among old New York families.

Fifth Avenue was then the chief residential street of New York and a nationally recognized symbol of wealth and good living. Its name first appeared on a map commissioned by the New York State legislature in 1811, but it was not until years later that the roadway was ready for use; as late as 1869 the uptown stretch of avenue on which John Mason's property fronted was described as "a muddy dirt road which ran alongside a bog."[9] The migration of society up the avenue north of Twenty-third Street began shortly after Madison Square, originally a six-acre potter's field, opened as a park in 1847.

The Hamersleys' neighborhood served as the social center of New York until after the Civil War, a period that coincided with an early phase of the city's mania for building long blocks of tall, nearly identical townhouses faced with a soft, chocolate-colored sandstone. These "brownstones" were the area norm, but there was also to be found there the occasional residential flight of fancy. Jennie Jerome, the future Lady Randolph Churchill and mother of Winston, spent part of her childhood nearby in a marble-trimmed, brick palace built in 1859 by her father, Leonard Jerome, at Madison Square and Twenty-sixth Street. One of the earliest examples of a new type of urban housing—the "French apartment house," designed for the housing of multiple families—went up in 1870 at Fifth Avenue and Twenty-seventh Street.[10]

The Hamersley home was situated in close proximity to many of the institutions favored by the city's elite. The Union Club, where Louis and his father were so often to be found, stood at the avenue and Twenty-first Street. Closer to hand, at Fifth and Twenty-sixth Street, was Delmonico's, New York's most stylish restaurant and social venue in the late decades of the nineteenth century. An Episcopal church was located nearby, but Lily and her husband eschewed this local house of worship and traveled downtown to Eighth Street and Broadway to pray in the long-held Hamersley family pew at fashionable Grace Church, where high pew expenses excluded all but the wealthiest churchgoers.

Despite its central location, the Hamersleys' stretch of Fifth Avenue had begun to lose its luster by the time Lily and Louis started their married life. As the city grew, its fashionable hub continued to move relentlessly uptown, and hotels, antique and bric-a-brac shops, and stores catering to sportsmen were springing up in their neighborhood as its one-time residents moved northward. The Hamersley home conformed to the standard brownstone layout: four stories above a high basement, each with two or three windows facing onto the street. Dining room and kitchen occupied the basement, library and little-used parlor the first floor. The second story accommodated Gordon, the family patriarch; housed in his comfortable front sitting room were the two desks comprising his and Louis's office. The third floor was given over to Lily and Louis, the floor above to servants.[11] The phenomenon of young married couples sharing a house with parents was widespread in New York before the concept of apartment living caught on. While it afforded everyone a modicum of privacy, it implied a more modest lifestyle than did the flamboyant family palaces then beginning to sprout uptown.

The Hamersleys made do with a minimal staff of servants. At its head was Becky Jones, who ran the house, shopped for food, and did some of the cooking. Outside help was brought in to see to additional cooking, cleaning, and laundry. A German valet and "body servant" to Gordon doubled as butler, serving three meals a day at table. After Louis's marriage, when Louis spent more time with Lily and less time with his father, it was the valet/butler who was often seen to accompany Gordon on his long daily walks. A coachman and groom tending to horses and wheeled vehicles were housed in the stable shared with John Hamersley's family several blocks away. The one new employee to join the household with the arrival of Lily was a lady's maid. Her responsibilities included laying out her mistress's clothes, helping her to dress and undress, and applying her skillful hands to the essential domestic tasks of hairdressing, needlework, and dressmaking. A lady's maid, it was said, did what most women do for themselves, and was the ultimate upper-class status symbol.[12]

It is easy to imagine the displacement caused by Lily's entrance into the Hamersley ménage. Louis and his father had shared a New York City bachelor life for nearly twenty years, filled, no doubt, with the kind of trivial but religiously observed rituals common to long-married couples. Becky Jones, while never overreaching her servant's standing, prided herself on her role as venerable family confidante. "The son Mr. Louis came to me for advise," she recalled in her memoir. "He would consult his father first and then come and reveil every thing to me and then would say, 'Beccky, what do you think of So & So?' He would set down for hours and hours and talk. He and his father would talk and then would call me to their private room and talk of things that know body ever new but themselves would. Leave it for me to decide, I would say. . . ."[13]

Now it was time for Becky to give way. "I went up to the old gentleman's room," she recalled, "and said, 'Mr. Hamersley, please give the madam charge of the house' . . . and they did. I stayed. She run her part and I had my part but it made Mr. Gordon feel bad. The old gentleman did not feel to home after the weding."[14] This is hardly surprising. Tempered by Gordon's probable joy at Louis's finding a compatible wife must have been a hitherto unknown loneliness that came with the lost intimacy of earlier years as well as a diffuse feeling of lowered status within his own home. Yet everyone did his best. In July 1880 the *New York Times* reported that Gordon Hamersley and his brother "and families" were staying at Long Branch. Not until June 1882 did the newspaper register the subtle power shift within the domestic circle in recording that "Louis Carré Hamersley and family" were at Saratoga. Ancestral leadership had passed to a new generation.

Lily may have privately chafed at constraints placed on her by the need to concede pride of place to the elder Mr. Hamersley, but she appears to have been a dutiful daughter-in-law and to have won Gordon's affection. A reporter for an early New York society paper who professed himself "averse, as a rule, to referring to wedding presents," considered Gordon's gift to Lily after her marriage sufficiently exceptional to warrant notice. This was a handsome table set of two hundred pieces of solid silver crafted by the respected firm of Black, Starr and Company, finished by Tiffany, and valued at $30,000. Included in the gift was an accompanying chandelier with gold settings ordered from Paris.[15] Such munificence would not have been extended to Lily had she been the cause of any tension in the Hamersley household.

Lily had not the slightest difficulty in breaking into the upper stratum of New York City society and immersing herself in its whirl. And while Louis's wealth and connections were all-important in defining her status, Lily had one influential family tie of her own: a cousin, George Henry Warren, who had been born in Troy but lived most of his adult life in New York and was a lawyer prominent in financial and social circles. Warren was a first cousin of Lily's grandmother, Eliza Paine, and her sister Phebe Tayloe (thus Lily's first cousin twice removed), but he was closer in age to Lily's mother than to his generational cousins. *The New York Times* reported the April 1879 wedding of Warren's daughter Harriet to Robert Goelet, III, son of another long-established New York family, as "a brilliant affair in old New-York Society."[16]

Within her own generation, Lily's transition to New York was eased by the support of her friend Lucy Clews and her husband, Henry. Clews, while running his successful brokerage firm, was also active in reform city politics and charitable work; Lucy played a traditional role as society wife. Lily's social progress as a transplanted bride can be traced through news items in the *New York Times*, where, in the course of eight days at the height of the city's social season in February 1881, Mr. and Mrs. Louis Hamersley's names were listed as attendees at several newsworthy social events:

> *7 February*: "Well-known Persons at Mrs. Mason Jones's— Mrs. Hayes Among the Guests."
>
> *10 February*: "Other Events Last Night ... Mrs. William Astor last evening entertained at dinner, at her own house, a party of 29 well-known people."
>
> *14 February*: "Patriarchs' Ball."[17]

Mary Mason Jones, hostess on 7 February to the wife of the president of the United States as well as to the Hamersleys, was a maternal aunt of Louis's—and a paternal great aunt of Edith Wharton's. In writing about upper-class New York life during this era, Wharton later drew fondly on the memory of her audacious aunt Mary, a matriarchal figure at the center of her extended family clan, for the character of Mrs. Catherine Spicer Mingott, the benevolent grandmother in her Pulitzer Prize-winning novel, *The Age of Innocence*. It was Mrs. Mingott, "whose monstrous obesity had long since made it impossible for her to attend the Opera," who made available the opera box that introduced the novel's central characters. She was lauded for her "moral courage" in constructing a cream-colored stone mansion "in an inaccessible wilderness near the Central Park,"[18] a reference to the real-life, white marble chateau modeled on Fontainebleau that

Mrs. Jones built in 1871 at 1 East 57th Street on one of those still unfashionable uptown real estate parcels inherited from her father, John Mason. Mrs. Jones's ball, given to launch a granddaughter into society, was held in the large ballroom above the elegant parlors of her home. Placed in front of the glittering ballroom mirrors, noted one journalist admiringly, "were numerous baskets of the choicest roses and other flowers, arranged in blocks and various pretty designs. The chandeliers were decorated with smilax and studded with roses."[19]

The Hamersleys' inclusion among the select dinner party guests at the home of Mrs. William Backhouse Astor, Jr. meant that Lily had achieved the highest level of status attainable in New York society. For Mrs. Astor was the acknowledged leader and arbiter of the elite social set. Endowed with impeccable ancestry and great wealth through marriage to one of the richest men in America, she had begun in the late 1860s to pursue the "social responsibilities" of New York women of her class: giving and attending dinners, presiding at balls and private receptions, gracing weddings, and paying calls.[20] By force of character and with the acquiescence of her social equals, Mrs. Astor had assumed the right to determine who and what were acceptable and to institutionalize the traditions and regulations of New York's upper crust.

The Patriarchs' Ball, the third event on the Hamersley's social agenda for that February week, had been the brainchild of Ward McAllister, a well-born transplant from Savannah, Georgia, who settled in New York in the 1850s. After serving a workmanlike apprenticeship as a member of reception committees and an attendee at dinners and balls, McAllister took upon himself a larger role: to shape the corporate identity of rich New Yorkers in an era when the city was a center of rapidly expanding wealth and a hotbed for the blatant social climbing of obscure arrivistes. He and Mrs. Astor developed a symbiotic relationship in which McAllister's pronouncements benefited from the distinction of Mrs. Astor's patronage, and McAllister, in turn, served for all intents and purposes as Mrs. Astor's "advance man" and publicist in upholding her monarchic prerogatives. To McAllister is credited the coinage of the term, "the Four Hundred," an oblique reference thrown out by him during a March 1888 newspaper interview as representing the number of fashionable people constituting the uppermost layer of New York society.[21]

McAllister's vehicle for controlling access to the social elite had been his introduction and promotion in 1872 of an annual series of three subscription balls underwritten by "the Patriarchs," an association of powerful New York men "who had the right to create and lead society" and were brought together for the two-fold purpose of lending the weight of their names and funding the balls. Each of the original twenty-five Patriarchs—including Lily's cousin George Warren and Louis's uncle John Hamersley—was entitled, in exchange for his support, to invite four socially flawless women and five men including himself to every ball.[22] Lily and Louis were regular attendees at the balls, and Louis, who had been thrust into the social spotlight by his marriage to Lily, was himself named a Patriarch in 1880.[23]

The couple was also seen at the balls of the Family Circle Dancing Class, a less formal cousin of the Patriarchs instituted by McAllister to appeal to younger members of society. What's more, Lily became something of a favorite with McAllister, and was reported to be his early partner at an 1882 Family Circle ball for the "german,"[24] one of the more complex rituals associated with the time-honored structure of balls. This dance, which could go on for as long as two hours, required couples called upon by a leader to be "up" and dancing; they then separated and selected new partners with whom they executed complicated figures before giving way to a new arrangement of dancers. Lively participation insured an evening's success and choice of the leader was crucial—the best leaders being those who could mix the participants in an entertaining and spirited manner. McAllister selected the leaders for the germans at both the Patriarch and Family Circle Dancing Class balls and their names figured prominently in newspaper reportage of these events, as did the names of the first-called dancers onto the floor. McAllister's choice of Lily as an early partner was not only an endorsement of her good looks and social preeminence, but a tribute to the vitality he felt she could bring to this public role that set a party's tone.

The frivolous social life of New York's upper class was perhaps not the best model to hold up to an impressionable young woman just entering this elevated stratum in her own right. The city's elite, according to historian Frederic Jaher, was unique among East Coast urban centers in "its admission of new wealth, female domination, extravagant lifestyle, internal rivalry for social sovereignty, desire for publicity, and indifference to civic responsibility." It was known to be intellectually and culturally apathetic, and as one New York hostess put it, would "have fled in a body from a poet, a painter, a musician or a clever Frenchman." Sustaining status in this milieu was a fulltime job; indeed, one local socialite insisted that there was "no profession, art, or trade that women are working in today as taxing on mental resource as being a leader of Society."[25] Lily had not been raised to be superficial, but the New York spirit was catching.

During the early years of her marriage, Lily began calling herself "Lillian" or "Lilian," a name that she may have imagined had a more highborn ring and looked more elegant in newspaper reportage than the diminutive Lily or her given name, the old-fashioned Eliza. She continued to call herself Lillian on and off for the rest of her life, but never did so consistently, nor did anyone else, and Lily was the name by which she was generally known.

The new Mrs. Hamersley sat for a formal oil portrait not long after her marriage—a *de rigueur* ceremonial milestone that marked her status. A sketch executed by the fashionable portrait painter Daniel Huntington as a study for the painting suggests Lily's beauty at that time. Huntington's earlier subjects had included presidents Abraham Lincoln and Martin Van Buren as well as Lily's great aunt and uncle, the Tayloes. In the finished painting of Lily—now lost—she was arrayed not in her chemise as in the sketch but in a gown of dark rich red velvet and lace. Louis paid $1,250 for the portrait on its completion in 1881.[26] It was exhibited that year in the annual exhibition at New York's National Academy of Design, of which Huntington was then president.

Louis, who was known to be very fond of horses, was elected in January 1883 to membership in the prestigious Coaching Club, of which Jennie Jerome's father had been a founding member in 1875.[27] The organization's annual late-May outing—a parade of gleaming "four-in-hand" coaches driven by their smartly attired owners up

Sketch by painter Daniel Huntington in preparation for portrait of Mrs. Louis Hamersley, 1881
COURTESY COOPER-HEWITT, NATIONAL DESIGN MUSEUM, SMITHSONIAN INSTITUTION/ART RESOURCE, NY

Fifth Avenue into Central Park and beyond—marked the close of the fashionable New York "season" that ran from November through June. Elizabeth Drexel Decies, fourteen years younger than Lily, later recalled being allowed to watch the annual parade in the company of her governess—an event other than which her "childish imagination could conceive of no greater bliss." She vividly evoked the parade's sounds and sights, including the tops of the arrayed coaches that "looked like so many flower-gardens, for every woman had put on her most be-trimmed hat and loveliest dress in honour of" this important event. In particular, she remembered Lily Hamersley, who to her youthful eyes had but one "rival to the claim of being the loveliest woman in the 'Four Hundred.'" She was nearly always dressed in white, according to Decies, "an affectation that annoyed other women, but it suited her opulent rose and gold beauty better than any other colour. She used to create a sensation when she appeared at the coaching parade in white from the ostrich plumes trimming her big hat to the French shoes on her tiny feet."[28]

Lily's daytime routine followed the prescribed agenda of all women who moved in New York society. At its heart was a merry-go-round of calling and leaving cards that represented upper-class women's institutionalized method of social networking prior to the advent of the telephone. Lily held regular reception days when she was known to be "at home,"[29] a technique for grouping the visits of acquaintances and avoiding the surprise of drop-in guests. Other pursuits included luncheons and teas as well as shopping and visits to the dressmaker and milliner.

Life in the Hamersley household followed a similar course to that it had known before Louis's marriage and included plenty of back-and-forth visits with Louis's widowed uncle and cousins next door. In deference to Gordon's deafness and in the on-going effort to assure him of his primacy in the household, dinner invitations were mostly tendered to other members of the extended family and to old friends with whom he would feel at ease. These meals had to have been woefully short on spontaneous conversation. Louis's loudly spoken prompts to his deaf father about whatever subject was at hand were abandoned when they had company in favor of what Gordon called "tablegrams"—little slips of paper on which Louis wrote word clues for his father about topics under discussion. Although Gordon now spoke infrequently, he continued to be keenly interested in what Louis had to report.[30]

Creating an appropriate backdrop for Lily as a New York society woman was expensive for Louis. As a cousin's husband recalled, "I think the most conspicuous thing was that he spent more money after his marriage than he ever did before." He remembered Louis's buying "horses, carriages, I think silverware, jewels"—although upon reflection he couldn't recall that he *had* bought jewels. "I can say," he concluded, "that Louis was not given to spending money very particularly before he was married, and after he was married he certainly spent much more money; he told me that he had spent his income, and, I think, that once he told me that he had spent a little more than his income; and I dare say, that he did; in lots of things . . . he was influenced by his wife—I know I [am.]"[31]

The Hamersley marriage was described as a happy one. "They always appeared to be on very good relations, the best relations that could exist, as far as I could judge—that ought to exist between a man and his wife," noted one friend. Lily was considered to have the more forceful personality of the two; if she requested her husband "to do things that he would not be likely to do, he did it," commented Gordon's valet. She was not as gentle as he was, he added, but he and other servants agreed that the pair was openly affectionate. They "never got angry," according to Lily's maid.[32] They spent a great deal of time in one another's company and were often seen out walking arm-in-arm. Did Lily love her husband? "Nobody knows. She was a modest, faithful wife at all events," noted one journalist, and Louis "in his behavior was ever polite, his morals excellent and his disposition kind."[33] The two were, in their way, a model couple.

Lily's cousin George Warren, perhaps goaded to do so by Lily, involved Louis in an enterprise that would take on tremendous importance for his wife as it would for others among the social elite of New York. This was the founding of the Metropolitan Opera House, a rival to the Academy of Music that had opened in 1854 with the financial backing of the then first families of New York. The academy zealously restricted access to its 30 privately subscribed boxes, which were semi-enclosed and bordered the academy auditorium, thus enabling a privileged opera-going few to display their socially preeminent status before equals as well as inferiors. More recent social lions and aspiring New Yorkers wanted their chance in the spotlight as provided by box "ownership" and set about to secure it.

In 1880 a number of wealthy and influential but boxless New Yorkers—including such successful corporate financiers and industrial entrepreneurs as Vanderbilts, Astors, and Goelets—floated the idea of building a "new and superb opera house." This venue was to have sufficient boxes "to accommodate the large and increasing class of patrons who are eager to obtain the best seats and willing to pay correspondingly choice prices for them so that they are accommodated" and have "ample opportunity to see and be seen."[34] Warren represented the interests of this upstart group in an April meeting with directors of the Academy of Music to discuss how their needs might be met within the academy, as well as the risks inherent in trying to financially support and ensure top-quality musical talent for two competing New York City opera venues. The best the academy could offer was a reconfiguration of its auditorium to provide 26 additional boxes at its rear, so plans went ahead for the construction of a new house with a horseshoe-shaped arrangement of stacked tiers surrounding three sides of its auditorium that would highlight the occupants of 123 opera boxes.[35] Louis Hamersley was recorded in 1882 as among the first seventy stockholders in the Metropolitan Opera House.[36] He subscribed $10,000 for 150 of the 10,500 shares of stock issued in the venture, and at a March 1883 stockholders' meeting was assigned box number 33 in the new opera house that was to open in October of that year.[37] The box was in the center of the most prestigious second tier of 36 "parterre" boxes reserved for stockholders only. Occupants would not only have satisfactory sight lines but, as importantly, would be virtually on stage themselves— visible to everyone seated in the auditorium.

Louis and Lily took on two projects in which they shared a mutual interest in the fall of 1882: the design and building of city and country houses. Both were ambitious ventures and would involve considerable expense—much more money, in fact, than Louis could afford to lay out on his own. Thus it is clear that Gordon Hamersley was an important partner in his son and daughter-in-law's building schemes and was expected, in both cases, to foot the bill. Lily had expensive tastes, but Gordon was as willing as Louis to give her what she wanted. Besides, real estate was real estate as far as father and son were concerned, and both projects were no doubt viewed as good long-term investments in the ever-rising property market.

The first Hamersley undertaking was a family home to be designed by popular architect John B. Snook and constructed at Fifth Avenue and Fifty-fifth Street on one of the newly stylish uptown plots Louis had inherited from his mother.[38] The second was a country house on a handsome sixty-acre plot overlooking Long Island Sound in Sands Point, Nassau County, some thirty miles from the city. This undeveloped parcel, far removed from the urbane resorts frequented by many of the Hamersleys' contemporaries, was to accommodate not only an important house, but also "stables and gardener's lodge and a whole lot of things usually following in the sequence of a country residence." Bruce Price, referred to in contemporary documents as the "builder" rather than the "architect" for the project, was at an early stage of a career that would bring him distinction as a seminal figure in the development of the indigenous American shingle style of architecture. He found Louis "a very agreeable client" with "a very pleasant manner" and met five or six times with him and his wife and father. Louis handled the business aspects of both undertakings but deferred to his wife on all facets of design development, including the arrangement of rooms and placement of windows.[39]

The tranquil pattern of the Hamersleys' life began to unravel in December 1882. After giving a dinner party noteworthy enough to be recorded in the annals of the 1882–83 New York season,[40] Louis and Lily went to visit Lily's family in Troy shortly before Christmas. While there, Louis developed bronchitis and was unwell enough that a doctor had to be called in. He seemed to recover but by early January was once again ailing, this time with pneumonia. He was ill for nearly a month, was usually feverish, and was delirious for a forty-eight-hour period—"the ordinary stage of the disease about the fourth or fifth day," according to Dr. Walter Gillette, his physician. Gillette was a new doctor for Louis, who previously had been a patient of the same family medical practitioner as his father. His specialty was "diseases of women," and Lily had earlier consulted him on her own behalf. Louis had called him in when his wife was ill in the fall and was apparently taken with his professional demeanor. In addition to the milk, beef tea, eggs, and toast that Gillette prescribed, he recommended that

Louis "be kept perfectly quiet; that no one should be permitted to see him but those who were in attendance upon him administering to his wants." Lily personally cared for her husband, rarely leaving his room.[41]

Louis was not told when his father was stricken with pneumonia and laid up on the floor below not long after the onset of his own illness. Gordon's doctor, too, issued a "no visitors" edict, and other family members and old friends were turned away from the Hamersley home. Following ten or twelve days during which he was attended by round-the-clock nurses and "very seldom had his reason," Gordon Hamersley died on 24 January 1883 at the age of seventy-seven.[42] The only familiar face to be seen at his bedside during his last days was that of Becky, his faithful housekeeper, who rarely slept during this dreadful period.[43] Louis was too weak to attend his father's funeral.

Louis mourned his father's death but was at the same time anxious about his own health. On Dr. Gillette's advice he and Lily went south. They left in February, traveling with a retinue that included a nurse, Lily's maid, and the valet/butler. Lily, in an unusual show of female autonomy, insisted that she hold the family purse strings during the trip, paying train fares and other expenses because, as she later explained, "I wanted to see if I could do it."[44] In assuming this role she exhibited what a French observer writing about American life noted as the "very singular . . . financial relations of man and wife . . . in this country, where the wife most frequently bears to her husband the relation of disbursing agent."[45]

The Hamersleys stopped in Washington and Atlanta on their way to the comfortable Uplands Hotel in Eastman, Georgia, a winter resort in a pine-forested region popular with those suffering from pulmonary complaints. Here Louis began to regain his strength. The talk in Georgia, his nurse later recalled, was all about the building of houses, and indeed this does seem to have been Louis's preoccupation at the time. He fired off a number of letters to Snook, the architect for his New York City home, about stair posts and molding details, doorknobs and furnace flues. He sent along a sketch of a griffin that he thought would "suit" a mantel if heightened considerably. He inquired about the difference in cost if he decided to put off building a stable adjoining the house until after he sold the lot next door, as he was afraid its presence might prejudice a sale. He expressed his eagerness to get back to work on both his building projects as soon as he returned home, but mentioned in confidence to a business associate that he and Lily, debarred from New York social life because they were in mourning for his father, planned to spend the following winter in Europe.[46]

Louis, Lily, and their attendants began the trip north from Georgia in mid-April. The weather in Eastman was growing warm and the region's winter resort season was at its end. From Washington, where the Hamersleys stopped for a few days, Dr. Gillette received an urgent summons from Lily. His patient was unwell again. Would he please come to Washington? The doctor did so, and found Louis half-dressed and lying on his bed. He complained of backache, loss of appetite, a general feeling of languor, and some slight fever. Despite his ailments, Louis rallied enough to spend two or three hours in the evening going over the plans of his new city house with his attending physician.[47]

Louis felt almost himself for a few days upon his return to New York, but then began a steady decline. He died on 8 May 1883, shortly before his forty-third birthday. The cause of death was given variously as typhoid fever or typho-malarial fever, a definition still used in the late nineteenth century to label a mixed infection that exhibited characteristics of both diseases. Ironically, it is likely that Louis contracted the disease that killed him in the health resort to which he had traveled to find respite from his earlier medical troubles. Many other guests at Eastman's Uplands Hotel were taken ill with symptoms suggestive of typhoid fever shortly before or after their April departure. The mortality rate for the disease, of which the causes were not well understood, was then somewhere between 10 and 15 percent, and most Eastman victims recovered. There was, however, at least one other death among the hotel's guests attributed to conditions at the hotel. Blame was assigned to two possible sources: the draining of some marshy land "and the laying bare to the rays of a hot sun of a large mass of vegetable matter that rapidly decomposed and sent out noxious vapors," and the hotel's cesspool, which emitted disagreeable odors in the vicinity of its outlet.[48] Dr. Gillette visited his patient two or three times daily during the two weeks of Louis's final illness.[49]

Lily was prostrated by her husband's death. She took to her bed, and when somewhat recovered, endeavored to spend as little time as possible in the house she had shared with Louis and his father. She passed several days with the Hamersley uncle and cousins next door before escaping to London in mid-June.[50] Louis's lawyer filed his client's will for probate on 18 May—and then Lily's legal troubles began.

CHAPTER 4

The Hamersley Will Case

Descendants of John Mason, Louis's maternal grandfather, had been aggrieved at the Mason will settlement of 1854 that assigned valuable Manhattan land parcels to Louis's father and to Louis. They seethed anew when they learned of Louis's will, a document that in essence excluded all members of the Mason family from any potential interest in the Hamersley estate. In July 1883, two months after the will was presented for probate, legal representatives of the extended Mason family filed notice that it would be contested. There was a great deal of money at stake. Louis's own assets of around $350,000 had been significantly augmented by his inheritance from his father, who left everything he had, valued at $2,838,000, outright to his son.[1] Thus Louis's estate amounted to something in the range of $3,200,000—much of it in steadily appreciating New York City real estate.

The background to the drawing up of the will submitted for probate, which promptly came to light, can only have given the contestants hope. For Louis's final will had been executed on 10 February, less than three months prior to his death and shortly before his and Lily's departure for Georgia. More importantly, as far as the contestants were concerned, it differed in almost every respect from a will in preparation on Louis's behalf drafted two months earlier, before the death of his father. Two different versions of the unsigned early will, along with the interlineations and marginal jottings of both Louis and the longtime family lawyer who drew it up, were entered into evidence during the subsequent court proceeding.

The terms of Louis's early will varied from draft to draft and were complicated in the ways that only testamentary documents can be. The testator's first consideration was to insure his wife's support in widowhood. According to one draft she was to have the income of the sum of $200,000 during "the rest of her natural life or during her widowhood" and of $400,000 if Louis's father's death preceded his own. Another draft generously bequeathed to Lily either of these sums outright "as the case may be" if she married again—"to be taken and be accepted by her in lieu and bar of dower and of every other right or claim to my estate both real and personal."[2] The right of "dower" mentioned here was a vital consideration, for embedded in early common law and guaranteed by statute in New York and most other states was a widow's right to at least a lifetime interest in one-third of her husband's estate. Thus if Lily exercised her dower right, she was destined, no matter what the exact stipulations of her husband's will, to become a comfortably well-to-do woman.

The eventual beneficiaries of Louis's wealth were to be his as yet unborn children—in particular, his male children, who would carry forward the Hamersley name. In one draft, his real estate and personal property were to go into trust for the use of his father and then of Lily, who was to enjoy them until the coming of age of the youngest of his children who lived to attain the age of twenty-one. ("All wrong" was written in the margin next to this entry.) Daughters were each to receive $100,000 by the terms of Louis's draft wills. The residue of his estate, which presumably would be in the range of several million dollars by the time of his eventual death, was to be divided equally among his sons, unless he had no sons, in which case it was to be divided among his daughters. If one of his children died leaving children they were to receive shares in proportion to their parent's share.[3]

Hopes for a possible inheritance as far as the Mason family contestants were concerned were vested in the next clause of the early will drafts. This passage stipulated that, if no children were born to Louis and Lily, generous lump sum payments or trusts were to go to assorted Hamersley, Mason, and Jones cousins. The residue was to benefit his cousin James Hooker Hamersley, known as Hooker, who was to have the use of its income during his life. Upon his death everything was to be divided equally among Hooker's male children. Should Hooker have no sons, the principal was to go to charities affiliated with the Episcopal Church. As his sole executor Louis named in his early will drafts his father. If his father were unable to fill this role the executor was to be his uncle John Hamersley, and then his cousin Hooker.[4]

The signed will of 10 February evidenced few of the intricacies exhibited in the drafts of the earlier will, but managed to stun everyone in its simplicity. Besides the formulaic opening and closing lines, this will was only three paragraphs in length and left *all* of Louis's estate in trust for "the use of my dear wife during her natural life." On Lily's death the estate was to go directly to Louis and Lily's children and their descendants. In the event that the couple had no children, his money was to go to the male issue of his cousin Hooker "then living and to the male issue of such of them as shall have previously died." Should his cousin have no sons "him surviving or surviving my wife, then on the decease of my wife I give devise and bequeath the whole of my said estate real and personal to such charitable and benevolent corporations located in the State of New York . . . as my dear wife shall by her last will and testament . . . designate." As in his father's will, there were no other dispositions: no small monetary gifts or personal effects left to friends or relatives, no charitable bequests, no lump sum payments or annuities to loyal servants. Named as executors and trustees were Lily; George Williams, president of the Chemical Bank; and Jacob Lockman, the lawyer who had served Louis and his father in real estate matters and had prepared Louis's final will document.[5]

Louis had a favorite saying: "Them's my sentiments."[6] In drawing up his last will he expressed his sentiments in the most passionate way he knew how. He loved his wife, wanted her to benefit from his wealth, and had immense confidence in her judgment. If, by chance, he and Lily remained childless, he wished to perpetuate the family name, and the only means of doing so was through Hooker, his one Hamersley male cousin—although at the age of forty Hooker was still a bachelor and seemed intent on remaining so. His father's death had given Louis freedom to follow his inclinations without fear of showing disrespect, and he had done so.

Louis's will was judged to be both odd and unorthodox. It was considered so primarily because the testator's death occurred so shortly after its execution and because the possibilities it anticipated carried into such an uncertain future. Mason family members, who felt that they had a standing claim on Louis's assets, were understandably affronted that a bride without children and married for less than four years should for the rest of her conceivably long life harvest all the benefits of what they still thought of as Mason wealth. But what galled them most was being cut out of Louis's estate altogether thanks to the so-called "charitable clause": Louis's instructions for disposition of his large fortune to charity if his Hamersley cousin had no male heirs at the time of Lily's death. Louis hated notoriety. Had he known the trouble this clause would precipitate, he might have acted differently.

New Yorkers in the Hamersleys' social milieu were rarely in the habit of giving for philanthropic causes. William H. Vanderbilt, for example, allotted three-quarters of 1 percent of his $200 million estate to philanthropy in 1885, while William Backhouse Astor, Jr. willed $145,000—one-third of 1 percent of his fortune—to public service organizations when he died in 1892.[7] To disregard family and throw away wealth in the manner Louis had chosen was an insult of inconceivable proportions. Thus there were sixteen angry members of the far-flung Mason clan who entered into the legal contest to break Louis's will.

Family pride could hardly be deemed sufficient reason to invalidate a properly executed will, nor could family greed. The Mason lawyers therefore advanced fanciful arguments to justify their legal action that were ruthlessly cruel to both Louis's memory and to the reputation of his wife. They unashamedly argued "that at the time of the alleged execution of said paper writing, the testator, Louis C. Hamersley, did not have testamentary capacity, and was not competent to make a will." They also claimed "that said paper writing was not the free act of the said testator, but was procured by undue influence practiced against and upon said testator by some person or persons unknown to these contestants." Other arguments were based on technicalities: that Louis did not orally declare the questionable document to be his last will and testament; that he did not specifically ask the appointed witnesses to sign it.[8] The case opened before Judge Daniel G. Rollins in the New York City division of the New York State Surrogate's Court in March 1884. In twenty court days over the course of the next fourteen months, during which thirty-eight subpoenaed witnesses were interrogated, the contestants' lawyers tried to make their case.

Louis's cousin Hooker, concerned that by its suit the Mason family might succeed in wresting "the entire Hamersley patrimony from the Hamersleys," requested early in the proceeding through his lawyer to join the lawsuit as another plaintiff. He felt entitled to a generous share of Louis's estate as the universal devisee and legatee named by his cousin in an 1876 will—a will predating Louis's marriage that Hooker brazenly maintained would still be valid if it hadn't been destroyed by Louis's designing wife. As for his cousin's final will, the one filed for probate, Hooker's attorney stated his opinion that Mrs. Hamersley must have dictated it to a reluctant husband. "I think that it is not difficult," he insisted, "in the mere provisions of this instrument to see a woman's hand. Upon its face it is woman's work."[9] The surrogate court judge denied Hooker's appeal to join the case. Hooker's father, Louis's uncle John Hamersley, who had never had any differences with Lily during her marriage, announced himself in favor of probating the will. He did, however, appear in court to request that the judge "construe" or interpret the meaning of the offensive charitable clause, a clause he considered "too vague, indefinite, uncertain and general to permit legal effect to be given to it."[10]

There were witnesses called upon during the course of the will hearing prepared to volunteer that Louis was "dull," that "his mind was such as to render him liable to be dominated by a superior mind," that he gave in and did everything that Lily asked him to do. Their testimony was countered by that of advocates eager to speak to Louis's towering intelligence and self-assertiveness. There were those who were comfortable in suggesting that Lily emotionally abused Louis, that she intentionally isolated son from father and from other family members, and that she was likely to have lied to Louis about the impending birth of a child.[11] This last accusation could only have been painful to Lily, for it was suggested more than a decade later that she had suffered at least one failed pregnancy during her first marriage.[12] (It was this, perhaps, that had first driven her to seek the services of Dr. Gillette, the medical specialist in diseases of women.) Pregnancy was, however, a taboo subject in polite society during the late nineteenth century, a period when pregnant women were expected, at least during the latter half of pregnancy, to live in retirement and to avoid "for the sake of decency" gatherings at which young people might be present.[13] Lily made no attempt to defend herself against the allegation, nor did she overtly refute any of the other charges against her.

Several reluctant witnesses could barely conceal their contempt for the legal proceeding and wearied of the repeated intimations as to the testator's diminished mental capacity and Lily's diabolical influence over her husband. One, in response to an attorney's insinuating query as to whether he had ever heard Lily call Louis names, blandly replied, "She called him Carré or Louis." The lawyer, not at all satisfied with this response, tried again. "Have you ever heard her use epithets in reference to him—calling him a fool?" "Don't be a goose," answered the witness agreeably. "I have heard that." A clerk in the office of the lawyer who drew up the final will, and who had been called upon to witness its signing in the Hamersley home, impatiently insisted that Mr. Hamersley "was just like everyone else. He didn't fly around the room or anything."[14] It was an uphill battle for the contestants' legal team.

Lily herself was called into court on 30 April. She entered the hearing room on the arm of her father and took the witness stand, looking tall and stately, beautiful, and very pale in her deep mourning. According to reporters who eagerly followed the case, she fanned herself feebly with a black fan, "exhibited unmistakable tokens of recent suffering," "frequently leaned her head wearily against the stone pillar back of her, and seemed as if about to faint." She revived quickly, however, and gave her testimony in a "refined and ladylike" voice, speaking so low that she sometimes needed to repeat herself in order to be heard. Twice she was overcome by emotion and had to pause to recover; during one breakdown, she retired to a side room in the company of Dr. Gillette, who attended her at the hearing, and took a reviving dose of medication from a vial he offered. Despite her apparent fragility, Lily's face was characterized by one newsman as "strong," with "fearless" eyes and a mouth that "indicates firmness and decision of character." The witness was inclined, he added, to gaze defiantly at a questioning lawyer and "confined herself . . . to somewhat curt, but amply responsive, answers to the interrogations of counsel."[15] The questions put to her were courteous enough, and were designed to elicit details of the Hamersley family's last months together and Lily's knowledge of previous wills drawn up on Louis's behalf.

Journalistic accounts contrasting Lily's apparent emotional and physical vulnerability with her expressions of calculated resolve suggest that there may have been an element of self-dramatization in Lily's court performance. Obviously, she was in a difficult position, and needed to express grief in an era when physical weakness and fainting were the expected responses of women under stress. At the same time, the occasion demanded that she exhibit righteousness, candor, self-confidence, and a determination to see to it that Louis's last wishes were carried out. She reconciled the contradictions; the effectiveness of her presentation can be judged from the limited press notice it received.

Lily was also lucky, for her day in court coincided with the first appearance of another witness: Becky Jones, the loyal Hamersley housekeeper. From that point on it would be Becky who, from the newspaper reporters' point of view, was the star attraction and focus of public interest in the proceeding.

Becky had been hard to find. She didn't want to be in court and despite having been subpoenaed failed to appear. New York policemen were sent to her home in upstate New York to escort her back to the city, but Becky eluded them. It was some time before they were able to locate her hiding out in a granary in Saratoga, and even then, she didn't acquiesce meekly. On the train ride to New York City, Becky recalled in her autobiography, she tried to escape. Deceptively leaving her small parcel containing one calico dress on the car seat when her captors "went out to have a smoke," she "walked along leisurely as if going to the toilet and everything was well so I opened the car door and made out down on the steps and gathered my skirts as close as possible and jumped. And when I landed I was in the rail road ditch in mud to my knees. It was an awful shake up but I came out all right."[16] Despite her valiant efforts to evade capture, this sixty-two-year-old fireball was now called as an unwilling witness on behalf of the Mason contestants.

Becky was a verbal caricaturist's dream. She was portrayed as dressed in a black silk dress. "Her hands were encased in black kid gloves; in one she held a large black fan and in the other a book entitled 'A Christian's Secret; or a Happy Life.'" Physically, it was noted, "she is small in stature, her face is angular and her nose is peaked. Her quick, jerky movements, the sharp manner of delivering her words and the expression of mingled cunning and flightiness which rested on her features made her appear not unlike Dickens's Miss Flite, who used to haunt the court during the trial of the famous case of Jarndyce vs. Jarndyce" in Dickens's novel *Bleak House*.[17]

Despite the drama of her chase and capture, Becky's spirit was far from broken when she was introduced into the courtroom. She stated her name, as required. She swore to tell the truth, as required. Then she kept going. "I will tell the truth," she announced,

> what I say shall be the truth and nothing but the truth; but I shall not say anything. . . . I will tell you what I have to say; I am going to say and do just what I know Mr. Gordon and his son, if they were here to speak, would tell me; he would say, "Becky, keep still," and I am going to do so; it is no use asking me any questions for I will not answer you. . . . I respect the dead and I will not say anything. . . . The idea of bringing an old woman like me to testify; I ain't going to, and that is all there is about it.[18]

The surrogate judge and lawyers representing both sides of the case puzzled over Becky's unwillingness to fulfill her legal obligations. Whether she had "taken the position that she has taken out of sheer obstinacy and mistaken fidelity and devotion, or whether as the result of some serious mental disturbance" couldn't be determined. Reasoning that perhaps Becky could be induced to testify "from the persuasion and at the instance of persons whom she regards as friendly to her,"[19] Lily was asked to write to Becky, which she did. She began by sympathizing with Becky's distress, adding that her own appearance on the witness stand had been one of the hardest things she had ever done. "I know," she continued,

> what those in the court-room to-day did not know, that your wish not to talk is because you honestly believe father and Mr. Louis would not wish it. I am sure this is your reason, but remember, Becky, that your duty to them, to their memories, is that you do your duty to me. And it is not right to make the court think, as they may, that I have asked you to keep silent, you and I know this is not true, but others might think so.
>
> When you go to Court again, Becky, answer quietly and truthfully the questions put to you.[20]

Becky would have none of it. She barely glanced at Lily's note, claiming that she "never could read Mrs. Hamersley's handwriting," and the letter had to be read privately to her by the contestants' counsel.[21] Still she refused to cooperate. She was threatened with imprisonment for contempt of court, but as "her little black eyes glittered defiantly," she declined to add another word. On 19 May Becky was unceremoniously escorted from the courtroom and taken off to "the common jail until she purge herself of contempt." Before her departure, the "contumacious" witness thanked the surrogate judge for her sentence, adding, "I am so glad I am going to get out of the lawyers' way at last."[22] She would remain in prison for the next forty-two weeks.

Becky continued to be an on-going source of news for the journalistic corps during her incarceration. She eagerly followed the proceeding and was decidedly more forthcoming in the presence of reporters than she had been in the courtroom. She was caustic in her comments about the Hamersley family who lived next door to her employers, particularly when it came to Louis's cousin Hooker. "That little goat," she called him. "I'd like to tell what I know about him. Do you know that before the case came to trial at all I was given a paper with what they wanted me to testify to written on it?" "If I should testify," she added cryptically, "if they only knew it—it wouldn't do them any good. I would do 'em all harm."[23]

What Becky might have said never came to light. Her autobiography concluded with the theatrical account of her effort to evade the officers sent to escort her to New York and the will hearing. It appears, however, from her courtroom responses and from reported conversations with journalists that there were no particular family secrets Becky had to impart. She simply chose to abide by Gordon Hamersley's frequent reminder to her to "keep your tongue still. Don't let it wag about family matters."[24] Nor did Becky ever let on as to what she thought of Lily, although the two women seem to have been on good terms. One of Gordon's end-of-life nurses recalled that while she was in the gloomy Hamersley household its young mistress "was always talking to Becky whenever I saw her," and Becky's only recorded reference to Lily in the press was entirely respectful—that she had heard that "Mrs. Louis C. Hamersley will never go to court again. I don't blame her," she added. "I'd rather stay here forever than to go there again."[25]

The Hamersley housekeeper appears to have quite enjoyed the months she passed in prison. She was comfortably housed, was a center of attention, and royally received her journalist and other visitors. She had her portrait painted—commissioned and paid for by the press corps. She had the run of the jail and was always popping into the kitchen to talk with the cook. News stories included details of her cell décor, of her companionable cat, and of her meals, such as a breakfast of "raspberries and cream, one loaf home-made bread, five hot rolls, three hard-boiled eggs, two cups of Java coffee, large sirloin steak and a glass of country milk," all of which were consumed "ravenously." Becky's loyalty struck a chord with the public and she received a quantity of letters, most of them from women. One, which she showed to a reporter, was signed by "three lady friends in Philadelphia" who lamented that there were not "more like her. They said she was an honor to her sex, and they were glad she had gone to jail, instead of giving in. . . . 'For such pluck as yours,' they wrote, 'signed the Declaration of Independence and threw the tea into the water at Boston.'" Becky appreciated the expressed sentiment, although "she shuddered at the thought of throwing away good tea."[26]

The months of Becky's imprisonment bestowed on her a status

that she had never before experienced. On 28 March 1885 she was released from prison on order of the General Term Supreme Court and quietly vanished. As a lawyer for the contestants in the case conceded, "he did not know where she was, nor did he care to know."[27]

Although Becky had had nothing to say against Lily, one court witness threw out a few hints suggesting that the honeymoon period of Lily and Louis's marriage might have been over by the time of Louis's death. This was William Spiegler, Gordon's German valet and butler, who had spent two years in the family household. It is hard to think of a reason why twenty-five-year-old Spiegler would have wanted to weaken Lily's case unless it was, perhaps, general pique, as he had been let go by Louis during his and Lily's Georgia sojourn because Louis felt little need for a valet. What Spiegler had to say did not cast Lily in an altogether flattering light. He implied that he had been privy to some disagreements between husband and wife and recounted that in their last winter together he had heard Lily tell her husband to "shut up" more than once at the dinner table, a directive that Louis obeyed. He had also seen her destroy some of Louis's little "tablegrams" to his father, "chuck[ing] them in the fire or in the fire-place to be swept up." Spiegler thought that the relevant conversations in both cases dwelt on "property" matters, and it is possible that Lily had wearied of the Hamersley men's single-minded preoccupation with business. More injurious to Lily's cause was what Spiegler claimed to have overheard Louis tell his father one morning when they were alone at breakfast: "that he was obliged to give up to his wife for peace sake, and that he could not stand it any longer."[28] While it is impossible to know what issues might have arisen between Louis and Lily, it is likely that they had something to do with money.

Another of Spiegler's overheard conversations purportedly related to Louis's will, and Lily's recommendation to her husband that he "leave $50,000 for charitable purposes all told."[29] In eliciting this statement the contestants' lawyers were trying to make the point that Louis discussed his will with his wife and that she exerted excessive influence on the final product. What it demonstrated was that she had been brought up in a philanthropically inclined family and that she had absorbed its values. Had Louis included that figure in his will it would have amounted to 1.57 percent of what Louis left behind—more than twice the amount assigned to charity in the will of William Vanderbilt. Lily's suggestions in this instance were possibly what motivated Louis to leave all charitable decisions to Lily in the unlikely event that there were no Hamersley children.

Spiegler was the last witness to appear in the will proceeding. His insinuations made little difference to the case's outcome, for after going to such trouble and expense, the Mason family contestants lost their battle. Judge Rollins determined in January 1886 that the original terms of the will were valid, and the document was approved for admission to probate. This announcement turned out to be premature, as the death of a legal guardian of minor contestants meant that the case had to be reopened until a new guardian was appointed. But the satisfactory outcome of the case for Lily now seemed assured, and in June the will was again formally approved for probate. Surrogate Rollins rejected all of the contestants' arguments about Louis's mental capacity to make a will and the physical conditions under which the will was executed. He rejected, too, the allegation of "undue influence" on Lily's part that might have determined will provisions. "The mere influence of affection and regard," opined Rollins, "can not suffice to invalidate a testamentary paper. . . . It is manifestly one of the paramount objects of the statute [of wills] to afford full and free opportunity for the influences of affection and regard to display themselves. If the very existence of those motives to the bestowal of testamentary bounty must be held to make such bestowal illegal and invalid, the statute is self-contradictory and preposterous."[30]

Rollins also dismissed the Masons' and John Hamersley's requests to construe the clause authorizing Lily to name charities that would benefit from Louis's wealth after her death should Hooker Hamersley have no son. This was in line with the position of George De Witt, who represented the executors named by Louis to administer his estate and argued that the court should not anticipate difficulties and "decide upon contingencies that may never occur." It seemed obvious to everyone that, no matter what ruling was made in regard to Lily's access to Louis's estate, the will would come again before the Surrogate's Court upon her death and that any attempt to settle secondary issues now would be a waste of time. "In any way we can look at it," contended De Witt, "a construction now is of no advantage to any one, unless the delay which must arise from such a course will be of some satisfaction if not advantage to the Contestants. Indeed, it seems to me that delay is the object sought for by the Contestants' counsel. They seem possessed of a vindictive desire to prevent Mrs. Hamersley from enjoying her Estate."[31]

The judge's decision did not mean that the will dispute quietly faded away. An appeal on behalf of several of the contestants was promptly lodged with the State Court of Appeals, but the Surrogate's Court directed the estate executors to exercise all the powers and authority of executors in an ordinary case while it was pending. An out-of-court financial settlement of what was believed to be around $100,000 eventually encouraged most of the contestants to drop their litigation,[32] but as late as December 1890 individual members of the Mason family continued to press their claims in the hope of receiving some kind of handout. Until these contests were resolved, it was necessary for Lily to undergo the legal formality of publicly requesting Surrogate's Court approval for each disbursement from estate income. By December 1886 she had applied for and received three lump sum payments of $75,000, $25,000, and $50,000.[33] There would not be a final settlement of the estate until 1891.

CHAPTER 5

New York Widow

ᴊᴏ

Lily, who had gone into mourning with her husband after the loss of Louis's father, naturally took up the trappings of this social ritual on her own behalf as a grieving widow. Despite increasing support for less ritualized demonstrations of mourning, visible manifestations of sorrow and respect for the dead were still generally expected from the bereaved. Abby Longstreet, author of a frequently updated guide to social etiquette in New York, recommended that widows assume mourning garb for a full year after the death of a husband—attire that would include a black dress of the plainest crepe and a little black crepe cap bordered in white. "During three months her long veil is worn to conceal her face," instructed Longstreet. "Afterward, she may wear a short tulle veil, with her crepe drapery thrown backward." Widows could display this extreme expression of respect as long as they chose, counseled Longstreet. "In New York, widows seldom dress in gay colors, and not a few of them wear only black dresses as long as they live, or until they are again wedded."[1]

As an old-fashioned woman who sincerely mourned her husband, Lily followed tradition and dressed in black. She also eschewed social life in keeping with the guidance of etiquette advisors who counseled, "usually two years are devoted to a more or less severe exclusion from general society."[2] The bereaved widow detached herself so completely from New York City social life during the next two-and-a-half years, in fact, that little is known about her activities except that she was frequently unwell and that she spent her summers in Europe.

Lily made one grand gesture in the early months of her widowhood. This was the promise of a memorial altar honoring her late husband for a new cathedral being planned as the focal point of a recently split-off Episcopal diocese in Albany, the capital of New York State. The cathedral project was the brainchild of Bishop William Croswell Doane, a powerful high-church prelate who had been assigned to administer the new diocese in 1869. Doane envisioned a house of worship in the manner and on the scale of the great Gothic cathedrals of Europe, and Lily's projected gift was a fitting tribute to Louis Hamersley as well as a token of Lily's religious faith. The letter outlining her commitment was sealed with other documents behind the cornerstone of the new cathedral, laid in June 1884.[3]

Hooker Hamersley, Louis's cousin, came in for a good deal of good-natured ribbing and press attention following Louis's death thanks to the wording of Louis's will. Born in 1844, Hooker was amiable, mild-mannered, and widely traveled—having visited nearly all of the capitals of Europe by the age of twelve. An 1865 honors graduate of Columbia University, he held a law degree from the same institution. After practicing for ten years he gave up his legal career in order to oversee his family's own substantial wealth, to devote himself to philanthropic activities, and to write, attracting favorable notice with a book of poems labeled a "minor work" by reviewers.[4] But in order to benefit, albeit indirectly, from Louis's will, Hooker had to marry and sire a son. "His people, in the most artfully artless way," it was said, threw "the prettiest and sweetest of the debutantes in his way" but had little success "in persuading him to abandon celibacy."[5] It was, of course, news when Hooker Hamersley took a wife in 1888, some five years after the death of his cousin. Two children were born to the newlyweds in short order, but, alas, they were daughters (one of whom died in infancy), and it was not until 1892 that the arrival of a son, Louis Gordon Hamersley, relieved Hooker of the private and public pressures to reproduce that had bedeviled him for nearly a decade. After that it was his own and his wife's social comings and goings as well as his good works that brought him into the public eye.

Hooker's fatherhood afforded Lily a certain relief in deflecting the attentions of charitable societies hoping to be included among her beneficiaries if Hooker remained without a male heir. "Every day's mail," reported one newspaper in 1886, carries to her documents setting forth the goodness of some hospital, church, mission, or other charity institution. She receives the printed reports of all the Bible, tract, and missionary corporations; sermons in pamphlet form pour in on her; marked papers from the professional revivalists inform her of the wonders of their works; and there seems to be a general determination that she shall not lack for information as to where the fortune would do the most good.[6]

The article listed Lily's postal address. "She might not see all the mail matter," it concluded mischievously, "but it would be there all the same."[7]

Becky Jones continued to crop up as a newspaper personality thanks to the notoriety she had garnered in the will contest. She retired to Ballston Spa and settled into Cozy Castle, the home purchased with her savings in which she generously housed a number of relatives over the years. Becky was a giving friend to those who knew her, but the circumstances surrounding her past act of loyalty to the Hamersleys led to a local perception of her as an oddball—even as something of a witch. This caused Becky to steadily retreat into herself and made more conspicuous her growing eccentricities. Her outdated clothing was a subject of gossip, as was the unusual paint scheme—red, yellow, white, and black—she selected for her parlor and sitting room. She was laughed at for her habits of wearing differently colored stockings on each leg and of daily alternating her shoes from one foot to the other to distribute wear. She was ridiculed for her delight in attending funerals, no matter whether she knew the deceased or not, and for always carrying an onion in her handkerchief so as to be sure of crying on cue.[8] She was reported to have turned down a fifty-dollar-a-week offer to undertake a lecture tour after her months in prison (which Becky thought ought more accurately to have been labeled a "preaching" tour).[9] This led a number of her neighbors to the conclusion that she must have received a large bribe to insure her silence during the will contest, and Ballston Spa boys were not averse to digging around her yard in search of her supposed fortune.

Becky lived comfortably, even traveling on her own to Europe in

1889. It was assumed that, if she had not accepted any bribes, then she must have been left a generous annuity by her Hamersley employers. This, as we have seen, was not the case. Yet Becky did receive checks on a regular basis for the rest of her life.[10] Since they did not come from the Hamersley estate, one can only assume that it was Lily who personally saw to the needs of the old family retainer in providing Becky with the financial security not directly bestowed on her by either Hamersley father or son. It was, indeed, her due.

In 1892 Becky merrily divulged to a *New York Times* reporter that upon her death her tombstone was to read, "Rebecca Jones, better known as the Obstinate Becky," and when she died, in 1905, those were approximately the words carved upon the tablet marking her grave. The final chapter of her story was written in 1922, when an envelope addressed to the postmaster arrived in Ballston Spa instructing the recipient to "hand this letter to any relative of the late Miss Becky Jones—a sister, a nephew if one be living." The correspondent, who then owned the oil portrait of Becky commissioned by the press during her months in prison, wanted to entrust this memento to its subject's family before her own death.[11] The painting was passed along to a nephew of Becky's and is now in the collection of the Saratoga County Historical Society.

Lily's great aunt Phebe Tayloe, who had so often provided a home for Lily, died in Troy in November 1884. She had been in failing health for three years and relocated to the city of her birth where she was cared for by Lily's mother, Elizabeth Price. The *Washington Post* observed in recording her passing that Mrs. Tayloe's death "closes the doors of a house that have stood open for more than half a century for the elite and crème de la crème of Washington, and of the prominent and distinguished men and women who have played the most important part in its history during that time, to enter and enjoy its elegant hospitality."[12]

Mrs. Tayloe's death set in motion the execution of an agreement she had negotiated in the 1870s with her stepchildren as a memorial to her late husband by which most of the treasures in the Tayloe home were donated to the Corcoran Gallery of Art, the Washington museum founded in 1869 by the couple's friend William Corcoran. Mrs. Tayloe left $10,000 in her will to maintain the earmarked items and to facilitate their relocation to the Corcoran, where they were to be kept "apart from other works of art" and designated as the Ogle Tayloe Collection. One hundred and eighty-six articles were individually itemized in a catalog of the collection published by the gallery in 1895, which also lumped together an agglomeration of "Coins, Medals, Cameos, and Curios, exhibited in Cases."[13] Other bequests, including real estate, went to Mrs. Tayloe's stepchildren and their descendants; $10,000 was set aside to fund two Christian education scholarships within the Society for the Increase of Ministry of the Protestant Episcopal Church. Lily's mother was named as her aunt's executor and residual legatee.[14]

Elizabeth Price was punctilious in fulfilling her obligations as executor of Mrs. Tayloe's estate—to the extent of insisting in 1900 upon the return of the Tayloe Collection by the Corcoran Gallery to the originally assigned Tayloe heirs. The justification for her petition was that, contrary to Mrs. Tayloe's wishes and stipulations, the items were not exhibited in a designated gallery and not all items included in the donation were on public display. In 1902 the gallery relinquished the collection to Mrs. Price for redistribution, keeping by negotiated agreement only two paintings—one of them a celebrated Gilbert Stuart portrait of George Washington.[15]

Lily faced unusual difficulties in determining how to reestablish herself socially after the period of seclusion she observed following Louis's death. For one thing, she had to contend with the on-going antagonism of her late husband's relatives, who represented a powerful segment of New York society and continued to express their fury at the outcome of the drawn-out will case. For another, the innuendos thrown out regarding her character as well as the outright accusations of deceit and manipulation leveled against her during the will proceeding had inevitably undermined her social standing. The hearing had been even more damaging to the memory of Louis Hamersley. Malicious words and phrases used by family members to represent him as mentally incompetent in their effort to break the will were gleefully reiterated in the press and came to define this private, gentle man in the absence of more tangible biographical data. It is time the record was set aright.

The timing of Lily's public reappearance in the New York milieu that had become her home was dictated by the conclusion of the court case, the validation of the original terms of the will, and its initial approval for probate in January 1886. She was spotted at the opera for the first time after her husband's death in February of that year, dressed in black, and was present at almost every evening performance during the last weeks of the season. But, for the most part, Lily continued to avoid society. She confined her early activities to benevolent work: serving on women's committees with good deeds on their agendas and socially impeccable ladies on their rosters. Thus she tried to strengthen and extend her network among the upper-class women who powered the city's elite, knowing that their support would be crucial in the more rigorous assault of the social ramparts she hoped to undertake later on.

Lily's name turned up on two committee lists in March. She was recorded as one of several "lady managers" of the New-York Cooking School, an institution with a three-pronged mission: to initiate society women into the mysteries of consommé *à la royale*, baked carp with Spanish sauce, and apple meringues; to instruct the wives and daughters of working men in plain cooking; and to prepare girls for domestic service.[16] Although the school's emphasis on training servants implied a conservative grasp of the working potential of lower-class women, the endeavor was well-intentioned, and as a philanthropic undertaking was a typical effort to effect social progress at this time. Lily's involvement appears to have been short-lived; her name did not appear again in connection with the school.

Lily was also among the "ladies prominent in New-York society" who constituted the patronesses of a March flower show organized by a society florist to garner publicity for himself and to benefit a few unspecified charities. The extravaganza, held at the Metropolitan Opera House, was described in the press as "the most beautiful and artistic flower show the metropolis has ever seen."[17] Lily had been asked to lend her name to the event because she, like the show's other patronesses, owned—or was the wife of an owner of—one of the house's fashionable opera boxes.

The Metropolitan Opera House had achieved preeminence not long after it opened in the autumn of 1883—swiftly eclipsing the rival Academy of Music in social prestige and forcing the academy to close in 1885. The combined wealth of the Metropolitan's box-owners and their willingness to spend it drove the house's success, and it was the opportunity to parade one's social ascendancy, more than love of music, that stimulated most benefactors' financial largesse. True opera lovers complained about the behavior of well-heeled patrons perched in the boxes bordering the auditorium: their tendency to arrive late at performances, to leave early, and to chatter through everything except the most show-stopping of arias.[18] But management had made a Mephistophelian bargain with its wealthiest backers—social exposure in exchange for monetary support—and the organization could not survive without them.

Lily had not relinquished box number thirty-three, the one assigned to Louis as an original stockholder in the opera house, during her widowhood. Having rented it out by the season to recoup expenses, she now found it useful as a social launching pad. The occasion she chose to do so was the opening night of the 1886–87 opera season when, ensconced in her box, she advertised herself overtly for the first time as a rich and marriageable widow.

"The opera box is used as a key to open many doors," pronounced New York's *Town Topics*,[19] the most widely read society paper in the country at the time. Indeed, being seen in a well-placed box in the 1880s was perhaps the most certain means for a woman to validate her high standing in the fluid and intrinsically competitive world of New York City's upper class. Boxes "created a frame around their occupants, drawing attention to their social status."[20] They also afforded a setting for the public parading of wealth through the wearing of elaborate clothing and jewelry, as "full toilet" was *de rigueur* in this section of the auditorium; a woman seated there not in evening dress, cautioned a popular guide to social etiquette, "would appear like an ugly weed in a gay garden of brilliant blossoms."[21] Showing themselves in boxes also increased the likelihood of affluent women's becoming subjects of interest to reporters who were now expanding the role of society journalism in the public press.

It has been argued that the "society page," which experienced a contents revolution during the last two decades of the nineteenth century, invented "society."[22] Generations of discreet newspaper jottings about upper-class social life suddenly gave way to a more aggressive style of reporting fueled, in part, by the influx into large cities and resorts like Newport "of unprecedented numbers of new millionaires not well enough brought up to deplore the uses of publicity."[23] The urban aristocracy, spurred to do so by its newer members, made itself an object of mass interest, and newspaper coverage of its doings stimulated an increase in circulation. At the same time, journalistic attention created the kind of idealized society figures that in our day would be called celebrities and publicly endorsed conspicuous displays of consumption.[24] The battle was "not so much to the strong as to the best-advertised,"[25] and women were particularly adept at polishing their means of self-presentation—clothing themselves in interesting personalities and novel departures in dress to attract journalistic attention.[26] They tried to exercise control over what appeared in print (and some among them were known to collect fees for the "pars" or paragraphs they provided to newspapers and journals about society's doings),[27] but their romancing of the press also put them at risk of attracting unwanted scrutiny. Like tightrope walkers, the publicity-conscious tried to maintain balance in a precarious milieu that required self-discipline, good judgment, and flair. Lily proved to have all three.

The opening performance of the opera season was a gala event on the New York social calendar. "To-morrow night the Metropolitan Opera-House will blaze with glory," effused a journalist on 7 November 1886. "Every prospect foreshadows a season of exceptional success, artistic and social." To enable members of the elite to recognize one another, and to give other opera-goers a key to the collective comings and goings of those in the rarefied ranks of box-holders, newspapers published floor plans of the socially important parterre and first tiers in the opera house indicating the names and box numbers of their assigned occupants. Lily's box denoted prize seating and was sandwiched between the boxes of Cornelius Vanderbilt II, head of the New York Central Railroad, and Charles Crocker, Troy-born but California-based founder of the Central Pacific Railroad. Lily's cousin George Henry Warren owned two boxes for the accommodation of his family and their guests.[28]

"One cannot sit in an orchestra seat at the Metropolitan without feeling somewhat like an astronomer," noted one observer. Up above, "all the bright, particular stars shone in the social firmament,"[29] and individual recognition was given to those whom journalists felt it was warranted. One star singled out on this opening night was Mrs. Louis Hamersley, who looked "remarkably handsome."[30] Benefiting from the magical effect of flickering gaslight on fabrics and jewels, she appeared "fairly dazzling in a low cut gray satin gown that glimmered and glistened like silver, while she wore around her lily-like throat three strings of priceless pearls and a necklace of diamonds, each stone as big as a hazelnut."[31] Like other box owners and occupants, Lily had decorated the interior of her box as well as the anteroom that connected it to the public corridor at its rear and served as a reception room for male visitors between acts. These efforts, too, came in for praise. Her box was reported to be a model of luxuriance, having "been fitted up in a most gorgeous way with crimson hangings, rich tapestries, palms and ferns and sconces, wherein burned wax candles." The tiny parlor behind it—"a centre of attraction to the young men present"—featured walls freshly hung with rare flowers and an elaborately carved combination of sideboard and icebox that yielded up wines for the enjoyment of her guests.[32]

The sensation caused by Lily's opening-night opera debut was not a fluke, and society reporters continued to single her out and to describe what she wore at subsequent opera performances. As a special correspondent for the *Washington Post* observed on 21 November, "It may seem a rashly sweeping and conclusive assertion, but I am conscientiously going to make it. The most beautiful woman in New

York fashionable society is the Widow Hamersley. All the other belles commonly mentioned as beauties are merely pretty . . . but Mrs. Louis C. Hamersley has come forth at the opening of the present season as a specimen of perfect loveliness." It was not simply "her perfection of face and form" that warranted admiration. "Her costumes are wonders of artistic construction, and she has not yet worn one of them twice. Her jewels, too, have thus far been changed every night. I do not recall," continued the *Post*'s correspondent, "an instance of costlier or more elaborate toilet preparation for a social season in New York by any belle, and if she carries through the winter's succession of balls, receptions and dinners the policy which she has thus far pursued at the opera, she will by spring become the most celebrated woman in America. She has evidently gone in for a great triumph."[33]

Lily could not count solely on haphazard press coverage to get her name before the public during the 1886–87 winter of her yearned-for social rebirth. To increase her chances of success, she assiduously followed what were becoming established rules of self-promotion among those seeking to assert high social status by informing newspapers of her activities. In March 1887 the *Washington Post* noted that the "queenly, accomplished and in all ways lovely" Mrs. Hamersley—a woman "of independent disposition but . . . never given to sensationalism"—had boldly hostessed an elaborate dinner party during Lent (setting modish but religiously conservative tongues wagging because of its religious timing), "and then sailed away for England." In early May she was reported to be back in New York; in early June she was spotted on the box seat of a coach at an informal Coaching Club meet; and later that month she was sighted at Tuxedo Park, a gated fall and spring sanctuary for socially elite New Yorkers under development some fifty miles northwest of New York City.[34] Lily was getting around, and as importantly, the world that mattered to her knew about it.

During the summer of 1887 Lily bought a summer home in partnership with her father in Luzerne, New York. Despite the mournful associations connected with the village as the place of death of their daughter Cora, Commodore Price and his wife had continued to favor the little resort for their summer holidays. Lily was in Luzerne with her parents that summer, attracting press attention when a lighted bedside candle ignited her bedclothes as she slept. ("Fortunately, Mrs. Hamersley woke and extinguished the fire at the expense of a few burns to herself. In a couple of minutes she would have been roasted alive.")[35] It was during this visit that the real estate transaction took place. Although the deed for the lakeside property, which included two summer cottages, was drawn in both Lily and her father's names, a news item in a local paper stating that the property "has been sold to a daughter of Commodore Price" suggests that Lily made the greater financial commitment to the acquisition.[36] Commodore Price was, after all, now eighty-one years old, not a conventional age to be undertaking new real estate ventures. The investment on Lily's part may have signified the loving gesture of a generous daughter toward her parents as well as an expression of her intent to spend at least a portion of her own future summers living out of the social spotlight in the restful beauty of the region. By early October the larger of the two houses on the property had been torn down in preparation for new construction. Hazelwood Cottage, which would reflect the ornate style of the nearby resort hotel and attract attention as the grandest private home in the village, was to be ready for habitation the following summer.[37] Lily's life, however, was to change completely during the intervening months.

The Duke of Marlborough

∞

In the spring of 1888 rumors began circulating about a possible marriage between Lily Hamersley and George Charles Spencer-Churchill, the eighth Duke of Marlborough. "It is very generally known by the initiated in London," reported New York's *Town Topics* in April, "that His Grace of Marlborough comes over here to see Mrs. Louis Hamersley, and to marry her, if she will let him."[1] The American press and the newspaper-reading public greeted the news of the duke's presumed objective with derision. Was this an appropriate attitude to take toward an English aristocrat of his elevated status? Many of those who knew something about this particular duke thought that it was.

The title of "duke," representing the highest rank in the British peerage below royalty, had been in the Churchill family since 1702, when Queen Anne designated John Churchill, the commander-in-chief of her armies, as the first Duke of Marlborough. Because Churchill left no surviving male issue, the title descended at his death through his daughter, the wife of Charles Spencer, Earl of Sunderland, who added Churchill to his surname in honor of her family in 1817 (although some later descendants shortened the hyphenated name to the simpler and more redolent "Churchill"). Marlborough ranked tenth in precedence among English dukes in order of creation. Thus the incumbent title-holder was a very big fish in the rank-driven puddle of Great Britain, and his doings were matters of collective curiosity.

Lily's putative suitor was born in 1844 and succeeded to the ducal title and the estate of Blenheim that came with it in 1883. He was called "Blandford" in recognition of his courtesy title, the Marquess of Blandford, which had been the second of his father's several titles and was conferred upon him, in keeping with the traditions of the aristocracy, as his father's eldest son and heir apparent when his father succeeded to the dukedom. Blandford and his brother Randolph, five years his junior, as well as six sisters were the surviving children into adulthood of John Winston Spencer-Churchill, the seventh duke, and his wife, Frances (Fanny), daughter of the third Marquess of Londonderry.

Blandford's father had inherited the ducal title and property in 1857, before which, as the Marquess of Blandford, he served as the elected Conservative representative in the House of Commons for the Oxfordshire constituency of Woodstock in which Blenheim is located. John Winston was the first in his line after the first duke to become a national figure of any consequence.[2] He devoted his life to government service, believing, as did Anthony Trollope in this age when the aristocracy held most of the reins of power, "that to sit in the British Parliament should be the highest object of ambition to every educated Englishman."[3] A steady and persevering politician, and known in private for his "grace, courtesy, and kindness," John Winston's public career was later recorded as that of "an earnest, plodding, and rather dreary figure."[4] His political focus was the Anglican Church, and his major accomplishment in the House of Commons the passage of the "Blandford Act" facilitating the sub-division of large church parishes. He passionately promoted other campaigns on behalf of his faith, among them the proper observance of Sundays, which entailed cracking down on the sale of liquor and a prohibition against military band-playing in parks on the Lord's Day. Pursuing these preoccupations into the House of Lords as the Duke of Marlborough, he sponsored there "a motion for a Select Committee to inquire into the Spiritual Destitution of England and Wales" and argued in favor of more religious instruction in schools. His last appearance in the Lords before his sudden death from heart disease was to make a long speech in support of a "Deceased Wife's Sister Bill" that advanced religious scruples against marriage to the sister of a dead wife.[5]

The two sons of this dull but capable man were of a different ilk, and the adjectives "erratic" and "brilliant" could be applied to both. The younger brother, Randolph Churchill, has received more extensive attention as an historical figure. Entering the House of Commons as Conservative member from Woodstock in 1874, Randolph's rise was meteoric. Despite a reputation "as an unstable and unprincipled adventurer,"[6] the audacious, fiery politician was by the age of thirty-six Chancellor of the Exchequer and leader of the House of Commons. For a while he was, after four-time Prime Minister William Gladstone, the best-known political figure in England, and it was rumored that he was predestined to become a future prime minister himself. A political miscalculation in resigning from office in 1886, and against his expectation, being allowed to do so, ruined his career. The rest of Randolph's life was an anticlimax. He was no longer in the limelight and passed his days as an investor in financial adventures and misadventures, an aficionado of horseracing and owner of racehorses, a traveler in foreign lands, and a visitor to other people's country houses.

Much of Randolph's political success could be attributed to his 1874 marriage to nineteen-year-old Jennie Jerome, the American-born daughter of colorful Wall Street speculator Leonard Jerome. Jennie was darkly beautiful in a flashing, almost Creole, way, with eyes, recalled Mr. Gladstone, "as limpid as those of a gazelle."[7] She was universally popular: a loyal friend who was "as delightful to women as to men,"[8] a pianist of near-professional skill, an able writer, and more politically savvy and active than most women of her day. The marriage of Jennie and Randolph was a love match that produced two sons, Winston and Jack. The pairing was ultimately unhappy and became little more than a marriage of social and political convenience. The couple often lived apart but nominally shared a household, staunchly supported one another, and never considered divorce. Jennie was one of the earliest American wives to achieve social success in London during the last third of the nineteenth century and was held up as a paradigm of transplanted American beauty and accomplishment.

Randolph's brother, Blandford, "had material in him for half a dozen reputations."[9] He was "a man of acute and powerful intellect," a student of science, mathematics, electronics, and engineering,[10] a patron and connoisseur of art, a versatile musician, a linguist who spoke fluent Urdu as well as French, and a capable writer who contributed to a number of highbrow journals. According to Henry Labouchere— popular politician, publisher of the weekly magazine *Truth*, and longtime friend to both brothers—the Duke of Marlborough "was far and away the cleverer" of the two, "whilst his charm of manner was altogether indescribable."[11] Moreton Frewen, married to a sister of Jennie Churchill, spoke of him as having "really a brilliant, scintillant mind, capable not merely of absorbing the most esoteric questions, but with a storage capacity quite without parallel in my experience for pigeon-holing the knowledge, and years later again calling it into being and utilizing it."[12] Unfortunately, this man of limitless promise comes down to us in history as simply "the wicked duke."[13]

"Sex was clearly a nuisance to him," blandly observed Churchill biographer A. L. Rowse of the eighth Duke of Marlborough.[14] And it was the duke's sexual liaisons that got him into trouble—not the liaisons themselves, but the amount of damage they caused and the publicity they aroused, both of which were unacceptable within the aristocratic circle in which he moved.

The duke had been on the wild side in his youth. Educated at Eton, from which he was expelled over an incident with a slingshot, he became a lieutenant in the Royal Horse Guards, a prestigious cavalry regiment based in London with the not usually onerous task of protecting the monarchy. The regiment, in which commissions were available through purchase prior to 1872, was popular with elder aristocratic sons killing time until inheriting their peerages, and members had plenty of leisure time in which to sow their wild oats. As a young man Blandford was close to Albert Edward, the Prince of Wales and Queen Victoria's heir apparent, who later was said to have "admitted something of the influence of the wayward, but often wholesomely stimulating example of quite the most intellectually gifted among his earliest friends."[15]

The Prince of Wales was an energetic and genial man whose mother refused to give him any royal responsibilities during her long reign. Growing restless in his circumscribed role, he became the central figure in a social clique known as the "Marlborough House Set" after the name of his residence in London (which had once belonged to the Churchill family). This circle was in every way more liberal in outlook and more continental in attitude than the queen's repressive court, and its early members were raffish scions of well-placed, usually noble, families with few responsibilities who looked to their leader to determine their parameters of diversion. Despite the prince's affection for the charming and beautiful Princess Alexandra of Denmark, whom he married in 1863 and who bore him six children within seven years, he began in the early 1870s to look beyond his marriage for amorous entertainment—a peccadillo his devoted wife was aware of but chose to ignore. His friends followed suit, and a "curious moral vacuum" developed within his social nucleus in which both men and women freely took on extramarital partners. The conventions governing their liaisons "were as strict and complicated as those of chess, and a mistake meant banishment."[16]

A cardinal rule within the prince's set was discretion. There was never to be any scandal, nor were homes to be broken up, in the course of amatory flirtations. Young, single girls were not fair targets; only married women were in play and only married women played—preferably ones of high social standing who "carried ancient names," "were hung with their own family jewels," and had already provided their husbands with sons to inherit their estates.[17] Women suffered no loss of status for their active participation. As a case in point, it has always been assumed, although never proven, that Jennie Churchill had an affair with her longtime friend the Prince of Wales, and it is generally accepted that her second son, Jack, was fathered, not by Randolph, but by one of her many lovers.[18]

Blandford transferred into the Queen's Own Oxfordshire Yeomanry in 1868, achieving promotion to captaincy in 1869, when he retired. That same year he married Lady Albertha Hamilton, a daughter of the powerful first Duke of Abercorn, in an imposing double ceremony at Westminster Abbey that also united Maud, a younger Hamilton sister, with the fifth Marquess of Lansdowne, later Viceroy of India. A goddaughter of Queen Victoria and her husband, Prince Albert, for whom she was named, Albertha, or Bertha, was celebrated for her beauty but not for her intelligence or wit. She was known to be fond of practical jokes: laying out bits of soap on the cheese tray, balancing inkpots above doors, knotting pajamas, and mixing up the chemical experiments of her husband. She was also "said to be much given to nagging."[19] It was not long before Blandford tired, not only of Bertha, but also of the wedded state. Writing in 1873 to Randolph, who was awaiting parental permission to wed his beloved Jennie, he tried his best to discourage his brother from taking the fatal step. "Had you been five and thirty or forty I could have pitied you," he counseled, "but five and twenty with life before you instead of behind you I tell you that you are mad simply mad." Drawing attention to his own unhappy situation, he passionately warned Randolph that marriage "is a delusion and a snare like all the rest, and in this disagreeable addition, that it is irrevocable."[20] Blandford was persistently unkind to his wife and became known as "a great scamp and an absentee husband."[21] The couple's marriage, during which the long-suffering Bertha produced the requisite heir and three daughters, became one of lengthy separations marked by ever more infrequent reconciliations.

In 1876 a scandal threatened to jeopardize the reputation of the royal family that was, according to Prime Minister Benjamin Disraeli, "almost as troublesome as the crisis then brewing in the Balkans."[22] Blandford was at its center. A letter from his then-mistress, Edith, Countess of Aylesford, to her hard-drinking, maritally wayward husband (conveniently off shooting tigers with the Prince of Wales in India), informed him that she and Lord Blandford intended to run off together. The Earl of Aylesford was furious. There was talk of a duel, and what was worse, the earl threatened his wife with divorce. Randolph Churchill, out of loyalty to his brother and the Churchill name, tried to avoid what he called "a fearful family disaster" by pressuring the prince, who warmly backed Aylesford, into dissuading his friend from his expressed resolution to divorce.[23] In doing so, he in essence blackmailed the queen's heir by threatening to make public the prince's compromising letters to Edith, of whom he had been an earlier admirer.

The Prince of Wales, enraged at Randolph's attempt to intimidate him, let it be known that neither he nor Princess Alexandra would accept invitations to houses where the Churchill brothers were received. To escape unwelcome publicity and attendant social ostracism, Mr. Disraeli recommended "the dignified withdrawal of the family from metropolitan and English Life,"[24] and the seventh Duke of Marlborough accepted the position of Lord Lieutenant of Ireland, taking Randolph, who served as his unpaid private secretary, and Jennie with him. It was four years before they returned to England, and another four years before the prince would again enter Randolph's home. Randolph's political rise and the prince's fondness for Jennie were factors in the reestablishment of cordial relations. The prince and Blandford never renewed their early friendship.

Lord Aylesford did eventually sue his wife for divorce on the grounds of adultery. She, eager to escape a dismal marriage, countersued. The queen's procurator-general, empowered to act in such matters when both parties were guilty of the same offense, intervened and both divorce petitions were refused, forcing the couple to settle in 1878 for a benignly acceptable judicial separation. Aylesford emigrated to Texas where he died of alcoholism in 1885. The outcast lovers, Blandford and Edith Aylesford, continued their affair. They lived openly together in Paris for several years as Mr. and Mrs. Spencer, parented a son in 1881, whom they named Guy Bertrand,[25] and separated not long afterward. Lady Aylesford, despite Blandford's public acknowledgment of paternity, optimistically called the boy Lord Guernsey as if he were the authentic son and heir of the Earl of Aylesford, on whose behalf she had born only daughters. Her claim to her son's right to inheritance from her husband on his 1885 death was disallowed, but the newly minted Duke of Marlborough, who had come into his father's title two years earlier, was required to give evidence at the hearing on the case.

Bertha, Blandford's wife, petitioned for divorce from her wayward husband in July 1882, accusing him of adultery, desertion, and cruelty. She had put up with a great deal, but the publicly bruited birth of Lady Aylesford's son by Blandford had been the last straw, and she felt that she had no choice but to formalize the break-up of her failed marriage. Her divorce was granted before Blandford's 1883 succession to his title but not finalized until shortly afterward. Thus Bertha was entitled to take the title of Duchess of Marlborough, but chose not to do so. It was later said that her family forbade her to accept a subsequent proposal from a gentleman of lower rank than the one she held,[26] and she never remarried, remaining the Marchioness of Blandford throughout life.

The stigma attached to divorce at this period in English history is difficult to comprehend from the vantage point of the twenty-first century. Most couples whose marriages failed simply separated with or without legal recognition and without thoughts of future lawful remarriage. In 1876, the year in which the Earl of Aylesford was making divorce threats, the divorce rate per 1000 married couples in England and Wales combined was only one-half of 1 percent, affecting some 208 marriages and reflecting a lower percentage rate than in the purportedly more puritanical United States. The powerful Anglican Church, which believed in the indissolubility of marriage, was virulently opposed to divorce; its attitude was reinforced by the purely secular argument that "the permanence of the nuptial tie is all but universally admitted to be of advantage to the state." Under a double standard in which men were expected to be "a little profligate," wives rarely instituted proceedings, and until passage of the hotly debated Divorce Act of 1857 were able to sue for divorce only when their husband's adultery was aggravated by incest or bigamy. Their property and earnings had no legal protection against seizure by their husbands until 1882. The Divorce Act was a first step toward abolishing gender inequality in marriage and marked the beginning of a shift in "the balance away from the traditional view of women as property, and toward the concept of marriage as a contract for the development of mutual comfort and domestic happiness."[27] When the Marchioness of Blandford was awarded her divorce, such actions were still rare as well as socially taboo, and Marlborough's position in the English aristocracy was severely compromised as a result of his wife's successful petition.

In the period immediately following his accession to the dukedom, Marlborough lay low. His mother and youngest sister, Sarah, often made their home at Blenheim, where the duchess presided as mistress of the palace and paid some of its expenses. The new duke quietly set about to retrieve his social respectability; appeared in the House of

Lords; and continued to write, contributing serious articles to journals between 1884 and 1887 on such diverse topics as independent politics in England, land transfer, international legal tender, and bimetallism—a monetary system based on gold and silver. As an old Eton schoolmate, who recalled him as a "kind-hearted, generous, and highly intelligent" student, noted at this time, Marlborough's talents had "flourished a little late, but if the yield of fruit should be very abundant, none of those who were intimately acquainted with him will feel surprised."[28] He "studies politics with aids to knowledge that few men possess," noted another observer. "He can both write and speak. Existence is still before him, and with concentration and the ballast which experience ought to supply he will make his mark and become a force to be reckoned with."[29]

Marlborough's enhanced reputation was shattered in late 1886 when he found himself once again in the kind of messy public trouble for which he had been known in the past. Lord Colin Campbell, the youngest son of the Scottish Duke of Argyll, and his wife, the former Gertrude Blood, sued one another for divorce after a brief marriage. Among the husband's charges in what was to become the longest, most sexually explicit divorce trial to date in British history were that his wife had committed adultery with four separate co-respondents: a military officer, Campbell's personal physician, the chief of the London fire brigade, and the Duke of Marlborough.

Marlborough had met the stunning Lady Colin in the spring of 1880. She was an unusual woman: an exhibited painter; a singer who performed frequently at charity events; a sportswoman who was fond of riding, swimming, fencing, fishing, and bicycling; and a professional writer. Her first magazine article, "My *Real* Turkish Bath," was published when she was seventeen; a popular children's book followed not long afterward. Her most commercially successful volume, an 1893 revision of an earlier guide to *Etiquette of Good Society*, would go through several editions during her lifetime.[30]

It appears certain that Marlborough and Lady Colin were involved in an ongoing if non-exclusive love affair that began shortly after her July 1881 marriage, but the duke, like the other co-defendants who appeared in the eighteen-day divorce proceeding, lied like a gentleman in the witness box and denied any sexual relationship. The jury called upon to decide the case determined that neither husband nor wife was guilty of the adulterous charges of which they had accused one another, and the divorce petitions were denied. Settling for the usual judicial separation, the couple henceforth lived apart. Lord Colin became a barrister and migrated to India where he died in 1895. His wife, a social pariah in conservative aristocratic circles after the sensational trial, supported herself by her writing. She showed no inclination to remarry upon the death of her husband.

The startling connection of the Duke of Marlborough's name with the messy Campbell vs. Campbell divorce suit contributed to the unusual level of public interest in the legal case, and a record attendance filled the London courtroom to glory in its salacious details. Even the *New York World* sent a correspondent to London who cabled back daily reports, and Marlborough became a household name in the United States, one with the most distasteful of connotations.

The duke was reported at the conclusion of the case to be "in despair" over his entanglement in the dispute. "There are reasons for believing," commented one journalist, "that, if he had not been involved in a new scandal, he would have renewed the attempts he made tentatively some time ago to enter on the discharge of those political duties for which, if he has not all the morality, he has certainly the ability. This latest scandal of course forever excludes him from political employment."[31] Marlborough's political future was not, however, his foremost concern at this point. He had other problems requiring his attention that were, literally, closer to home.

Blenheim Palace, the seat of the Duke of Marlborough, was a grand conception. Situated in Woodstock, eight miles from the university town of Oxford and sixty-five miles from London, it was built in the early years of the eighteenth century for John Churchill, the first duke to bear the Marlborough title. Its construction was largely paid for by a grateful government to celebrate the duke's 1704 military victory over Louis XIV, the powerful king of France, at Blindheim, or Blenheim, Bavaria. The commanding placement of a colossal marble bust of the great French monarch whom Marlborough defeated over the south portico of the palace served as an odd if compelling reminder of his accomplishment.

The creator of Blenheim was besotted with his palace during his lifetime. He chose an architect of Dutch extraction, Sir John Vanbrugh, to realize his vision, and although the palace was still unfinished at Marlborough's death in 1722, the duke was constantly buying for it during his lifetime: commissioning tapestries, ordering fabrics, and collecting furniture and artworks from all over Europe. By 1724 the writer Daniel Defoe, author of *Robinson Crusoe*, had visited Blenheim and commented upon the magnificent scale of Marlborough's undertaking. "It requires," he noted prophetically, "the Royalty of a Sovereign Prince to support an Equipage suitable to the Greatness of this Place."[32] Rivaling Versailles in size, Blenheim is today recognized as the grandest home in Britain, far outstripping in magnificence those of the royal family, and is revered as one of the proudest manifestations of the country's heritage.

Sarah, the first Duke of Marlborough's formidable wife, unwillingly took over the building project when her husband died, and subsequent members of the family continued to improve and enlarge the property. By 1817 and the death of the fourth duke, there were some 187 furnished palace rooms in use. The fifth duke, who spent as liberally as his predecessors, found he had dispensed more than his income and had to sell his own library to pay debts. "He lived in utter retirement at one corner of his magnificent palace," it was reported after his death in 1840, "a melancholy instance of the results of extravagance."[33]

The seventh Duke of Marlborough, father of Blandford and Randolph, was of a hospitable nature, and upon his succession to the dukedom he revived what had become a flaccid Blenheim social life under his immediate predecessors and entertained on an expanded scale. He discovered during the 1870s, however, that he was no longer a wealthy man, and he was forced to enter upon a period of economic retrenchment. This meant deferment of the kind of on-going maintenance required to keep a palace the size of Blenheim in good repair, and the first duke's great memorial began to look a little shabby.

The seventh duke was not alone among the British landed

Blenheim Palace, seat of the Duke of Marlborough

aristocracy in finding himself with less spending money than he had heretofore enjoyed. His income derived almost entirely from rents on the 20,000-odd agricultural acres surrounding Blenheim and its park. Compared to the vast real estate holdings of some of his peers, such as the Duke of Devonshire's 180,000 acres, Marlborough's properties, and thus his returns, were modest. He was now battered, as were other great proprietors whose wealth was held in rural land, by the effects of a European agricultural depression brought on in part by the influx of cheap agricultural imports from North and South America, Australia, and New Zealand. Rents fell, as tenant farmers could no longer command the same level of prices for their products as they had in earlier years. Regions heavily invested in cereal or "corn" crops (wheat, barley, and oats) were particularly hard hit; southeastern England, where Blenheim is situated, suffered a diminution in rural rent returns between 1874 and the mid-1890s of some 41 percent.[34] The long-term results of the agricultural depression for the essentially agrarian elite were severe. "The whole territorial basis of patrician existence," observed historian David Cannadine, "was undermined and the easy confidences and certainties of the mid-Victorian period vanished forever."[35]

Many members of the landed aristocracy had other than agricultural resources available to them—from urban ground rents and investments in such industrial enterprises as mines, railways, and docks—to offset their agricultural losses. The seventh Duke of Marlborough did not. To meet the expenses of keeping up Blenheim and the Marlborough title, he began selling collections acquired in better days by his forbears from impoverished continental aristocrats.

This was no more than the expansion of an agenda cautiously pursued by his own father, the sixth Duke of Marlborough, who had disposed of some of Blenheim's less-celebrated accumulations, yet the scale and historical significance of the seventh duke's transactions were new phenomena in the market for treasured antique objects. He engineered the passage by Parliament of the Blenheim Settled Estates Act in 1880, which allowed him to sell off an important library and a collection of Limoges enamels without consideration for future generations, who by laws of primogeniture and entail were entitled to receive his property intact. Although money realized through sales had to go back into the estate's coffers, income derived from its investment was available to meet on-going expenses.

Other landed aristocrats were deaccessioning too, a process made easier by the passage of the Settled Lands Act in 1882, modeled on the earlier legislation tailored for the seventh Duke of Marlborough, and between the 1880s and the First World War the formerly "great accumulators" became the "great dispersers."[36] The sales were a shock to the complacent English conviction that its inheritance laws functioned adequately to preserve great private estates as quasi-public institutions, and purchases of English ancestral treasures by the newly minted rich, often from across the Atlantic, attracted negative press attention.

As the agricultural decline continued, so did the downward slide of Blenheim's income, and the eighth Duke of Marlborough, when he came into possession of his inheritance, had even less money to work with than had his father. His income in 1888 was estimated to be in the range of £25,000 a year. There were, at this time, perhaps 250 of his countrymen who had yearly revenues of more than £30,000; his returns placed him in a lower tier of 750 persons with annual incomes of between £10,000 and £30,000.[37] Thus the duke was not one of England's most affluent individuals, yet he was charged with the responsibility of maintaining at Blenheim a physical plant that would financially challenge many wealthier peers.

The outlay required to keep up Blenheim and its splendors was immense. In response to an 1886 query as to how many rooms there were in the palace, Marlborough replied that he wasn't sure, "but I know I paid a bill this Spring for painting a thousand windows."[38] He was also quoted as saying "that it cost him £7,000 a year to maintain the castle and the grounds in any kind of shape when they were unoccupied," and that £800 were required annually "to keep the place in putty alone."[39] In addition, there were ducal perquisites and a style of living to be paid for that Marlborough, like other noblemen, felt it incumbent upon himself to uphold "not as a fashion but as a duty." Such outward show of high-born privilege was taken for granted, not only by members of the peerage, but by the less moneyed classes, who tolerated an elevated level of aristocratic expenditure because of the generally public-spirited role assumed by men of title in their private and public lives. "It may be said," noted an American in 1912 of the English aristocracy, "that in the main this has been an aristocracy born to duties first, to privileges afterward, and it is because . . . they have lived up to this standard that they still hold the place and power they do."[40]

Although the Settled Lands Act allowed for the sale of agricultural land by the life tenants of landed estates, land prices continued to fall steeply as a result of the rural depression; indeed, as Marlborough pointed out, "were there any effective demand for the purchase of land, half the land of England would be in the market tomorrow."[41] To raise income, Marlborough continued the process begun by his recent ancestors and in 1884 announced his intention of selling off yet more of Blenheim's accumulated assets, among them three hundred paintings, many by well-known artists, that had been personally assembled by John Churchill. Public reaction was hostile. Not only had sentiment been galvanized by losses of what had been belatedly recognized as national treasures through other contemporary sales, but Blenheim was regarded as something of a special case. That it had been constructed largely at state expense was common knowledge, as was the fact that its owner received an annual £5,000 government subsidy in keeping with a commitment made to the first duke in the days of Queen Anne. Thus Marlborough's home was considered to be more of a public institution than most, and the dispersal of its contents was deeply offensive. Nevertheless, the sale went forward, adding over £300,000 to the Blenheim treasury.

The duke, who admitted to liking "things neat about him when he can get them," plowed the income back into his estate, restoring and improving it in keeping with his own exacting conceptions of fitness and taste. Tapestries commissioned by the first duke that had been hanging in the state rooms were cleaned and restored; a panel missing from a tapestry series on the first duke's victories in the Low Countries was found in Paris and purchased for the palace. The lawns of the park were leveled and re-laid. Money went into permanent farm improvements, and a scientific laboratory was built to accommodate the duke's experiments in electricity and chemistry.[42]

The English people may have begrudgingly swallowed the Blenheim art sales, but revelations about the duke's involvement in the Campbell vs. Campbell divorce fiasco were the last straw as far as his personal reputation was concerned. What lay ahead for the wicked duke? A February 1887 conversation between Marlborough and "a gentleman who is on intimate terms" with him was reported at some length in a British journal:

> "I asked the Duke," said [the gentleman], "if it was really true that he was in love with Lady Campbell and if he had intended to marry her if she had got her divorce. He replied with perfect frankness . . . and declared that neither assertion was true. Moreover, there was an insuperable obstacle to their marriage, namely, they were both too poor. The Duke is in straitened circumstances and he really cannot afford to marry a woman who has not a large fortune of her own. He told me that he supposed the only chance left open for him, since he had been so cut by English society, was to marry an American heiress."[43]

There was but one way to test these waters, and that was to cross the Atlantic and have a look around.

CHAPTER 7

Marlborough in America, 1887

The Duke of Marlborough traveled to the United States in the late summer of 1887, disembarking in New York on 28 August. This was Marlborough's second trip to the city, which he had first visited in 1875 and which he remarked seemed much changed. "I really don't know how long I shall remain," he disclosed to a reporter. "You see, I just came over for a pleasure trip. . . . I shall take in all the watering places within easy reach of New York and probably Niagara Falls as well. It may take me six weeks to do it all properly, maybe more. Further than that my plans are not arranged. In fact, circumstances will chiefly guide me."[1] The following day the titled tourist left for Newport, Rhode Island, the coastal watering place to which New York City society transported itself *en bloc* during the summer months. There Marlborough could share with the inhabitants of ostentatious "cottages" a quasi-outdoor social life that echoed the customs, prejudices, and pecking order of its urban counterpart.

The duke's American tour got off to an inauspicious start. His divorce, his court appearance in connection with Lady Aylesford's attempt to have her son recognized as the legitimate heir to the Aylesford title, and his prominent role in the Campbell vs. Campbell divorce case had attracted adverse press attention, and his reputation in the United States was that of a notorious rake. *Town Topics* advised American husbands to "get your wives ready, for His Grace will have been a whole week at sea." There could be no doubt, it added, as to the validity of Marlborough's title, and "a man could almost afford to trust his wife alone with His Grace" for the privilege of having his name in one's card tray.[2]

Compounding the distasteful associations connected with Marlborough was widespread disgust at the recent antics of another titled Englishman, Hugh Cecil Lowther, fifth Earl of Lonsdale, who had spent a disruptive month in New York City less than a year earlier. Newspapers had avidly tracked this married lord's scandalous liaison with a London burlesque actress whose husband, arriving on the same steamship as the two lovers, was arrested for threatening to kill or cripple his estranged wife and who noisily sued the earl for alienating his wife's affections. As far as the public was concerned, there were too many parallels between the behaviors of the aristocratic visitors. Polite society collectively shuddered at the latest noble incursion, and it was a widely expressed opinion that Marlborough could hardly expect "that a press and public who drew the line at his fellow-countryman, Lord Lonsdale, in his open attempt to flaunt his vices before the eyes of every one . . . would go very far to meet a man of his reputation in the divorce courts."[3]

Marlborough's nearly two-week sojourn in Newport stirred up a veritable hornets' nest. Although the more decorous members of Newport's transplanted summer community shunned the disgraced duke, those who tended to get their names in the paper lionized him. Foremost among these was Marietta Stevens, a commanding figure in New York society and gossip-sheet regular who entertained Marlborough as her houseguest during most of his visit. Mrs. Stevens was the daughter of a Lowell, Massachusetts, merchant and had come into great wealth as the second wife of Paran Stevens, a hotelier with property interests in Boston, New York, Philadelphia, and Mobile, Alabama. Widowed since 1872, Mrs. Stevens was known as New York's most "slap-dash and democratic society leader," a rough-edged, "impulsive woman, never hesitating to give full expression of her opinions about everybody and everything uppermost in her mind for the moment." Her unalloyed social ambition made her the frequent butt of press derision, but her occasional vulgarities were more than offset by her financial generosity, her loyalty to friends, and her memorable parties to which guests were "invited more for their brains and beauty than their bonds and bank accounts."[4] In 1878 she had achieved a social coup in marrying her handsome daughter Minnie (who, like Jennie Churchill, was reported to have had an "intimate friendship" with the Prince of Wales) to a titled Englishman. Minnie's husband, Lord Arthur Henry Paget, was the fifth son of the Marquess of Anglesey and his family had close ties to the royal family. Mrs. Stevens, who knew the Duke of Marlborough through her English connections, took it upon herself to act as his Newport sponsor.

"Never," reported *Town Topics*, "has there been a more disgraceful scramble and scuffle of servile social lickspittleism than the Duke is made the occasion of." While Mrs. Stevens displayed her catch and entertained him "with a certain bluff freedom of her own," some members of the Newport elite outdid themselves "with the slavish sycophancy of lackeys" in offering up extravagant dinners, receptions, and yachting parties to the visitor. Among the affairs Marlborough attended was a gathering at the opulent new villa belonging to Lucy and Henry Clews. "The hostess herself was in a positive ecstasy," it was reported, and "seemed to float rather than walk."[5] The competitive Newport to-do generated a glut of unflattering press attention that publicly dishonored both Marlborough and his sponsor, Mrs. Stevens.

Mrs. Stevens countered the press attack with the kind of verbal fusillade expected of her. (As Marlborough remarked to an acquaintance of her outburst, "Gad! She talked like red peppers.")[6] The duke responded to the public mud-slinging as well, penning an ill-considered prose-and-poetry "memorandum" that was duly printed and reprinted in American newspapers. "It is not improbable," asserted the duke, "that I shall collect a few of the best reported specimens of the gutter gazettes of this country and have the same framed for the edification or benefit of the thousand or more American tourists who are kind enough to honor my country house in England every year with a visit." He went on to carp in free verse about the "flights of mendacity" of the "American eagle" in a manner that was above the heads of most readers, but was intuitively interpreted as an exercise in aristocratic pomposity and literary pretension.[7]

Marlborough's troubles with the press did not end with his

injudicious "mem." On 15 September a letter attributed to the duke appeared in *Truth*, a weekly New York newspaper of indifferent repute and apathetic circulation that borrowed its name from the popular British journal of the same title. In fine phrases, the alleged author of this communication expressed his "gratitude at the excessively kind and hospitable manner in which I have been received by my friends in America." He wanted, according to the letter, to contradict the widespread misunderstanding about the famous memorandum and call attention to the fact that it had been "an impudent forgery" and that his supposed signature in connection with it "had been used without the slightest authority."[8]

Despite the flowery language and the conciliatory sentiments expressed in the latest public statement attributed to Marlborough, the missive printed in *Truth* really *was* a forgery, perhaps intended to secure the duke's good will, but Marlborough was furious with the fabrication and could not let it go unremarked. A 16 October letter to the *New York Herald* made his sentiments clear. "That vile rag called *Truth*," he wrote, "had the audacity to publish a letter . . . signed by my name, which I never saw or heard of till some time after." "Criticisms," he added, "however blackguard, are one thing, but calmly forging an individual's name is another. . . . I do not wish," the duke astutely concluded, "to take legal steps against these people, as it would only be giving them the publicity they wish for." Davidson Dalziel, the publisher of *Truth*, promptly sued Marlborough for $25,000, accusing the duke of "wickedly and maliciously intending to injure the plaintiff in his good name and credit."[9] Although public interest in the suit quickly died out, it did cause a flutter of exposure for *Truth*, as Marlborough had predicted, and was a source for him of more unsavory and unwanted newspaper coverage.

After visiting Boston and the Berkshire hills, Marlborough drifted in early October back to New York, just then beginning to stir from its summer social torpor. It was during this period of collective calm that he first met Thomas Alva Edison, the scientist and inventor who had devised the incandescent electric lamp in 1879. As an enthusiastic student of electricity, the duke had corresponded with his American contemporary, and now ventured out to meet him in person in

Harrison, New Jersey, where Edison was working at the Edison Lamp Company.

The duke was ushered into the private office of young Alfred Tate, the inventor's associate and private secretary. "While waiting for Edison to receive him," wrote Tate later, "the Duke began to discuss with me the technique of incandescent lamp manufacture, a subject with which I thought I was fairly familiar. But the Duke amazed me. His familiarity with every minute technical detail was a revelation, and I wondered where and how he had become such a complete master of this comparatively novel art. He referred to Blenheim," he continued,

> and told me that he had installed a telephone system [thought to be the first private system of its kind in England] which enabled him to call up all the various departments on his estate from his bed. This sounded better. It seemed to harmonize more closely with my preconceived ideas concerning the preoccupations of the Idle Rich. But on the other hand it was very confusing when viewed in the light of the Duke's superior knowledge of an art in which I had imagined myself to be proficient.[10]

Although much had been made of Marlborough's womanizing past when he first arrived in the United States, there was surprisingly little press comment thereafter about his encounters with American women at the social centers he frequented. Young debutantes were thrust at him, and the name of a particular lady seen hanging on his arm at some social function might go recorded, but all was chronicled without cynical speculation as to their wealth or the duke's possible intentions toward them. Yet the duke's recorded allusions of the preceding February to his need for money and the possibility of securing it through an American marriage had been broadcast in the United States and could not have helped but fuel some public speculation. Press silence on the subject was due in part to Marlborough's discretion. It could also be attributed to the announcement in early October of the duke's purported engagement to Cornelia Wadsworth Ritchie Adair, a wealthy, twice-widowed American from Geneseo, New York, then living in Ireland and London who "was and is yet well known as a great beauty and of surpassing brilliancy."[11] The rumor proved false, but it served a useful purpose in alleviating curiosity about Marlborough's marital future.

Marlborough headed west to St. Paul, Minnesota, and Chicago in late October, returning at the beginning of November to New York, where he slipped quietly out of public view. The privacy now accorded him by journalists must have come as a welcome relief, for Marlborough had certainly endured more than his share of their attention during his trip. But he learned from his mistakes and mastered the art of the interview, a purely American invention that was found offensive by most foreigners subjected to its format of formal, often personal and aggressive, questioning. A mid-November interview with a representative of the *New York Herald* was seriously reported,[12] and journalists praised Marlborough's eloquence in discussing British and American politics.

The duke left for home on 26 November—not escaping, however, without one last flutter of unsolicited press notice. Rumors were floated that Dalziel, the gossip sheet publisher who had sued the duke for defamation, sought to wring the last ounce of publicity from his stunt by having the duke arrested and "to give him as much annoyance as possible by making the arrest on board the steamer a short time before the hour of sailing." Marlborough's American friends got wind of the threat, perhaps through the good offices of the publicity-hungry Dalziel himself, and Henry Clews accompanied Marlborough on board the steamship *Umbria*, ready to provide a bond of $50,000 for the duke's release if an arrest were made, which, unsurprisingly, it was not.[13] As Marlborough made his final farewells, he declared to Clews that his trip to the States "had given him great delight and revealed to him a great deal in American life whose existence he had never suspected." He "certainly would," he added cheerily, "return in the spring."[14]

CHAPTER 8

Courtship and Marriage II

ॐ

Marlborough's 1887 pledge to return to the United States the following year was interpreted as meaning that he wished "merely to pursue his observations and study of the country."[1] That he might have other motives for revisiting America occurred to no one, and little more was said in surprising early 1888 reports of his intended visit than that he was hurrying back "to continue his wooing of a fair, younger and, above all, wealthy widow whose charms attracted him when he was here last year."[2] The suggestion that the duke's romantic object was a woman marked "out for a great deal of notice during the past few years" was, however, easily decoded by those who were socially au courant.[3]

"There is probably a good deal more truth in this gossip than gossip usually contains," surmised a journalist in late March, "and the friends of the lady in question who speak of the matter at all, say that so far as she is concerned, the marriage will probably take place."[4] A month later *Town Topics* boldly named the object of the duke's admiration. "It is not believed, however," added this usually reliable source, "that matters have been satisfactorily adjusted between the two prospective contracting parties. The Duke is very anxious to effect the alliance, but the widow is decidedly coy."[5]

No one could later recall just when and through whom Lily Hamersley and the Duke of Marlborough made one another's acquaintance during the duke's visit of the previous autumn. The introduction might have taken place at a dinner party at the home of mutual friends such as the Henry Clewses. It might also have been through Mrs. Paran Stevens or Ward McAllister, both of whom prided themselves on their matchmaking skills. In any event, Lily and Marlborough were never in New York at the same time until close to 2 November, when they separately attended the performance of *Tristan and Isolde* that inaugurated the winter season of the Metropolitan Opera. The three weeks before the duke's 26 November departure left little time for their friendship to advance beyond the stage of polite formalities.

But the fire of romance had been ignited, and after the duke's return to England he and Lily carried on what became an increasingly personal and goal-oriented correspondence. In the absence of physical proximity, there was no role for amorous gesture in advancing the budding relationship. Only initial impressions, recognition of the potential for meeting reciprocal needs and aspirations, mutual respect for what were perceived as underlying qualities, and some degree of dispassionate frankness can have driven the couple's growing long-distance intimacy.

The duke, according to members of New York men's clubs, had "talked very freely of American girls who have married on the other side" during his 1887 visit, and had mentioned the popularity of several American brides in English society.[6] He was quoted as saying that there "was no kind of disguise or circumlocution" in male attentions addressed to young heiresses in London, and that when an heiress came out in society she began to receive proposals at once. "Oftentimes," he said, "a girl has received as many as two hundred in the first month. The candidates do not expect to be accepted, but they are willing to take their chances."[7] The duke, after, it was reported, "a strict and searching investigation into Mrs. Hamersley's pecuniary eligibility,"[8] had simply followed English custom in making his overtures to the wealthy widow.

Lily was hardly an adventuress. Decorous in her personal relations, she was nevertheless far from naïve, and would certainly have been aware of the motives behind Marlborough's advances. She read the newspapers, was attuned to contemporary gossip, and knew of the duke's reputation and financial shortfalls. At the same time, she was

Duke of Marlborough, 1892

newly rich, and ambitious. How could she have been impervious to the merits of the kind of public status offered her by marriage to a duke? "Considering the matter simply in a general way," noted one American journalist philosophically, "it is not probable that any woman could resist the temptation which this condition of things would hold out."[9]

Lily had, moreover, her personal situation to consider. She was nearly thirty-four years old, had been a widow for five years, and had not yet found another man she wished to marry. She had, of course, close friends of both sexes, some of whom held high status. But the families of "old New York" were closed to her because of the lingering consequences of the Hamersley will case, and it had proven easy for acquaintances to ignore her when issuing invitations to social events at which members of the extended Mason/Jones/Hamersley family might be present. Her awkward position was unlikely to change, and marriage into the uppermost tier of the English nobility would offer her a fresh start.

Lily's income apparently proved sufficient to mark her out as an appropriate marital partner as far as Marlborough was concerned. The duke's quarry also had good looks, dignity, a graceful manner, and an easy way in conversation. Her family background was impeccable. She was not, like so many American heiresses, the daughter of a successful dry goods merchant, but of a high-ranking military officer. Thus she was descended from the American equivalent of what was known in England as the "traditional gentlemanly class"—a time-honored source of titled wives.[10] Her reputation was without taint and she lived quietly. Marriage to Lily would strengthen Marlborough's ambivalent social position if he wished to redeem his reputation in the eyes of the British public.

It must be more than wishful thinking to assume that something other than chilly self-interest motivated this couple—a spark of mutual attraction that gave them the courage to contemplate marriage and the confidence to believe that whatever exchanges they were willing to make with one another would be worthwhile. Marlborough arrived in the United States on 6 May 1888 at Lily's invitation to pursue his matrimonial suit.

Lily was not socially idle during the late winter and early spring months during which she and the Duke of Marlborough were corresponding about a possible future together. She continued to see that her name made it into the papers, prompting two mid-February press announcements that Mrs. Louis Hamersley would be entertaining, and on 26 February, that she had given "a large dinner party."[11] She was spotted at a musicale hosted by a man-about-town in his handsome studio, and was the hostess of a musicale herself on 15 March.[12] It mattered to her now that she be recognized as a prominent personality, and reporters fell into line. As the *Brooklyn Eagle* reminded its readers,

> Mrs. Louis Hamersley is one of the handsomest women in
> New York, and is to be seen during the season at her box in

the opera calm, fair and beautiful, generally in white, with heaps of snowy furs drawn about her and a huge fan of white curled ostrich plumes in her languid hand—she herself looking amid all this white like a snow bank, for her shoulders and arms will bear comparison with anything. Add to this great beauty the fact that she owns some five or six millions, and the natural result is that her opera box is constantly filled with the most attractive men in the town.[13]

This journalistic tribute would have afforded pleasure to Lily, appearing as it did on the day that the Duke of Marlborough steamed into New York.

Marlborough, as he stepped ashore, must have felt some anxiety about his welcome from a press corps that had given him such trouble during his previous visit. He had little to worry about. For one thing, his name had not appeared in newspapers in connection with marital scandals in the five months since his departure. More importantly, New York City newspapermen who had had some personal contact with him during his 1887 trip had succumbed to his charm and would increasingly treat the duke with the respect they felt he had earned. In fact, his earlier visit, as well as that of the next few weeks, served to "revolutionize American opinion concerning him." Members of the press and others who had expected arrogance liked Marlborough for his modesty and amiability, because he didn't "bear a single eye glass," and because his accent was not so dissimilar to that of a cultivated citizen of their own country. "He is in some respects," noted one journalist, "the least pretentious man in New York." They liked him too for his curiosity, his "intelligent and earnest desire to get the real facts concerning the commercial and mechanical advancement of the nation," and for his interest in and knowledge about substantive subjects.[14] (He contributed a signed article on politics to the *New York World* during this trip and would publish an English journal article on electricity based on his American observations the following year.)[15] While out-of-town newspapers that knew him only by past repute as well as New York journals reliant on muckraking to sustain their circulation continued to taunt Marlborough, the press for the most part treated him benignly. The duke was, nevertheless, an important visitor, and there was a reporter on hand to greet him as his steamship docked.

Was it true, he was asked, as stated in some of the papers, that he was to wed Mrs. Hamersley? "What bosh the papers do print," was the good-natured reply. "The same report appeared in the English papers, but my friends did not pay any attention to it. The report is untrue, as I have never even met the lady." He would not, he said remain in the country for the Newport season, but had "only run over for a short trip to California to see the country."[16] That was the end of the interview, and to a large degree, of press curiosity. Although his comings and goings were noted and rumors of a possible marriage continued to circulate, Marlborough and Lily's circumspection meant that the couple was not often glimpsed together, and their independent activities fired little press speculation.

Despite his remark to the press that he was California-bound, Marlborough was never far nor long away from New York City during the next two months. He had made a formal proposal of marriage to Lily, but his intended bride required more time than he had perhaps anticipated to be reassured about the possible ramifications of accepting his offer. Despite any personal inclinations, she weighed his proposal dispassionately and insisted on an exact understanding of his legal situation vis-à-vis remarriage and the protection of her own financial interests. Negotiations and guarantees in connection with both took time.

The opinions of eminent English lawyers were solicited on the duke's behalf in defense of his right to remarry, which, according to press reports, had been distinctly forbidden by the divorce decree granted to his wife in 1883. Marlborough, however, had the facts at his fingertips, and later shared them in some detail with a reporter. "The present English law," he explained, "was changed during the premiership of Lord Palmerston," the British prime minister at the time of passage of the Divorce Act of 1857. "While it is perfectly true that some of the ultra-church people did all they possibly could to secure the introduction of such a clause in the law prohibiting a man or woman, from whom a divorce had been obtained, from remarrying, it is equally true that no success attended their efforts." Palmerston, a notorious ladies' man who was cited in a divorce proceeding himself when he was in his late seventies, "strenuously opposed the addition of any such clause," added Marlborough, "on the broad ground that such action was simply putting a premium on vice."[17]

The legal arguments advanced were sufficiently convincing to put Lily and her lawyers at ease on this crucial point. In regard to money, the prospective bride would settle no money directly on Marlborough, in opposition to long-standing English custom, and it was understood that she would retain absolute control of her own wealth. She did, however, insure her life for a considerable sum and make undisclosed commitments to financial participation in the duke's life—most likely in regard to the maintenance and enhancement of Blenheim.[18]

Lily had more to contend with than legal niceties in weighing the duke's proposal. Many of her friends disapproved of the prospective match, and cited not only Marlborough's past reputation but also his supposedly heavy debts in their efforts to discourage her from taking the decisive step. Of greater concern to Lily was the reaction of her family. For her parents, rather than expressing enthusiasm for such a prestigious match, were bitterly opposed on religious principle to the idea of their daughter marrying a divorcé. "Mrs. Hamersley," declared Lily's mother's cousin and former Troy mayor, George B. Warren, "has been earnestly requested by her parents and relatives not to marry the duke, but she is as uncontrollable as a horse without a bit in his mouth." It was the general consensus in Troy that by marrying Marlborough Lily would estrange herself from her parents, and family members were believed to have asked leading New York clergymen not to officiate at her marriage if an application to do so were made to them.[19]

Marlborough could not devote all of his time to pursuing what might prove to be an unsuccessful suit, and he was marked out socially during his visit as one of "the guests much sought after for dinners."[20] His presence was reported on a yachting trip sponsored by the New York Yacht Club, he was seen at a steeplechase race in Westchester County, and he was invited by his brother's father-in-law, Leonard Jerome, to join him for a flat race and luncheon at the clubhouse of a racetrack at Sheepshead Bay, Brooklyn, of which Jerome was a founder. The duke, it was observed, "said absolutely nothing to the few men who were on intimate terms with him here" about his unresolved courtship,[21] and most of them remained in the dark about his tentative plans.

Marlborough did, however, confide in Jerome. On 18 May, the day Marlborough left for an upstate New York fishing trip with Jerome's brother Lawrence, Jennie Churchill's father disclosed Marlborough's intentions in a letter to his wife. "The Duke," he wrote, "has gone off this morning with Lawrence and a party to the Adirondacks trout fishing, to be gone a week. I rather think he will marry the Hamersley. Don't you fear any responsibility on my part. Mrs. H. is quite capable of deciding for herself. Besides I have never laid eyes on the lady but once. At the same time I hope the marriage will come off as there is no doubt that she has lots of tin."[22]

Through frequent reiteration it has become accepted as fact that Marlborough and Lily were introduced to one another and their marriage promoted by Leonard Jerome. This seems unlikely. There is, moreover, no reason to disbelieve Jerome's own assertion that he barely knew Lily. For Jennie Churchill's father, although respected and admired in New York for his financial acumen, his honesty, his generosity, and his sporting interests, had a somewhat raffish reputation. A "man's man" who was "nevertheless gallant and devoted to a rather tolerant type of society woman,"[23] he had little interest in society per se, and would have been an unlikely guest in most of the drawing rooms frequented by Lily's more conservative social set. It is clear from his letter, however, that Jerome did know Lily by reputation as a woman of formidable self-assurance and that he approved of Marlborough's choice.

Unseasonably hot June weather increased speculation about the covert romance. "It has been a matter of comment," noted one journalist, "that so fashionable a woman should tarry so late in town, in the midst of all this heat."[24] Marlborough and Lily maintained their silence, but Lily found it difficult to dissimulate with everyone about her plans. She "indignantly denied to one friend the possibility of her becoming a duchess, while to another, in a most mysterious manner she remarked, 'Do not be surprised at anything that may happen this summer.'"[25]

Lily endeavored, meanwhile, to finance her escape from New York. On 26 June, in keeping with the legal requirements attending the still unsettled Hamersley estate, she requested a payout of $100,000 from the Surrogate's Court in order to "maintain her establishment in a manner suitable and befitting to her station in life, and to meet future and existing liabilities." Her last court petition had been in December 1887 when she asked for and received $75,000, bringing to $375,000 the total amount extracted to date from estate income. She had, Lily declared in her petition, spent it all.[26]

It was also on 26 June that concrete intelligence of an imminent marriage between Lily and the duke first appeared in print. The source was said to be a Newport summer resident "high in society," and others in the resort confirmed "that there may be some truth in the reported marriage."[27] On 29 June Lily's mother denounced in the press the idea of her daughter's rumored nuptials as a "ridiculous canard."[28] Either Mrs. Price was promoting the secrecy surrounding the occasion or, more likely, she had been spared the final details concerning a union of which she disapproved. For, on the same day, Lily Hamersley wed the Duke of Marlborough. In doing so she became the highest-ranking American woman in England and the first American duchess since 1838, when the husband of Louisa Caton of Baltimore, Maryland, inherited his father's title and became the seventh Duke of Leeds.[29] Wagging tongues on both sides of the Atlantic finally had something concrete to wag about.

The marriage may not have come as a surprise to the newspaper-reading public, but the plebeian wedding venue did. The highborn duke, whose first marriage had taken place with such pomp in the lofty elegance of London's Westminster Abbey, unobtrusively linked his future with that of Lily in the mayor's office at New York's City Hall. The ceremony took place at one fifteen in the afternoon, giving the evening papers just time enough to break the story. Details at this point were sketchy; most of the text below the *Brooklyn Eagle*'s front-page headline, "A New Duchess," was devoted to a description of the several gowns comprising Lily's trousseau, all of which had been provided by the New York dressmaker Madame Donovan, and all of which were "in the very latest Parisian style."[30] By the next morning the marriage was international news, and local papers and wire services vied to outdo one another in relating the facts—often conflicting—of the previous day's proceedings and to provide background details, color, and editorial comment.

There were a number of reasons why the duke and Lily had chosen to wed quietly. One of these was certainly to avoid giving unnecessary pain to members of Lily's family, who had so vigorously opposed the marriage and who were not represented at the wedding. (The acute illness of Commodore Price at Luzerne was proffered as a compelling excuse for the absence, at least, of Lily's parents.) Another was to avoid journalistic attention and discourage reporters from any review of the duke's marital and amatory history. Lily's ambiguous status in New York society had to be considered as well. Finally, there was the duke's eagerness to hurry through official procedures in order to carry his bride back to England and properly introduce her during what remained of the London Season, the three-month period in spring and early summer when everyone of importance went to town for the parliamentary session before dispersing in early August to their country estates.

The original plan had been for a simple morning religious ceremony at Lily's Fifth Avenue home, after which the couple would immediately embark for England. At the last moment, however, a decision was made to preface the religious service with a civil ceremony—allegedly on the recommendation of the English consul in New York and in compliance with the duke's wish "to give to the marriage the importance and dignity with which I wanted it should be regarded in England."[31] This was hurriedly arranged, with New York City's wealthy and socially connected Mayor Abram S. Hewitt professing himself willing to do the honors.

Orchestrating the desired religious component of the nuptials to follow proved problematic. The duke, an English Anglican, and Lily, an American Episcopalian, essentially shared a denomination. The canon law governing Episcopalianism, however, was strict in disallowing divorced persons to marry when both parties to the divorce were still living—although exceptions might be made in favor of the "wronged" partner in such situations. As Marlborough had hardly been the wronged spouse in his divorce, no Episcopal clergyman in New York would consent to perform the marriage, and the duke had to look elsewhere. Thus it was a minister of the Baptist faith, which had no formal position on the question of remarriage after divorce, who finally agreed to conduct a simple religious service (and who was sardonically surmised to have received "perhaps the largest fee he had ever pocketed" for doing so).[32] Newspapers offered meticulous and vivid reports of this ceremony as being held variously at the bride's home, the Tabernacle Baptist Church at Second Avenue and St. Mark's Place, and the church parsonage.

There were perhaps fifteen invited guests at the two ceremonies comprising the Hamersley-Marlborough nuptials. Leonard Jerome accompanied the groom from his hotel to City Hall, and Creighton Webb, who had joined the duke on his western trip the year before, acted as best man at the civil wedding (and gave the bride away at the religious ceremony). Blanche Spedden Cruger, the friend who had often appeared beside Lily in her opera box during the past two years, was the bride's only attendant. Lily's physician, Dr. Walter Gillette, and her lawyer signed the marriage contract as its two witnesses.

Among the wedding guests was New York's social ringmaster, Ward McAllister, "whose saddened looks," according to a Troy newspaper, "told how deeply he felt the pain of having his famous fashion regiment reduced to 399."[33] (It is noteworthy that McAllister's phrase, "the Four Hundred," had gained currency in upstate New York barely three months after it was first coined in New York City.) McAllister's presence gives credence to his later claim for a degree of responsibility in engineering Lily's marriage; it seems unlikely that he, along with his daughter, would have been included in the select wedding party had he not advanced the project in some way. Missing from the guest list was Mrs. Paran Stevens, Marlborough's Newport hostess of the previous summer. This did not eliminate her as another possible facilitator of the couple's acquaintance; she had left for Europe in May and would be one of the newlyweds' first guests at Blenheim in August. Henry Clews acted as something of a master of ceremonies during the day;

his wife, Lucy, was delayed in leaving Newport and did not get to the city until late afternoon.

Newspapers devoted meticulous attention to the physical appearance and clothing of the two central characters in this not quite fairytale wedding. The bride was described as "just of the type calculated to impress the English. She is big . . . and blooming. Her hair . . . lies in lovely disorder all about her brow, which is really what one is justified in calling alabaster. Her eyes are large and fine, of dark grayish blue, with long, thick lashes. She has a high-bred, mobile mouth, and a look and carriage of great distinction." She was attired for the civil ceremony in a "very quiet toilet": a terra-cotta silk walking dress with dead-gold passementerie trimming and matching long gloves. A small turban-like bonnet of the same color ornamented with black beads was "set back well on her head, showing off to advantage her pretty face," and a bunch of lilies of the valley, her namesake flower, nestled at her waist. Her "hair was brushed carefully off her forehead and arranged in a Greek coil," noted one reporter, "and she impressed the beholder simply as a magnificent woman."[34]

The "little duke," who was "rather below the medium stature and of slight build," stood nearly a head shorter than his bride. He wore "a dark business suit with a four-button cutaway coat, with a white hydrangea in the lapel, patent-leather buttoned gaiters, and carried in his hand an English-made black silk hat, with bright purple lining, on which his monogram was worked." His hair, too, was "carefully brushed from his forehead," in his case "revealing an inclination to baldness in front."[35]

The atmosphere at City Hall was relaxed. "The Duke's 'I do' rang out firm and strong, but his bride could scarcely find her voice when it came her turn to reply." Once the official procedure was over, scribbled Mayor Hewitt hastily in a note to his vacationing wife after the event, "having exercised for the first time in New York the royal prerogative of creating a Duchess I demanded the Mayor's privilege of saluting the bride and received the first kiss."[36]

The religious ceremony took place after a break for lunch. The bride had had an opportunity to freshen up, noted a reporter, and now looked "lovely in a soft silk street dress, which perhaps reflected in a grosser way her agitated mind, in that in every light it bore a different shade." As Marlborough slipped a heavy, plain gold ring on Lily's finger, "his eyes for the first time during the ordeal encountered those of his bride, and they looked at each other for just a second."[37] That evening Clews hosted a "very pleasant and vivacious" dinner for the wedding guests at Delmonico's that broke up at eleven thirty, as there was packing to be done before the next morning's departure for England. Marlborough, after escorting Lily to her home close by, returned directly to his hotel.[38]

Some two hundred onlookers, tipped off by the morning newspapers, were on hand at the Cunard pier early the next day to catch a glimpse of the duke and his duchess as they arrived to board the steamship *Aurania*. Marlborough, like Lily, had sent his luggage ahead the night before, and left his hotel "alone on foot, carrying a small hand satchel, and sauntered a short distance up Fifth Avenue to the home of his bride." Forty minutes later he and Lily left the house, climbed into Lily's closed carriage, and set off. When their vehicle reached the dock, "a little man, not very distinguished in appearance, stepped out and assisted a tall, dark and very handsome lady to alight. 'That's them,' whispered the crowd, and sure enough it was. Arm in arm, in the most approved democratic style, the pair, apparently unconcerned by their reception, walked together up the gangway."[39]

Marlborough settled Lily into the captain's cabin, which was to serve as their parlor during the trip (and which, like the rest of their suite on board, had been reserved two weeks earlier by a third party).[40] He then wandered off in search of friends who had come to say good-bye—most of whom had attended the wedding the day before. A journalist spotted Lily "reading with seeming amusement the highly colored reports of her marriage" and reported that she "expressed herself as very happy and looked forward to a pleasant voyage." The duke was successful in corralling the assorted well-wishers and delivered them to the captain's cabin. As "the ladies mingled their tears, he and Leonard Jerome stepped out on deck, where the Duke lit a Turkish cigarette, which he puffed contentedly."[41]

Clews, in a statement to the press shortly after the couple's departure, expressed his belief "that the Duchess will be well received abroad and her dignity, her grace, and her tact will coin for her general approbation. She will open a new career for her husband in my opinion, and I think you will soon see him in political life." He praised his friend as equal to Randolph Churchill in talents while possessing "more of that quality which Americans class as level-headedness," and added inconsequentially that the duchess "shows her patriotism by her desire to have her victoria and some of her other American carriages sent over to England."[42]

Breeziness prevailed in press coverage of the wedding. Neither Lily nor the duke had sufficient status to command journalistic reverence, and there was something about their partnership that encouraged flippancy. Reporters outside of New York City pandered to what they perceived as the public's on-going aversion to the duke and what he represented. "All the talk about a romantic attachment," scoffed the upstate *Albany Argus*, "is mere rubbish, as the noble debauchee is incapable of such a feeling and the American widow could not by any stretch of imagination discover any loveable traits in such a specimen of the English nobility. . . . There is more genuine nobility in the most humble American family than in the polluted blood of the Churchills."[43]

New York journalists, however, gave further proof that their long-held animus toward the duke had mellowed. The most generous expression of the changed attitude came from the *New York Times*, which recalled the adverse criticism heaped upon Marlborough and his Newport hosts of the previous year. But, noted the *Times*, his American friends "stood by him, and the Duke, on his part, conducted himself with the most exemplary propriety and has succeeded in grounding the conviction in many minds that whatever he may heretofore have been, he is now a sober, sedate, and proper scion of the house of Marlborough, and will probably make the American widow a good husband."[44]

CHAPTER 9

Titles and Heiresses

ჯ

As a democratic nation, the United States was anti-titles. Yet Americans were fascinated by manifestations of rank, and a foreign title appeared to be an unambiguous indicator of social standing. Lily's marriage to the Duke of Marlborough generated a heightened interest in the title phenomenon, and American publishing outlets were generous in their efforts to shed light on the relative social weight of assorted European peerages, clarify issues of precedence, and specify proper forms of address.

Perhaps the most curious response to Lily's ascension to noble status was the publication in early 1890 of *Titled Americans: A List of American Ladies Who Have Married Foreigners of Rank*. This anonymously authored treatise was proffered to refute the impression conveyed by newspapers "and accepted by the public that Mrs. Louis Hamersley was the only American lady entitled to ducal rank." On the contrary, according to *Titled Americans*, there were some ten or twelve American-born duchesses sprinkled about Europe at that time, as well as nearly twenty American princesses and about the same number of countrywomen wedded to foreign ambassadors at various European courts.[1] A summary of the comparative worth of national peerages followed, a compendium that should have been mandatory reading for any woman contemplating marriage to an aristocratic nobleman from across the sea.

"There are nobles and nobles," intoned *Titled Americans* in stressing the fact that some European titles had more value than others. Titles had been granted, it continued, "with the most reckless profusion" by a number of countries in the past—often "for mere financial assistance, rendered not to the State, but to some member of the reigning family." In the general scheme of things, the author stated that Russian titles were worthless—certainly inferior to those of any other country in Europe. The custom of dividing landed properties in equal shares among all of a titled Russian's children impoverished the old aristocracy, and the offspring of later generations of ancestors who received titles as marks of official distinction had the on-going right to their use. Thus there were possibly thousands of Russian princes and princesses in circulation who would not be admitted to the society of St. Petersburg or any other European capital—among them a princess "who figures in tights and spangles as a bareback rider in a fourth-rate circus," a princely cabdriver, and a titled nobleman "who has served terms of penal servitude in several of the convict prisons of Europe."[2]

Portuguese, Spanish, Italian, and French titles, according to *Titled Americans*, were little better. Hereditary designations had been abolished in Portugal twenty years earlier but, prior to then, English and French merchants had been able to obtain lifetime Portuguese titles of count, viscount, and baron, "which in some cases they have subsequently proceeded to drag through the mud." Most Spanish peerages, with the exception of some thirty titles dating to the sixteenth century, were dismissed as upstart creations of the nineteenth century, and until "the year 1859 every petty sovereign, and even certain cities and towns," in Italy possessed the privilege of conferring nobility. Kings of Italy, as well as popes, reportedly continued to distribute titles liberally to those without criminal records who were willing to pay for them. When it came to French titles, it was recommended to be suspicious of their origins. Since the overthrow of the empire and abolition of the monarchy, people were said to have ornamented "their names with any titles that suit their fancy," claiming, if asked to defend them, that their "family papers were destroyed in the revolution of 1793."[3]

The titles of Germany and Austro-Hungary, however, were claimed to still hold social value. Although they were borne by all of a nobleman's children, the laws of entail and primogeniture by which property and honors descended only to the eldest son preserved the vigor of the ranking structure. Such regular pruning maintained the aristocratic merit of Britain's nobility as well, and it was averred that British titles "enjoy greater consideration, both at home and abroad, than those conferred by any other State."[4]

Titled Americans provided brief biographies of countrywomen who had married into European aristocracies, and for those maidens still seeking their opportunity, included a "Carefully Compiled List of Peers who are supposed to be eager to lay their coronets, and incidentally their hearts, at the feet of the all-conquering American girl."[5] Along with the names of these eligible bachelors appeared information on their present and likely future titles; projected income; professions, if any; and family seats.

Other writers addressed themselves to the appropriate use of British "Titles of Honor" in an effort to shed light on a system that was admittedly not "simple or easy or philosophical." Nevertheless, Americans were reminded that the British rules of precedence were steeped in more than eight centuries of tradition and law, as was its peerage, and it was "impossible to avoid dealing with it at times; it can be learned, and to say we will not learn it because it is absurd is in itself no less an absurdity."[6]

Lords-and-ladies trivia met the needs of the merely curious, but there were broader issues involved in what was becoming a mini-explosion of marriages between aristocratic British men and wealthy American women. Pundits in both the United States and the United Kingdom discussed the phenomenon in terms of sweeping generalities based on assumed personality traits and social skills as well as economics. Other subtexts in coverage of the trend reflected reactions in America to the general concept of its women marrying into the British nobility, and conversely, the response of the British aristocracy to what was increasingly seen as an unwarranted incursion onto its turf.

The 1874 wedding of American-born Jennie Jerome and Lord Randolph Churchill was often cited as precipitating the subsequent "invasion" of American brides into the British aristocracy.[7] This marriage took place, according to Jennie's nephew Shane Leslie, "when such an alliance was considered as experimental as mating with Martians,"[8] and pecuniary negotiations preceding their union underscored fundamental national differences in both women's access to money and their economic treatment within marriage. The inter-family deliberations about finances before Jennie and Randolph's wedding, leading to the compulsory marriage "settlement," were as foreign in concept to Jennie's father as they would have been to most American parents.

Randolph's father, the seventh Duke of Marlborough, whose title, estate, and most of what he had in the way of funds to support them would descend to his oldest son, was unable to offer his younger son much in the way of financial support as a married man. Thus he expected a generous monetary settlement from Jennie's father. What's more, he expected it to be given directly to his son, who would then dispense "pin money" to his wife to meet her personal expenses as he saw fit. This was the British way, and it differed from the financial independence legally afforded to married women in the United States. Mr. Jerome, naturally enough, wanted to settle money directly on his daughter, but, as a lawyer for the Duke of Marlborough explained to Randolph, "such a settlement cannot as far as you are personally concerned be considered as any settlement at all. . . . Miss Jerome would be made quite independent of you in a pecuniary point of view, which in my experience is quite unusual." It would be better, he advised, "that the settlement should be according to the law and custom here."[9]

The international differences over the assigning of financial power to married women caused some bitterness between the Jerome and Churchill families, but the matter was eventually resolved, if not amicably, then at least satisfactorily. "I can but think your English custom of making the wife so entirely dependent upon the husband is most unwise," Jerome observed in a conciliatory letter to the duke at the close of negotiations. "I have ignored American customs and waived all my American prejudices," he wrote, "and have conceded to your views and English customs on every point, save one. That is a somewhat unusual allowance of money to the wife." His action, Jerome noted, "by no means arises from any distrust of Randolph," but was based on principle.[10] As it turned out, Jennie's father, who suffered a number of reverses during his financial career, was unable to provide as much of an allowance to his daughter as he had wished. Nevertheless, his forceful stand on her monetary rights went some way toward reducing British prejudice and easing the path of future American brides who entered into matrimonial contracts on the other side of the Atlantic.

It was not universally the case, but most upper-class Anglo-American marriages were about money and the straightforward barter of wealth for title. American girls had the advantage over their English cousins here, because the rule of primogeniture was unknown in the United States and because American fathers generally exhibited little sexual discrimination when it came to passing on wealth. (Louis Hamersley had been unusually chauvinistic in structuring his wills to unevenly disperse wealth among unborn sons and daughters.) "In America," noted the English weekly *Truth* not long after Lily's marriage, "a man who has sons and daughters makes no financial difference between the two. In England, even when a man is not so silly as to pile everything on his eldest son, he gives his sons more than his daughters. The result is that there are more American girls with money than English girls, and outside novels, the fact that a girl can pay her own way conduces to marriage." *Truth* went on to make the radical albeit patronizing suggestion that fathers leave more money to daughters than to sons, "for a boy, if he be not a fool, can make money produce money, whereas a girl rarely can."[11]

The pace of Anglo-American marriages increased in the fourteen years between the nuptials of Jennie and Lily, although at a slower rate than it would from the last decade of the century on. The concept of wealth for title exchange became fully articulated, and cautionary tales about failed Anglo-American marriages made their way into American newspapers. One admonitory 1886 message focused on the Duke of Marlborough, whose celebrity as a result of the Campbell vs. Campbell divorce case had reportedly led to his being shadowed by no fewer than eight detectives working on behalf of suspicious husbands. The duke's situation was admitted to have a "sort of opera-bouffe comicality" to it, but was offered up as a useful reminder to stateside debutantes with aristocratic aspirations that they were better off marrying at home than throwing "themselves away upon miserable lords who have nothing noble about them except the beggarly titles they inherit."[12]

The time gap between the marriages of the two Churchill sisters-in-law provided ample opportunity to generate international bridal stereotypes. The most invariable of these dated to the 1870s, when it was maintained that wealthy American women in London tended to be beautiful and to be better dressed than their English counterparts. George Smalley, an American correspondent in London for the *New York Tribune*, used the Hamersley-Marlborough marriage as an occasion to make additional comparisons between the young women of his own country and those of England. He was not averse to patriotic advocacy. The American girl's "intelligence," he wrote, her "quickness, freshness, animation, fullness of character, often her brilliancy, always her individuality, were perfectly novel to [the English male] and perfectly delightful." He attributed American girls' ease with men to "the relations between the sexes," which "in youth are ten times more natural, genuine, and right in America than in England." The English girl, he continued, who was sheltered and schooled at home until she came out, was "taught to be timid." She had no "opinions, ideas, initiative of her own. . . . She is monotonous, and men like variety. She is a chrysalis, and to a chrysalis even a butterfly is preferable."[13]

Her sense of equality was lauded as perhaps the American girl's most distinguishing attribute. Unlike her English sister, she "never learned to play second fiddle."[14] "She was, and she felt herself, the social equal of those whom she met, and her bearing was such that others perceived this instantly."[15] From early childhood, observed an English woman journalist, she is "trained to habits of self-reliance and independence" that lead "her generally to place a high value on herself."[16] She comes to London, noted another writer, and tackles everything "with the same cheerful alacrity and certainty of success, sooner or later."[17]

Chauncey Depew, a New York railroad magnate, politician, and man-about-town (later a United States Senator), was interviewed as to "Why English Noblemen Seek American Brides" for *Titled Americans* in 1890. He, too, commented on the repressive effects of a cloistered upbringing on English girls and extolled their American counterparts as "full of dash, and snap, and go, sprightly, dazzling, and audacious." He lauded their "ready tact and marvelous adaptability," but tempered his praise by stating that the education of the American girl who gravitated to London was inferior to that of her English equivalent, who "becomes bright, and suggestive, and alert as she grows older, and able to converse with men intelligently on all vital questions." The American girl, in Depew's opinion, while quick at "repartee and chaff," was deficient in fundamental knowledge, a trait that put her at an eventual disadvantage against married English women, who were not only comfortable discussing serious subjects but were "the brightest and most venomous politicians" in the British Isles. "Our graduates of Wellesley, Vassar, Wells' College, and similar institutions," he added, "are the best educated women in the world; but a London lady said to me, 'They never come over here. We never see them.' "[18]

A British journalist spoke up for English girls as more refined, more delicate of temperament, and more romantic than their cousins from across the sea. The warm reception accorded to American women in England, he surmised, was in part owing to their more practical and "business-like" education, "in harmony with the hard and somewhat cynical conditions of their life." There was no "nonsense" about them, he concluded. "They succeed in London drawing-rooms as their brothers succeed in 'dry-goods stores' in New York, and for much the same reason. We have no doubt they make excellent wives to men who live in the full glare of society and prefer a clever, capable associate to a tender domestic companion."[19]

Did Lily conform to the stereotype of the American woman in London? Her bold manner of advertising herself when she reentered New York society after the period of mourning she observed for her first husband proved that she was no shrinking violet, and she obviously felt herself at ease in the exalted company of the British peerage as represented by the Duke of Marlborough. That she chose her second husband with her eyes open, largely orchestrated her own marriage, and insisted on the protection of her income before accepting Marlborough's marital entreaties spoke to her independence in making both personal and business decisions.

Lily's countrymen, despite ambivalence about what they perceived to have been her transparent exchange of money for title, were gratified by her accomplishment and expressed pride and satisfaction at her likely acceptability to the British aristocracy. But American attitudes toward money-for-title marriages shifted over time, and ever more glittering alliances led to grumbling about the blatant attempts of nouveaux riches families that had achieved preeminence through the open American social system to "aristocratize" themselves by marrying daughters into a class-dominated structure of hereditary privilege. By the turn of the century, women who wed foreign noblemen were denounced as "unpatriotic," and their marriages regarded as a betrayal of the country's underlying democratic principles.[20]

The aristocratic British reaction to the growing number of transatlantic marriages expressed itself in anxieties about the lowering of social barriers; the displacement of the landed elite from its position of economic and social preeminence; and a shrinking marriage market in eligible, aristocratic males.[21] This unease had as one effect a rise in British resentment against the infiltration of American women into the upper ranks of English society, and was most caustically expressed by supposedly well-bred women of the upper class. The heiress stereotype was fully delineated by the late nineteenth century, and the expression "gilded prostitutes" was understood to refer to those American "adventuresses," "forward hussies," and "sad poachers" who were perversely bartered for the coronets of impoverished aristocrats.[22] Despite the intensification of negative imagery, the pace of Anglo-American marriages accelerated, and the number of American-born peeresses increased from four in 1880 to more than fifty by 1914.[23]

Lily was, of course, an individual as well as a stock character in the phenomenon of the Anglo-American marriage. She disembarked on the other side of the Atlantic with optimism and plenty of baggage, much of it packed with the disreputable history of her newly acquired husband. There were surprises ahead, many of which she had not foreseen when she took on the title and role of duchess, and her English welcome was more nuanced than she could have possibly anticipated.

CHAPTER 10

Speculative Marriage

ぷ

Lily's social entrée in England was facilitated by the passionate activism of her new mother-in-law, Fanny, Duchess of Marlborough, on behalf of the Churchill family and the Marlborough heritage. She had been in favor of her eldest son's remarriage, and welcomed him and his wife into her home as houseguests when they arrived in London. Bride and bridegroom hurried to town shortly after the couple's steamship docked in Liverpool on 9 July for a family tea hostessed that afternoon by Theresa, Marchioness of Londonderry, the politically connected daughter-in-law of the Duchess Fanny's deceased brother, the third marquess.[1]

The Churchills turned out in strength again that evening to support Lily at the sumptuous ball given by Mrs. H. O. Oppenheim at which she made her first public appearance. The duke hovered attentively nearby, and "a strong cohort of his married sisters, ablaze with diamonds, furnished the new duchess with a kind of ornamental guard of honour."[2] Lily was led into the ballroom by her sister-in-law Anne, the Duchess of Roxburghe, who, although fourth in sisterly birth order, held the highest noble rank among the six Churchill sisters and had served as Queen Victoria's Mistress of the Robes from 1883 to 1885. Anne was the same age as Lily, as was her sister-in-law Jennie Churchill.

The new duchess was, needless to say, the object of intense scrutiny at the Oppenheim ball. She "must undoubtedly be a woman of strong character and great courage," it was opined, "for the manner in which she was stared at was such as only a well-bred London crowd is capable of."[3] Most observers praised the way in which she good-humoredly responded to "the criticism of the mobbing and staring people," and commented, too, on her pleasing looks. "Not beautiful," pronounced one, "but tall, with a fine carriage and good manner."[4] There were some skeptics. The *Washington Post* chose to quote "a lady very learned in social things, who goes everywhere" and whose "impressions may be taken as fairly representing those of the average English woman." Instead of wearing a "ravishing costume," groused this source, Lily "appeared at the ball in a white dress crushed and crumpled as though it had lain under a heavy load in a sea chest a long voyage. She had diamonds, but they were surpassed by many others in the room," and she bowed "to those introduced to her with a stereotyped smile."[5] It was noted that the duchess spent most of the evening in conversation with her new relatives. A number of well-wishers entertained Lily and her husband at smaller parties over the course of the next several weeks. Marlborough, it was remarked, "has not for years been so often in London drawing rooms as has happened during the last fortnight."[6]

There was one remaining piece of marriage business to attend to after Lily and Marlborough's arrival in London. In late July the couple wed with "extreme quietude" for yet a third time in the registrar's office of the parish of St. George's Church, Hanover Square.[7] This step was taken to counteract what was foreseen as a possible American legal argument that the duke's New York City marriage, although legitimate under English law, might not, if challenged, be construed as such within the State of New York. A number of out-of-state divorcés had stumbled up against a legal opinion laid down in 1854 (Cropsey vs. Ogden) that declared their subsequent remarriages in New York to have been unlawful.[8] It paid to tread carefully in testing the principle of comity, whereby the laws of states, and by extension, countries, crossed jurisdictional lines; it was doubly important to do so when it came to the delicate subject of divorce, and the newlyweds were taking no chances. The name of the bride as registered on the London marriage document was Lily Warren Spencer-Churchill, formerly Lily Warren Hamersley, widow, and her "rank or profession" was listed as Duchess of Marlborough. This designation, noted the *New York Times* sardonically, "if the previous marriage really proves to have been invalid, might cause some technical difficulty—and it may be interesting to add that [the bride] . . . gave her age as thirty," i.e., she declared herself to be four years younger than her real age. One of the witnesses to the civil proceeding was Marlborough's mother. News of the couple's London nuptials was immediately forwarded to Lily's relatives in New York.[9]

The duke and duchess made their way to Blenheim for a weekend stay on 20 July. This was Lily's first visit to the great house that was to be her home and where she would have to create her own place within a complex web of established rituals and relationships. She could not say that she hadn't been forewarned about the key role this property and its bucolic surroundings played in her husband's world.

"As a fact, there is no such thing as country life in the United States as we understand it in England," Marlborough had commented to a journalist at the close of his 1887 American visit. It was his belief that the life of wealthy New Yorkers in the places they went to flee the city, such as Newport and the Berkshire hills, "affords no contrasts between the ceremonies and habits of city life and the freedom of English country amusements." Members of the American upper crust, he continued, "apparently would not be happy if they lost the means of little social rounds of amusement and gossip which constitute the life of a big city." On the other hand, according to Marlborough, the primary association of all English "persons of leisure and refinement" was with the country home of his ancestors,

> his home farm and little game covers, and here the whole family throws itself into the amusements of the country in a way that an American has not yet learned to realize. The Englishman loves his farm: he delights in improving his stock; he looks forward to the cattle shows, and the local race meetings and his winter sport and hunting. The lady loves her garden; she is interested in the village school; she tries her best to interest herself in local matters of every description. . . . The contrast of rest to activity which we enjoy in the freedom of country life is a delicious experience which you have not yet learned to cultivate.

Both English men and women, he added, "would practically be bored with the same existence with which an American seems to be delighted."[10]

The English aristocracy regarded itself as essentially rural, and the Duke of Marlborough identified with the Englishmen he described. Like most others of his standing, he was only a part-time rural resident, but considered his country property his true home and took an abiding interest in pastoral life and the oversight of rural acreage. He professed in New York that the odds of a woman from the United States adapting to such an existence were small. "It is always said in Europe," he argued, "that the American woman is quite unsuited to country life, and one understands this better after a visit to this country."[11] Lily would certainly have known of Marlborough's observations before she married him. But could she, with her urban background, be happy as the wife of a country squire, no matter how elevated his status?

There was no traditional "welcome home" ceremony for Lily when she arrived in the village of Woodstock as a Blenheim bride— no gathering of townspeople to wish her well, no merry ringing of church bells, no blasts from the town band, no welcoming speech from the mayor. Instead, she and her husband were met with "splendid silence," and nothing but a letter of "friendly greeting" from the town clerk awaited the newlyweds at Blenheim.[12] This frosty reception, so different from the warm public greeting extended to Jennie Churchill on her first visit to Woodstock as a bride, was interpreted by Marlborough as a pointed snub and led to a feud of tempest-in-teapot proportions between the duke and the rector of Woodstock, one Reverend Arthur Majendie. The two men, it transpired, had been at odds since the death of Marlborough's father, when the rector chose the Prodigal Son as the text for the seventh duke's memorial service in what was understood by all to have been a veiled reference to his wayward heir. The eighth duke never entered the parish church again and dispensed with the rector's services as chaplain at Blenheim, appointing a more congenial chaplain in his place.[13]

A deputation of town worthies had visited Reverend Majendie in anticipation of Lily's arrival to request that the parish bells be rung in her honor. The symbolic gesture was, it advised, the "wish of the people," and might go some way toward promoting the mistress of Blenheim's interest in the poor people of the town. On hearing this, the mayor of Woodstock later related, the clergyman "changed color, and then refused." As an Anglican of High Church persuasion, Majendie explained, he altogether disapproved of the remarriage of divorced persons. "It was not personal to the Duke," he insisted. "I would have discountenanced any similar union. . . . I could not subserve my sense of duty to such wishes." Church higher-ups backed his position, and without the rector's support the idea of a public reception came to nothing. Marlborough was livid. Knowing the source of the prohibition, he forbade Majendie to drive in Blenheim Park, depriving him of the afternoon outings he had enjoyed for years and adding many miles to his journeys to the nearest railway station. The duke also replaced the rector as the provider of religious instruction at a parish school of which he defrayed the costs, and threatened to plant a wall of fir trees against the good man's house, just a few feet beyond the entrance to Blenheim, to cut off his light and his fine park view.[14] "His Grace," noted the mayor philosophically, "is not the one to stand a slap in the face without giving back."[15]

Lily, as a newcomer to England, had ties of affiliation with two communities that might be expected to extend a welcome to the transplanted bride: her husband's immediate family, and American women who had married into the English aristocracy. Jennie Churchill, as a member of both, was quick to extend friendship and went down to spend a few days at Blenheim shortly after Lily's arrival. The two women became close friends and supported one another through many unexpected upheavals. Jennie was in an excellent position to explain to her sister-in-law the idiosyncrasies of the Churchills as well as offer details of the duke's complicated relationship with his family.

Marlborough's divorce and history of well-publicized dalliances had exasperated his siblings, and his apparent insensitivity to the embarrassment his misadventures caused them meant that family interactions were sometimes prickly. His mother and sisters had invested their affection in Randolph, but as it was the duke's dynastic position that was responsible for their own social supremacy they paid him the respect they considered his due. The 1884–85 sale of Blenheim paintings frayed the already complex bonds between Marlborough and Randolph, who took exception to what he saw as the duke's stripping of the ancestral home of an important collection. Randolph tried to distance himself and his dependants from the duke after the transactions took place, but Jennie balked. She liked her brother-in-law, understood the importance of the ducal connection to her sons' future place in the world, and judiciously maintained her personal friendship with Marlborough. Her sons, Winston and Jack, however, had little contact with their cousin the duke's son or with Blenheim during the eighth duke's tenure.

The brothers' relationship remained tense at the time of the duke's remarriage, and it is not surprising that Randolph didn't take to Lily. "I have been rather bored here," he wrote grumpily to his mother from Blenheim during a visit not long after the Marlboroughs' arrival. "The Duchess Lily talks about Blandford and to Blandford all day long, flatters him and exalts him to his heart's content. He believes himself to be a beneficent genius." Randolph also had complaints about Lily's competence as mistress of the palace. "I never knew anything like the unpunctuality here," he groused. "Yesterday, we did not get breakfast till eleven, lunch until three, and dinner till nine; most tiresome."[16]

Luckily for Lily, it wasn't long before her mother-in-law developed a warm affection for the newest member of her family. The Duchess Fanny was a strong, warm-hearted, and judicious, if sometimes overbearing, woman. She had often stumped for Randolph during his election campaigns, and was considered an "admirable organizer" and one of very few society women able to "preside and speak at a meeting as well as their husbands."[17] Her rapport with Lily was in sharp contrast to her notoriously difficult relationship with her other daughter-in-law, Jennie, whose lifestyle she abhorred, and whom she urged at a difficult time in Jennie's marriage "to give up that fast lot you live with racing flirting & gossiping."[18] Lily neither raced nor flirted and had her own finely honed sense of personal and family dignity. No wonder tranquility reigned between the two women.

The six Churchill daughters were dutiful, and it was said that "the whole-hearted way in which they espoused each other's cause and threw themselves into their mutual interests was a great example of the old saying, '*L'union fait la force*.' "[19] There was, it was said, something of the masculine in the sisters that could be interpreted as "force of character," and while the women were all deemed "estimable and worthy," they were collectively labeled as *grandes dames*, each liable to reveal herself in the "occasional and unconscious raising of the chin." They all married wealthy and eventually titled men, and their marriages were said to be "dovelike" in their "peacefulness and utterly devoid of unpleasant incident."[20] In 1895 it was estimated that the sisters were jointly worth, through their husbands, some £16 million.[21] Like their mother, they took to Lily and gave her their full support.

Characteristics common to Churchill family members were typical of what some late-nineteenth-century English observers and later social historians have identified as the "aristocratic personality." Those of high rank, according to historian David Cannadine, shared a "sublime indifference to consequences" and a "total lack of interest in the thoughts and feelings of others."[22] The "pedestal" on which they were set, noted Adam Badeau, member of the American delegation to London in 1880, "is just as high, no matter what figure is placed on it." Aristocrats, he believed, "have no need, they think, to defer, with equals or inferiors. . . . Like everybody else they can be civil enough when it is in their interest to be so. But when none of these reasons exists—interest, preference, or necessity, they are often cold, supercilious, and arrogant to a degree unknown in what is called good company elsewhere." In summary, Badeau maintained that the influence of rank was "not refining" and inspired "an offensive pride" and "a certain brusqueness which almost never wears off."[23] The Churchill brothers, certainly, were known for their asperity, and neither of them suffered fools gladly. There was no one, it was said, who "could be more politely rude than Randolph" if bored or annoyed, and getting on the duke's nerves was likened to "having a fox-trot with a cobra."[24]

Men of the English aristocracy exercised influence in a manner that was wholly unfamiliar to Lily. Supported primarily by incomes derived from rent rolls, their lives were predicated on an assumption of leisure that allowed them to commit themselves to a cult of amateurism and a general denigration of the professions that enabled hustling Americans to lift themselves and their families into society (although there was no aversion to the entry of younger, unlanded sons into such careers). Most believed they had a "general role to play, not as experts but as leaders and representatives," and, thoroughly versed in the workings of government, they held the reins of national political and administrative power as members of the House of Lords, the House of Commons, and the sitting government.[25] When not engaged in these duties, they had a good deal of free time on their hands, and following the role model of the Prince of Wales, were an active force in society. A young American newspaperman who arrived in London at the turn of the twentieth century picked them out immediately: "hosts of tall, handsome, military-looking men, who seemed cast for no part but to appear in Bond Street or Piccadilly in the late morning wearing top hats, morning coats and spats; or at luncheon hour to step out of hansom cabs before clubs or restaurants; or at tea-time to grace the lounges of hotels to chat and flirt with fashionable-looking women."[26]

Marlborough had commented in an 1887 New York interview on the difference between America's urban elite, in which male members were devoted to professional and financial success and where "there is absolutely no class of idle men," and the elite of "a lazy capital like London," where leisured gentlemen played a conspicuous role. In New York, he added, "there is not the same craving for daily excitement that is met with in a large community of idlers, and I think that the people of this country have nothing to complain of in that they are free from this development."[27] Although the duke had once been one of London's idle men, he no longer thought of himself as among them.

The duke had given up any idea of a political career, but was increasingly devoting himself to business interests. He was largely self-taught in this area as he was in electronics and science, for his schooling had not offered much in the way of practical training. Indeed, the point of an English classical education was to produce disciplined "gentlemen" who, if they were not older sons destined to return to their estates, knew their Greek and Latin and were equipped with the kind of leadership skills necessary for life in the ministry, the commanding ranks of the military, or colonial administration. Thus it was only through experience and independent study that Marlborough and his cohort learned to retrofit themselves as entrepreneurs and capitalists in the changing world of the late nineteenth century.

Foreign politicians, English and foreign civil service officials, and financiers were the duke's preferred companions. He was in regular correspondence with members of European chanceries and stayed in touch with scientists whose work he followed. At Blenheim, he spent hours a day in his chemistry lab, preferring this occupation, noted a long-time acquaintance, "to the covert-side pastimes of an English country gentleman [hunting and shooting], though in these he was no discreditable performer." He was also a man of hobbies, among them the turning lathe, on which he produced a steady output of cigarette tubes in meerschaum and amber, ebony boxes, and caskets of ivory for his friends.[28] (Two of the duke's earliest gifts to Lily had been an inlaid table and box of his own manufacture.)[29] Another enthusiasm, one inherited from his father, was orchids,[30] and at the time of his marriage Marlborough was said to have probably the finest collection of these strange, whimsical, and graceful blooms in England.[31] A man with multiple interests, the duke was engaged on many fronts.

Lily met her stepson, Charles Richard John Spencer-Churchill, for the first time when he came to visit Blenheim in September 1888. Sunny, born in India in 1871, was then not quite seventeen years old. His nickname derived from his courtesy title, Earl of Sunderland, held as heir presumptive to his father when the latter was Marquess of Blandford. (During the years of his father's dukedom, Sunny became in his turn the Marquess of Blandford.) The youth was described as a "small, slender, rather delicate-looking boy" with "fine, clearly-cut features; a broad, high forehead; narrow chest; and a thin, almost meager, frame." He was said to take his looks from his mother's family.[32]

The bond between Marlborough and his son was strained. Sunny claimed as an adult to have been bullied and "entirely crushed" by his

Duke's son, Sunny, 1892

father as a boy; as Churchill family historian A. L. Rowse phrased it, "he is much more likely to have been neglected."[33] During his early childhood, Sunny's father had lived little at home—indeed, he did not see his youngest daughter (born in 1875) until she was two years old. His parental detachment was to some degree a natural result of upper-class child-rearing practices in England, where children were handed over to the care of nannies until they were old enough to be sent away to school—usually at the age of seven. There were also, in this instance, extenuating factors dictated by the 1883 divorce of Sunny's parents.

Neither courts nor aristocratic families had yet had much experience in handling the interests of firstborn sons of divorce who were heirs, like Sunny, to imposing titles and domains. The Marchioness of Blandford was given full custody of her daughters at the time of her divorce, but it was considered essential "for the welfare of the boy that he should be brought up in connexion with the great estate which he was to inherit" and that he "have the opportunity of becoming acquainted with the large body of people who at a future time would be his own tenantry."[34] Thus it was agreed that Sunny's paternal grandfather would have a formal role in raising his grandchild along with both his parents. The seventh duke's death shortly before the final decree took effect removed what was considered to be his stabilizing influence and reopened the matter. The Duchess Fanny petitioned to assume her husband's role in the rearing of her grandson, arguing "that the late Duke had consulted her on all details of the bringing up of the boy; that he had undertaken to maintain and educate the boy at his own expense; that he wished the child to be brought up at Blenheim under her care; . . . [and] that she was prepared to make herself responsible for the boy's maintenance and education."[35]

The duchess served for a while as a guardian to her grandson as a result of her petition, but at some point a decision was made to involve another male trustee in the heir's upbringing, and both Sunny's maternal uncle the Duke of Abercorn and his paternal uncle by marriage Edward Marjoribanks acted at one time or another in this capacity. In fulfilling what they perceived to be their trusteeship obligations, they brought a number of legal proceedings against Marlborough in the boy's interest during the 1880s. These challenged steps the duke was taking to produce income for the maintenance and improvement of his estate—including the sale of Blenheim paintings—as diminishing the son's patrimony. The cases were all decided in Marlborough's favor, but the duke was not one to brook interference, and the circumstances could be blamed for a degree of paternal coldness. By the same token, the constant attention paid by others to Sunny's alleged rights and entitlements, as well as the amount of time he spent in his mother's Hamilton family, whose members were hostile to the duke, were likely to have encouraged in the youth a measure of self-importance and an attitude of disrespect toward his father. Despite the complicated relationship between the two, Lily befriended her stepson, and Sunny began to spend more time than he had in the past several years at Blenheim.

The most serious and widely publicized threat to the ducal marriage occurred within months of Lily's arrival in England. Newspapers began publishing reports in the autumn of 1888 that the duchess had been seen walking and driving about in London with Lady Colin Campbell, the central figure in the Campbell vs. Campbell divorce case and Marlborough's reputed former lover.[36] Why Lily would have put herself in this situation is hard to imagine. The only possible answer is that her husband was still staggeringly arrogant when it came to getting what he wanted. Playing on his wife's imagined naïveté, he must have convinced Lily that a show of trust on her part regarding his purportedly platonic friendship with Lady Colin would improve the newlyweds' social situation. At the same time, it would give the duke what looked like innocent opportunities to see a woman to whom he was still attached.

Lady Colin turned up at Blenheim in October at Lily's express invitation for a visit of indefinite duration. It didn't last long. While Marlborough may have been adept at feigning indifference to Lady Colin's personal charms, the guest could not resist making it obvious to Lily that she and Marlborough were more to one another than fond friends. This was apparently typical behavior for the sensuous beauty, remembered as a man's woman who "amused herself recklessly," enjoyed playing the role of siren, and was more invested in her power over men than in the creation of enduring friendships with women.[37] Once Lily understood the situation, she was both angry and mortified. She did not accept extramarital affairs in the manner of the aristocratic sector dominated by the Prince of Wales, and unlike Marlborough's long-suffering first wife, made a magnificent fuss. The duke's mother and one of his sisters hastily made their way to Blenheim to intervene, arriving just after Lady Colin decamped. They were successful in effecting a reconciliation, but Lily was reported to be under a doctor's care after the confrontation, and subsequently took off on a brief solo excursion to the Riviera.

The press gave full attention to the incident, often in the "told-you-so" vein, and it was prophesied that "this wonderful match, the consummation of which caused two continents to contract their eyebrows," might soon come to an end.[38] Society gossips were delighted at the enormity of Marlborough's transgression. "I did not think Blandford would be silly enough to get talked about again so soon," wrote London hostess Gladys, Lady de Grey, to her sister-in-law, "and I imagined he would try and electrify the world by his exemplary conduct, but not at all."[39]

Not many weeks after Lily's return from the south of France, a brief article appeared in the *London World* to the effect that the duke had professed to have discovered certain traits of Lily's "temperament that are not to his liking, and as she is very high spirited there may possibly be some serious ado over the matter."[40] Whatever her husband's complaints may have been, Lily apparently took them to heart and made an effort to adjust her manner to please him. Her mother-in-law, who dined with the couple in February, reported Lily as "quieter" (presumably less exuberantly American than in the past) in a letter to Randolph. "I am sure poor thing she does her best to make [her husband] kind," she added. "But I do not envy her."[41]

The Gertrude Campbell incident and subsequent to-do may have marked the true beginning of the Marlboroughs' marriage. The duke recognized that his access to Lily's money was dependent on her continuing good will, and he was forced, perhaps for the first time, to give up a short-term object in pursuit of long-term goals. His wife had given him a clear signal that she was not to be trifled with, and as she tried to respond to his grievances, he made concessions to her expectations. A rapprochement was reached; at a private entertainment held several months later the duke and duchess were said to evince "a most exemplary absorption in each other."[42]

A subject of interest to the press, especially the American press, during Lily's early months in England was the duchess's weight. That the bride had put on pounds during her widowhood had been mentioned obliquely by New York newspapers at the time of her marriage—the *New York World* suggesting that the new duchess was "neither so slender nor so graceful as she was several years ago."[43] British newspapers made frequent reference to "her fine figure," but they, too, hinted that she was not slender. "The new duchess is reported to be on a large scale with a corresponding fortune," noted one journal.[44]

Standards of beauty change, of course, and the 1880s were a period of transition vis-à-vis the ideal female form. The frail,

Lily, first formal photograph as the Duchess of Marlborough, 1888

small-featured woman rendered in steel engravings of the American antebellum era had long since given way to a more vigorous, hearty model, influenced by the fleshy female nudes of French salon paintings and the voluptuous, sensual curves of popular actresses like Lillian Russell. The trend was backed by the medical profession, which advised that "plumpness was a sign of health and that both men and women should try to keep their weight up."[45] Paul Blouet, a French writer who traveled in the United States in 1887–88, admired American women for their "amplitude of proportions," equating them with those of stylish Frenchwomen.[46]

England was in advance of the United States in initiating a reaction against modish corpulence, and in the 1880s a new physical type gained vogue in Britain that found its ideal in the spare, athletic build of the beautiful Alexandra, Princess of Wales. Americans commenced their enduring battle against body fat in the 1890s, taking up British strategies for weight reduction, among them a pioneering notion for accomplishing it among women: exercise. William Banting, the author of a popular guide to weight loss first published in England in 1863, became so closely connected with the concept of "diet" (a word that didn't gain its modern meaning until early in the twentieth century) that his name was conferred on the phenomenon.[47] Thus an August 1890 headline in the *Philadelphia Inquirer*, "Duchess of Marlborough Banting," meant simply that Lily was on a diet.[48]

She had begun taking steps before her marriage to shed some of her excess weight. A New York doctor put her on a sensible diet that substituted fruit for sweets and forbade tea, coffee, and sweet wine. Exercise was a part of the regimen, and "while no limit was put upon the pleasure of driving or riding, she was expected to select the roughest, rockiest roads" to insure a good jouncing about, and to walk from five to ten miles a day in the open air. Unusual constraints, by twenty-first century standards, included prohibitions against the drinking of ice water, all liquid food at mealtime, bedroom heat, and more clothing than was needed to keep from taking cold.[49] As warm bathing was also proscribed, Lily instituted a scheme of "vapor baths." This entailed seating herself in a sort of steamer chair shaped like a tennis racket, encased in a rubber blanket and surrounded by the steam of a spirit lamp sweetened with delicate perfume. She was said to buy her scent in gallon jars.[50] By late 1888 the duchess was reported to have "reduced her weight amazingly," dropping from 160 to between 135 and 140 pounds.[51] An old friend from New York who visited her at Blenheim in the autumn of 1889 reported that he had "never known the one-time Mrs. Hamersley so brilliant and so beautiful as she is at present, and declares she has regained all the lissomeness of figure which was characteristic of her while she was still Lily Price."[52]

Stray bits of negative gossip regarding Lily's past found their way into the press shortly after her marriage. These were provided by Lily's so-called intimates and former servants and surfaced at a rate, estimated *Town Topics*, of about "a waste-basket full a week." Among the revelations were that Lily smoked cigarettes (something that few women dared to do in public), that she had a brother in an insane asylum, and that she had been "for years a victim of the opium habit."[53]

It is probable that Lily did make excessive use of opium at some periods of her life, but in this she was hardly alone. Indeed, opium, in the form of morphine by hypodermic injection and as the key ingredient in laudanum, paregoric, and a host of patent medicines, was until the 1890s considered a virtual panacea. It was deemed harmless when used in moderation and was taken to relieve the symptoms of a wide range of conditions including pain, insomnia, diarrhea, and "nervousness." Lily fit the late nineteenth century profile of Americans most likely to acquire the habit: married, stay-at-home women of the upper and upper-middle classes who became dependent on the drug through the direct ministrations of their physicians—who were blissfully unaware of its addictive potential. "Female complaints" were routinely treated with morphine; as one investigator noted, "uterine and ovarian complications cause more ladies to fall into the habit, than all other diseases combined."[54] Lily's New York doctor, Walter Gillette, routinely prescribed the drug, and another of his loyal patients allowed that under his care her mind was often "dulled by opium."[55] Feminine abuse of the substance was thought to be more widespread in the United States than in England, where alcohol was considered the self-prescribed drug of preference. At least, wrote one American acerbically, with morphine "the results are not so disgusting."[56] Opium use declined in the last years of the century as improved public health measures and non-addictive drugs, such as aspirin, were introduced, and overuse came to be regarded as a "disease" or an "addiction" with a confusing mix of physical and moral aspects.[57]

Lily tied up the loose ends of her New York past as she settled into her English life. A three-day "Duchess of Marlborough sale" held at a New York City auction gallery in early November 1888 was advertised "with a flourish of trumpets" and realized high prices.[58] It was suggested, however, that Lily had never set eyes on much of the furnishings and ornamental bric-a-brac sold in her name. As knowledgeable commentators pointed out, the sale was just another example of the incorrigibility of auctioneers and was made up largely of goods from dealers, who knew "by experience that the poorest article in the world will sell for a high price if a title is connected with it," and "the 'Duchess of Marlborough' is the killing bait thrown to New York people of wealth to make them flock together and swallow anything."[59] A carved oak dining-room set was identified as "about the only good furniture of hers to be seen," and other "articles which really belonged to Mrs. Hamersley spoke rather for her judgment in getting rid of them than for her taste in having bought them." Some of Lily's acquaintants "who visited the rooms before the sale, apparently from curiosity, seemed much shocked at recognizing certain objects as gifts made to her Grace on her first marriage."[60] Once the Hamersley home on Fifth Avenue was emptied of furniture, it was leased to a phonograph company as its headquarters.

Lily let go of her box at the Metropolitan Opera House in November as well, which sold for $15,000—$5,000 more than Louis Hamersley had paid for it in 1883. It is indicative of Lily's long-laid plans to escape New York that she had chosen not to vote with other box holders in January 1888 on the question of whether the then financially shaky opera company should continue into the following season. The ultimate decision to do so meant that box holders were assessed an additional amount above their annual carrying charges.[61]

Lily's remarriage severed her sentimental ties to Louis Hamersley, the generous husband who had made her splendid new life possible. With an eye to the financial obligations she had contracted as Duchess of Marlborough, she rescinded her 1884 pledge to donate a memorial altar in Louis's honor to the Episcopal Cathedral of All Saints going up in Albany, New York.[62] Bishop Doane, who had solicited and obtained Lily's commitment to his grandiose project, was informed of her decision when he called upon her during an 1889 visit to England. The religious inflexibility of the bishop may have had something to do with Lily's change of heart, as Doane was one of the most enthusiastic and vocal opponents in the American episcopate of the right of divorced persons to remarry (and was intimated to have declared that the children of such unholy liaisons should be considered illegitimate).[63] His attitude would not have endeared him to Lily in view of the numerous obstructions she and the duke encountered in their effort to contract a religious marriage in New York—obstructions in which Doane himself may have had a hand. The cathedral project continued, needless to say, without Lily's support, but was not completed at the time of the bishop's death in 1913. Still unfinished, it is the fifth largest cathedral in the United States and the twenty-ninth largest in the world.

Lily's father succumbed to pneumonia in Troy, New York, in November 1888, just short of his eighty-third birthday. The two decades passed by the old commodore in Troy had been an uneventful postlude to his world-ranging years as a naval careerist. The opening line of the commodore's will reflected his lifelong modesty. "First," it read, "after my death, I wish to be buried quietly, with few carriages and no funeral."[64] The news of her father's passing was cabled to Lily in England. She did not return to the United States.

CHAPTER 11

Chatelaine of Blenheim

ٮۄ

Lily's influence at Blenheim began to be felt not long after her arrival in England. "The 'new' Duchess of Marlborough," it was reported in November 1888, "has been receiving company at Blenheim this week, and the huge house, which has been partly closed during the past five or six years, looked once more cheerful and brilliant."[1]

Among the reasons for the palace's lively aspect were renovations the duke had undertaken in the years before his marriage to bring the building up to his rigorous standards. He had recently seen to the installation of a new heating system, the re-laying of 10,000 square feet of parquet floors, and the construction of a number of conservatories and greenhouses.[2] The most talked-about alteration was the introduction of electric lighting according to a scheme of Marlborough's own invention. Carried out over a period of two years, the system was unveiled during the weekend of 20–21 October 1888, when some 1,200 "incandescent jets," many of them disposed in magnificent chandeliers, first illuminated what was soon referred to as "the best lighted building in Europe."[3] Marlborough was justifiably proud of his accomplishment, and according to one visitor, it became his habit to treat all of his guests "who cared to listen to a most instructive lecture upon electricity down in a room in the basement of Blenheim Palace, in which the electrical machinery was stored. In the compass of about twenty minutes, and with an eloquence, grace, and precision of language which charmed every hearer, he would discourse upon the coming marvels of the electric age."[4] The house electricians who tended the system were accorded the respect due to "men of science" and held upper servant status equal to that of the Blenheim butler.[5]

Lily, as she had committed herself to do before her marriage, joined her husband in tackling the transformation of Blenheim. The first undertaking with which her name was associated was the repair of the three-acre palace roof; a September 1888 cost estimate for the necessary work came to £30,000.[6] A boathouse was added to the park as an embellishment to its artificial lake that incorporated a comfortable sitting room and open porch above a boat storage area at water level. Inscribed on the palace side of the building were the words, "Built by George Charles and Lily Warren Duke and Duchess of Marlborough anno 1888," while the lakeside dedication read, "So may thy craft glide gently on as years roll down the stream."[7]

The duchess may have reneged on her promise to bestow a memorial altar on the Episcopal cathedral going up in Albany, New York, but, like her mother and her great aunt Phebe Tayloe before her, she had an abiding interest in the church and in the enhancement of church buildings. So it is not surprising that she took an active role in the restoration and updating of the Blenheim family chapel during the winter of 1888–89. The architect for the project, comprising a new gallery, organ, stalls, and other fittings, was Thomas Graham Jackson, remembered today as the architect of more Oxford University buildings than any other designer in the institution's history.

Jackson recorded his impressions of Blenheim, which he first visited in connection with the chapel renovation. The house, he recalled, "struck me as amazingly fine; and the whole thing, with the approach through successive courts and the men in a sort of antique costume at the gate, had a superb effect." He was given a private tour of the family apartments by Lily, and noted that its "great rooms" were "grand, almost too grand for comfort. They are all vaulted in stone." In Lily's bedroom, he added, one could get lost in her "vast bed as big as a house, with a canopy of blue silk hangings that looks twenty feet high."[8]

Turning the huge expanse of Blenheim into a comfortable home might have seemed an insurmountable task, but the Duke of Marlborough prided himself on his ability to create a "pretty house" and made many changes. He was admired for his "wonderful taste and ingenuity" when it came to interiors, a domestic interest as prevalent among men as women in the Victorian era. According to an acquaintance, he "never minded what trouble he took over decoration. He would find an old piece of brocade and wait months to have it copied on account of the design and color, and the whole result was beautiful."[9]

Lily shared her husband's zeal for good furniture and art, of which she was considered to be "a connoisseur and critic of more than ordinary ability and acumen,"[10] and she worked with the duke to infuse warmth into their palace. The two frequented auction galleries and succeeded in doing something, it was reported, "to fill the vacancies caused by earlier ravages."[11] Examination of photographs of Blenheim's interior taken during the couple's tenure indicate no empty walls or absence of ornamentation attributable to Marlborough or his father's sales of palace contents. While a few treasures were admittedly lost in the process, the capital-raising transactions of this era appear to have had as a byproduct the editing of what had become a Victorian clutter of artwork and objects, and a disciplined approach to interior design was imposed upon the palace during the eighth duke's incumbency.

Gardening, wrote Edith Wharton in *The Buccaneers*, her novel chronicling socially ambitious American women's assault on the English aristocracy during this period, was "regarded in the highest circles not only as an elegant distraction but almost as one of a great lady's tasks."[12] The Blenheim gardens were said to be "a special pride of the duchess," and in 1889 there were sixty-five men at work on the palace grounds.[13] Lily was spending freely in her new role. Her income from the Hamersley estate in 1889, her first full year as a duchess, was $400,000.[14]

Tourists were not a constant presence during Lily's years at Blenheim. The park and the palace interiors had been open for viewing under one scheme or another since the eighteenth century, when Blenheim was a favorite site of pilgrimage and was among perhaps two dozen residential properties offering printed guidebooks. But it, like other country houses, became less welcoming in the later 1800s. The reasons for this were many: a vast increase in the number and class diversity of visitors thanks to the ease of rail travel; higher costs of upkeep and fewer resources with which to pay for them because of agricultural depression; and altered political relations between classes that diminished aristocratic commitment to the principle of noblesse oblige. Of the one hundred or so houses open to the public in the 1860s and 1870s, half were closed to outside visitors by 1914, of which two-thirds were closed before 1900.[15] During Lily's years at Blenheim, the palace was generally open from eleven to one o'clock twice a week (on Tuesdays and Fridays) in the late spring and summer months; the 350 acres of private grounds and gardens were open from eleven to two o'clock on the same days.[16] Entry fees collected by the lodge-keeper were given to charity on the theory, according to one commentator, that admission fees kept "the more undesirable visitors away" and "that if 'show days' were a necessity, they should be made a blessing to someone."[17]

Lily was, in principle, responsible for the running of her household. Blenheim, however, like other great houses, functioned according to what one contemporary called "a carefully regulated system, worked by capable machines, of which the lady herself is the nominal head. In reality, the system goes on without interference on the part of the mistress, whose control, though absolute in theory, is almost *nil* in practice."[18] The palace's indoor staff numbered over forty and was under the direct supervision of a butler and a housekeeper who hired and fired underlings, maintained standards, and dealt with the petty arguments that inevitably arose within their domains. Servants worked to a schedule that kept them out of the way of their employers, and Blenheim's network of narrow rear corridors and service staircases enabled staff to go about their duties without disturbing, or even being seen by, those on whose behalf they labored. It was typical for employers in large establishments like

Blenheim to know only the servants who personally attended them; lower servants were not always able to recognize their masters and mistresses by sight.[19]

In order to retain competent staff members, masters and mistresses were advised to let "their servants see that they take a lively interest in their welfare and happiness, and that they do *not* look upon them as *mere* servants, *who are here to-day and gone to-morrow,* but as a part of their family."[20] One manner of showing appreciation was the annual ball for servants and local tradesmen that by custom took place at great estates during the Christmas/New Year's season, and such events were a regular feature of Blenheim life. The audit room that served on ordinary days as the estate office where tenants came to pay their rent was given over on these occasions to dancing. Music at Lily's first Blenheim servants' ball commenced around ten o'clock in the evening, and the duke and duchess, along with two of Marlborough's sisters and his son, who were on hand for a family party, took part in the first two dances. The strains of Herr Slapoffski's Quadrille Band kept dancers on their feet until five o'clock the next morning, and "supper, which was of a most *recherché* character, and to which 230 sat down, was served in the servants' hall."[21]

The dinner for Blenheim estate laborers and their wives held the evening before had been a departure from tradition. It was the duke's Christmas custom to give a piece of beef to each workman (four pounds to married and three pounds to single men), but this year some 315 men and women came together for a common meal in Blenheim's Riding School, now twinkling with electric lights and festively adorned with evergreens. As Marlborough was quoted as saying in an after-dinner address, "this being the first Christmas the Duchess had spent in Oxfordshire, she was anxious that they should assemble at the Palace together." After the withdrawal of the duke and duchess from the party, "a convivial evening was spent, smoking was freely indulged in, and some good songs were sung, the singing of 'God Save the Queen' bringing a very pleasant and thoroughly enjoyable evening to a close."[22] In future years, estate employees were again presented with Christmas beef allotments rather than a celebratory gathering.[23]

Aristocratic women endowed through their husbands with the possession of large country estates, Lily found, had a prescribed role to play in English country life. While the proprietor superintended the administration of his domain, his wife was expected to support him through a program of local good works that meshed social consciousness and kindness with her husband's need to extend his local influence, safeguard property rights, and enhance the prestige of both landlord and estate. This feminine agenda was regarded as work at a time when upper-class women were precluded from pursuing recognized professions, and those who willingly took on the task prided themselves on their ability to extend their traditional nurturing role beyond the walls of their immediate homes.

There was no counterpart to the task of estate mistress on the other side of the Atlantic, and according to Vivien, Lady Decies, an American who married into the British aristocracy in 1911, there was "little doubt that responsibilities which an American woman must accept if she marries an English country gentleman are good for her. They usually give her a fuller and more useful life than she would spend as the wife of a man of equal position in her own country."[24] Lily's sister-in-law Jennie Churchill agreed with Lady Decies in principle. "The English woman," she told an interviewer in 1902, "takes herself very seriously indeed, and does much more work than her American cousin."[25]

The mistress's charitable acts were most often directed to known individuals, usually estate dependants. Some labeled this tradition of aristocratic philanthropy a manner of serfdom—in which kindnesses received were expected to be paid for in subservience. As a correspondent for the *London Daily News* phrased it, there were many who regarded "'good landlords' with utter abhorrence. They are beneficent, but their beneficence implies the forfeiture of every particle of freedom, and the submission of the people to whatever may be imposed upon them. . . . There is literally nothing for the people to do but plod quietly on as they are told, take what is given them, and be thankful. It is all well intended . . . but it is the abnegation of all manhood, of everything like citizenship."[26]

England was, however, still a "deference society," in which everyone knew his place and had fixed expectations of those both above and below him on the class ladder.[27] When the lady of the manor saw her role as a long-term commitment, and was compassionate in carrying it out, warm bonds often developed between donor and recipients that made acceptable the patriarchal social system it bolstered. Lily threw herself into her job and discovered that it suited her. "The Duchess of Marlborough," it was reported in January 1889, "has made herself exceedingly popular with the inhabitants of Woodstock."[28] She forged relationships with Blenheim's dependants and made the obligatory gifts to charitable organizations that served a larger constituency, such as a box of pears or a Christmas tree to Oxford's Radcliffe Infirmary.[29] Her good works were not restricted to the poor, and she "won golden opinions from all classes for [her] practical sympathy," it was reported, as well as with her provision of floral decorations and her enthusiastic presence at a number of popular entertainments in Woodstock.[30] "It is only right to mention," announced the mayor in connection with the duchess's support of one such event in 1892, "that no work of any description goes on in this neighborhood, either for the pleasure or for the more substantial benefit of the people, in which she does not take the keenest interest, and lend to it the most liberal support."[31]

Parks or "pleasure grounds" surrounding large estates and their private gardens played an important role in community life. Blenheim's park, 2,100 acres in extent, did so in its little corner of Oxfordshire. Its cricket field was home to the Blenheim Park cricket team (of which the duke was the nominal president and on which Sunny played when he was at Blenheim). Team members were drawn from Woodstock and surrounding villages and competed on Saturday afternoons during the season against teams from nearby towns and Oxford colleges. The estate had enough players among its employees in various departments to place two or three teams on the field, and there were occasional strictly local matches, such as "indoor vs. outdoor Blenheim servants," or Blenheim Estate vs. the Town of Woodstock.[32]

In winter, the park's frozen lake was opened for skating after reminders were posted at the gates warning visitors of spots where special caution was advisable because of thin ice. Hockey matches were mounted between Woodstock and Oxford teams, and there was night skating lit by the soft twinkle of Japanese lanterns hanging from bushes rimming the island in the middle of the lake.[33] The park was a frequent setting, too, for the outings of organized groups, and the May 1890 opening of a three-mile rail spur for the transport of goods and passengers between Blenheim and Woodstock, constructed mostly at Marlborough's expense, made the grounds easily accessible.[34] Excursion planners relied on the special character of the surroundings to attract patrons and charged admission that went to support the groups' activities. They counted on the occasional appearance of the duke and/or duchess to thrill attendees, and when Lily and her husband were on hand Marlborough was expected to offer a laudatory speech and Lily to present prizes to contest winners.

The agricultural show or fair, at which farm products were displayed and prizes awarded for the best entries in a long list of categories, was a highlight of the rural year, and the Woodstock Agricultural and Horticultural Association's early autumn fair was an annual event in Blenheim Park. It and comparable shows mounted in nearby villages were important, according to Marlborough, in encouraging "friendly rivalry" and enabling agriculturalists "to see the best that their neighbors could produce and that what they did produce was sometimes good enough to compete in the larger shows."[35]

Not all aristocratic landowners regarded owning tracts of agricultural land as an opportunity to farm, but Marlborough was genuinely attracted to agriculture and the improvement of farm products. Like others responding to the English agricultural depression, he was convinced that the future of the countryside lay elsewhere than in the growing of traditional cereal crops. He began before his second marriage to amass choice herds of Shorthorns and Jersey cows and launched into animal husbandry as well as dairy farming, an agricultural trend new to Oxfordshire that, thanks to the county's proximity to large urban markets, was proving profitable. He erected new barns and cattle yards, drained fields, removed hedges, and remodeled the Blenheim dairy around 1887, fitting it with modern machinery to produce butter that became a sought-after market product.[36] The output of the recently built greenhouses—rare orchids, other flowering plants, and winter fruits—also gained in economic value as the agricultural branch of horticulture, less immune to overseas competition than cereal cultivation, expanded.

The duke took more than casual interest in hackneys and trotting horses (trained to run in harness), as well as Shire horses (large, heavy carthorses with long hair on their lower legs that originated in the English Midlands). Sharing the British aristocracy's obsession with animal bloodlines as a means of improving stock quality, he exerted his local influence to encourage Oxfordshire farmers to turn their attention to increasing their capabilities for carrying and breeding high-end livestock. Their mutual goal, he argued, should be not in the production of "general purpose animals," but in cattle and horses of superior ancestry for export as the sires and dams of "future race[s] of fat steers and hardy horses that would be bred in other countries than our own, and of which we would be delighted to receive back the produce, at the cheap prices the foreigner can afford to sell them to us in our Free Trade ports."[37] As practical extensions of his philosophy, he served on the leadership council of the Shire Horse Society and bought a highbred Shire stallion, *Hydrometer*, which he made available to "approved mares"; his own tenant farmers benefited from reduced stud fees.[38] Marlborough wrote up his theories on animal propagation, and according to *Live Stock Journal*, "approached the consideration of subjects connected with stock-breeding with independence and courage. Several of the papers published from his pen," it added, "have led to most useful discussion in our columns."[39]

It wasn't long before Lily ventured into animal breeding herself on a domestic scale, winning first prize in the "Blenheim spaniel" category at the 1889 Woodstock agricultural show with her recently purchased *Norwich Lady*.[40] The chestnut and white Blenheim spaniel purportedly had its origin in 1704, when a spaniel with distinctive features stayed with the first duke throughout the day at the Battle of Blenheim. His duchess, Sarah Churchill, took up the type in honor of this incident, and there were always such spaniels at Blenheim thereafter. The 250-odd Blenheims raised in the vicinity of Woodstock at this time, known in dog-breeding circles as "Marlborough Blenheims," were stout, curly-coated, sporting dogs closer in resemblance to cocker spaniels than to the toy Blenheim spaniels then competing in nationwide shows.[41] Lily's association with the strain created a vogue for the animals, one that was not confined to England, and it was soon reported that a number of American breeders had taken up the rearing of Woodstock Blenheims from imported sires.[42]

Large animals dominated county and national agricultural shows, and in May 1889 Blenheim hosted the two-day annual fair of the Oxfordshire Agricultural Association—the second largest event of its kind in the country and the most important public event to take place at Blenheim during Lily's tenure. The fair had last been held there in 1879, and in 1889 it attracted 172 entries in the cattle division, 140 horses, 97 sheep, 50 pigs, and nearly 5,000 attendees. The town of Woodstock was gaily decorated for the occasion with flags and banners, "and the old benediction 'Success to Agriculture' was observed on more than one flag which danced a welcome to the throng of visitors."[43] The duke and duchess gathered a large house party, including Marlborough's sister Georgiana, a well-known horsewoman who won premium honors as the driver of her own mare in a contest held in the commodious horse ring erected for the fair. Marlborough, who handled a gelding in the same class, took the chair at a marquee luncheon as that year's association chairman. Responding to a toast, he courteously attributed some of the enthusiasm expressed for his endeavors to Lily. "Her Grace," he said, "had quite as much interest in it as [himself], and he was sure she would always feel the same with regard to any other interests connected with this place."[44]

Journalists covering the fair were impressed with the improvements in evidence at Blenheim. *Truth* declared the duke's farming operation to be "one of the most perfect establishments in the country," one that was "conducted with excellent judgment." The tiny village of Bladon, just outside the park, was reported to have been "extensively rebuilt with model cottages, which have replaced dilapidated and unhealthy structures and, indeed, extensive and judicious improvements of all kinds are being carefully carried out on the Blenheim estate."[45] Marlborough was proving himself a dedicated landlord and innovative agriculturalist, and Lily shared his enthusiasm.

CHAPTER 12

The London Challenge

To master the routines of Blenheim was one thing. To conquer London society was another. Lily landed in England with every intention of making a splash in the country's social seat, and her first step in that direction had been to procure an elegant London dwelling as an in-town base. The acquisition was made in her name and was announced at the time of her marriage. As she made no trips to England in the months before her wedding, the selection can only have been made and the purchase negotiated on Lily's behalf by the Duke of Marlborough. The house was located in Carlton House Terrace, a handsome double block of stucco-faced residences built about 1831 on the earlier site and grounds of Carlton House, home of King George IV from 1811 to 1820 when he was Prince Regent. Overlooking the Horse Guards Parade and the Mall, the terrace adjoined Marlborough House, the London residence of the Prince of Wales, and its houses were considered among the finest and best situated in the city. Lily spent freely on the redecoration of her home; the duke was commended for completely altering the appearance of the long and narrow staircase in its entrance hall by designing a wrought-iron stair rail that was much wider at the bottom than at the top.[1]

Lily did not arrive in England until July, so she missed most of the activities associated with the 1888 Season—the annual period from late April until the beginning of August when aristocratic families congregated in London for an elaborately orchestrated round of social events. Balls, receptions, garden parties, charity bazaars, concerts, coaching meets, the Henley rowing regatta, and a trio of important horse races were all on the agenda. Other ritualized opportunities for mixing included opera performances at Covent Garden and the horseback riding, daily parade of carriages, and after-church Sunday strolling that took place in Hyde Park. Parliament was in session then, and men with government responsibilities had work to do. But for women, the Season meant an opportunity to entertain and be entertained, to search out likely spouses for their children, and to shop. For most of the year, noted one observer, the fashionable West End district of London was " 'empty.' Blinds were drawn in the front of the house, a couple of servants acted as caretakers, and if some member of a family were compelled for any reason to be in London . . . she crept in and out of her own house as though she had no right there. The man put up at his Club."[2] From April to early August, however, patrician London was a lively place.

Lily assumed that her title would guarantee her reception into the uppermost crust of society once the stumbling blocks of her husband's divorce and damaged reputation had been overcome. But she was to discover in short order that, despite her elevated position in the peerage, there were barriers in London that she would be unable to penetrate.

A definition of what constituted "society" was hard to determine. The phrase "upper ten thousand" or "upper ten" lumped together the one in every three thousand people among the British population with land, title, wealth, and/or position in a loose category that demarcated society in its widest sense.[3] At the same time, the word "society" was applied more specifically to that group making up the most visible and talked about segment within this broad classification. Its center was unofficially defined as "the social area of which the Prince of Wales is personally cognizant, within the limits of which he visits, and every member of which is to some extent in touch with the ideas and wishes of His Royal Highness."[4] Indeed, the prince's endorsement was so critical to success at society's peak that American-born Minnie Paget, Mrs. Paran Stevens's daughter, could not understand why so much energy and money were expended in the United States in attaining and maintaining social preeminence. "Just what is it that you are all after anyway?" she was quoted as querying her American friends. "In

England," she said, "all the effort was to get the Prince of Wales as a guest, to have him frequent your house."[5]

The most prominent circle in society looked to the aristocracy for its leaders, but it was hardly homogeneous. On the contrary, thanks to the prince's initiative and authority, it was open to an unprecedented degree to what historian Barbara Tuchman labeled "a variety of disturbing outsiders, provided they were either beautiful, rich or amusing: Americans, Jews, bankers and stockbrokers, even an occasional manufacturer, explorer or other temporary celebrity."[6] It was closed, however, to those whom the Prince of Wales chose to exclude, and he was an unforgiving man. He had not relaxed his social injunction against Marlborough after the Aylesford affair some thirteen years earlier, and as he once told a friend who had served with the duke in the Royal Horse Guards, he "greatly disliked" his former companion because "he always reminds me of one of the most disagreeable episodes of my life."[7] Jealously guarding his role as "a sort of censor and inquisitor of society and of the Court,"[8] the prince insisted that the duke remain an outcast within his sphere.

There was some uncertainty as to how strictly the prince intended to enforce his ban after the duke's second marriage, and a few social lions tested it during the first weeks of the 1889 season. Among them was Marlborough's sister Lady Cornelia, Baroness Wimborne, a favorite hostess to the royal family and a clever woman considered "quite infallible in discerning between the aspirants for fashionable recognition who are likely to 'arrive,' and those whose chances are doubtful."[9] Lily and her husband were among the guests at Cornelia's early April ball to "meet" the Duchess of Teck, a cousin of Queen Victoria (and mother of Mary, who would wed the Duke of York, later King George V, in 1892). "It was hoped," noted one reporter, "that the prince and princess would come, but they did not."[10] As it was accepted wisdom that "society in London will never judge for itself if its rulers will relieve it of the responsibility,"[11] once it became apparent that the prince intended to be inflexible in this case, the doors of sycophants currying his favor were determinedly closed against the duke and his wife.

Queen Victoria's personal aversion to the Duke of Marlborough was known to equal that of her son. Furthermore, Her Majesty loathed the concept of divorce, and until making an exception in 1883 for Marlborough's first wife, Lady Blandford, had never allowed anyone who had been through the divorce court, either as plaintiff or defendant, to appear at royal functions.[12] It was smugly asserted by many that the queen's personal antipathy to Marlborough, in conjunction with her stance on divorce as a disqualification for royal acceptance, meant that she would bluntly snub Lily. The issue was moot in 1888, but became a topic of intense speculation in early 1889.

It was a curious anomaly that Queen Victoria's only real social power lay in her authority to restrict women's formal admittance to court, a power she exercised through rigid control of access to the four "drawing rooms" that took place in the first half of the year at Buckingham Palace. Presentation at one such event, under the patronage of a woman in good court standing, was a necessary prelude to invitations to other state social functions. Some suggested that the queen's jealously guarded prerogative had, "in point of exclusiveness, ceased to be critical."[13] But the royal gesture of acceptance still mattered, certainly, to old families like the Churchills and to lesser mortals who did not understand the complex changes taking place in English life.

The months before the 1889 drawing rooms allowed plenty of time for behind-the-scenes maneuvering over the question of Lily's court presentation, and a thinly veiled rivalry played itself out between the Churchills, on behalf of Marlborough's bride, and the Marchioness of Blandford's Hamilton family. Bertha's siblings—the offspring of the first Duke of Abercorn and his wife—were, like the Prince of Wales, dedicated to insuring the social exile of the dissolute aristocrat who had so wronged their sister, and were said to be "naturally annoyed at the fact that he had been set on his legs again in a financial sense" by his new wife.[14] In terms of collective influence and numbers, the duke's former in-laws outranked the Churchills. Although the Duke of Abercorn was an Irish title created only in 1868 (the duke also held an English marquessate), the Hamilton family was unusually close to the monarchy and unusually prolific—the first Duchess of Abercorn, Bertha's mother, leaving behind 169 living descendants at her death in 1905.[15] The duchess and Queen Victoria were intimate friends, and two of Bertha's nine surviving siblings served the royal family directly: Louisa, Duchess of Buccleuch and Queensberry, as Mistress of the Robes to the queen; and James Hamilton, the second Duke of Abercorn, as Groom of the Stole to the Prince of Wales. Maud, wife of the Marquess of Lansdowne, was Vicereine of India; George was First Lord of the Admiralty and a Conservative member of the House of Commons; and two other brothers were then or had recently served in Parliament. Through marriage into other great families, the Hamilton influence was widespread, and theirs was a dynasty to be reckoned with.

Bertha's family and its allies were not the only ones to raise the question of Lily's eligibility for court presentation. The issue resonated with humble members of the public, who were for the most part steadfast supporters of their monarchal system and likely to be even more conservative than their self-styled betters when it came to observing its social niceties. *Modern Society*, a "servants' paper" that specialized in gossip about the highly placed, published a strongly worded letter in March 1889 from a reader signing herself simply "an Englishwoman" that represented the view of many. "I think," bristled this upholder of hereditary privilege,

> a decided voice should be raised on the Marlborough presentation question, which is one of public interest and importance, on account of the precedent it would create. Mrs. Hamersley, like all the rest of the world, gentle and simple, knew the story of the Duke, of his conduct to his noble wife, of his mean desertion of the woman he had betrayed. . . . She openly chose to espouse a man under a cloud, knowing full well his position at our English court, and how can she expect to be presented, thereby getting her husband whitewashed into Society again? The Duke set Society and morality at open defiance, and it is only just he should suffer outside the pale, as a middle-class or poor man would have to do. The Duchess

showed so little feeling of anything but ambition in having the courage to come to this country and face all the disagreeables that must daily come before her, that it would only be justice to let her see her ambition cannot be satisfied by the breaking of old rules which have been hitherto stringently observed. This is just the thin edge of the wedge, and if the Queen receives herself or puts on the Princess of Wales the indignity of receiving such a presentation, she will open the door to a jumble of relationships that one cannot contemplate without a shudder.[16]

Not everyone agreed with this writer's point of view, and some expressed the opinion that "the poor American lady has nothing to reproach herself with."[17] It is likely, however, that the issue of Lily's court presentation was hotly debated around dining tables at all levels of society for several months.

Despite the charged emotions engendered by the issue, the Duke of Marlborough's mother resolutely pressed Queen Victoria on her daughter-in-law's behalf. Her request that Lily be received was one that the queen, regardless of her personal disinclination, could not refuse an old friend with a high position in the peerage and a politically prominent son in Randolph. The Hamiltons made certain, however, that Lily was subjected to an uncomfortable degree of humiliation before achieving her court welcome. An announcement that the Duchess of Marlborough would be presented at the first (considered the most prestigious)[18] drawing room of the year on 26 February occasioned great curiosity. But Lily was absent from court that day. She had, it was later said, "fully intended to be present," but did not receive the necessary tickets admitting her to the palace, nor was she given an explanation for their nonappearance.[19] The reason for her exclusion, it came out, was simple enough. The Marchioness of Blandford had chosen to flaunt her personal ascendancy and presented Frances, the middle daughter from her marriage to Marlborough, at this drawing room.[20] She could hardly have been expected to share the occasion with Lily.

Queen Victoria's drawing rooms were bound by strictly enforced conventions and were equivalent to the Prince of Wales's levées that introduced men to court. They were held in mid-afternoon, and while husbands might escort their wives to the venue, the only men allowed to enter the Presence Chamber were those with some official position at court. Debutante daughters of the peerage were automatically eligible for presentation, but other women had access only if they could find suitable sponsors. Full evening dress was required: unmarried women and brides wore white; other married ladies, although they were at liberty to wear whatever colors they chose, often affected white as well. Bared arms and neck were compulsory, although it had recently been decreed that a medical certificate "to the effect that the delicate health of a lady requires the protection of a high dress" could circumvent the regulation. Each presentee wore a nine-foot train and a headdress made up of a "lappet" and feathers. The lappet—two widths of tulle at least one yard in length and neither hemmed nor trimmed—was gathered at the top and fastened over the back hair. Standing at the center of this confection was a fountain of tall plumes (three for married and two for unmarried women) so arranged that they would be visible to the queen when the woman wearing them entered the throne room.[21]

The etiquette surrounding drawing room procedure was no less rigid than the obligations of dress. Ladies were admitted in groups and passed through a series of apartments roped off to prevent their pushing forward too eagerly. Bad behavior in these appropriately called "pens" by women eager to reach Queen Victoria before she relinquished her place to a surrogate (usually the Princess of Wales) was not unheard of—the daughter of an earl once revealing that "she had often known ladies stick pins into the bare arms of those in front to make them move out of the way."[22] The diplomatic corps was welcomed first and made its reverences to the queen, the ladies of her family, and the Prince of Wales and his brothers. The women to be presented followed, each of them entering the throne room with her train over her arm, which was taken and spread behind her by two gentlemen-in-waiting. The Lord Chamberlain announced a name, and its bearer approached the queen, made a deep curtsey, and accepted the queen's acknowledgment (a touch on the hand, or, if she were of sufficiently noble rank, a kiss on the forehead). She recaptured her train, gathered together for her by two other gentlemen-in-waiting, stumbled slowly backwards out of the room into a larger area in which other guests mingled, and could now announce to the world that she had "been at court."[23]

Lily's presentation finally took place on 1 May. The drawing room, as was usually the case, received widespread attention in the press. "There never was a more perfect day," effused *Truth*, "and the Mall looked lovely, with all the fresh young green leaves on the trees." The carriages that bore their overdressed female occupants to court "were smarter than usual, too, as though in honor of the splendid weather." The drawing room was described as "not so full as had been expected." There was "no great show of beauty," but "the gowns as a whole were decidedly above average." Few women, it was reported, availed themselves of the new court regulation concerning high dresses, "though there were numerous instances in which it would have been, to say the least, desirable that it should have been remembered."[24]

All eyes were on the Duchess of Marlborough, there under the sponsorship of her mother-in-law. She was the first woman to be presented after the diplomatic corps had entered the throne room, and because of her rank, had been extended the privilege of the "entrée," a distinction that meant she was able to circumnavigate the women waiting in the pens and come in by a special entrance.[25] "After the Queen had given her Grace the prescribed kiss," noted one observer, Her Majesty "shook hands with her most graciously, and kept her in conversation for two minutes, giving her a very kindly welcome to the English court."[26] This personal attention was perceived to be "an altogether exceptional favor, as the royal person scarcely ever notices any of the mob of toadying females who crowd to these shows."[27] The Prince and Princess of Wales bowed coldly to Lily but gave her no further salutation.[28]

"The staring, whispering, and remarks, that were by no means whispered, as she passed by, among the throng of *debutantes* and habituées," according to one reporter, would have disgraced the good manners of a much less august assembly! But all the other fine ladies had evidently made up their minds to gaze as much as they liked; and we are sorry to say that a good many of them were even resolved to speak their minds as well—and very censorious and unamiable those minds must, some of them, be!—though we are happy to add that the majority of utterances did full justice to the good looks of the American lady, and the excellent taste of her dress.[29]

As New York's *Town Topics* observed in recounting the event, "All in all, the recent Queen's Drawing Room was pregnant with interest . . . for the student of sociology."[30]

Lily's court gown was described as "magnificent." It was black, in token, it was announced, of Lily's mourning for her father, who had died six months earlier. This departure from the norm not only caused Lily to stand out in a sea of white, but as an outward show of bereavement would have been expected to please the queen, who wore nothing but black for nearly forty years in honor of her deceased consort. The press was inexhaustible in its praise of the garment—not one, but two, correspondents describing it at length in a single issue of *Truth*. Its satin bodice and train were brocaded in silk in an unusual sweeping palm leaf design; the skirt front was richly embroidered in a finely wrought pattern of wreaths in gold, silver, and cut jet over black satin; and plumes of black feathers caught the folds here and there, while diamond clasps glittered among the feathers. The train, lined with silk, was bordered all around with black ostrich-feather trim, while up one side clusters of three unusually long and splendid plumes stood erect at frequent intervals. Lily's chest and neck were ablaze with sparkling diamonds, some of which had belonged to Sarah, wife of the first Duke of Marlborough, and more jewels glittered at her ears and in her hair.[31] "To crown all," her bouquet of Blenheim orchids, shaded from mauve to white, mounted with variegated foliage, and tied up with a mauve ribbon, was judged to be "perhaps the handsomest of all the superb posies in all that brilliant crowd."[32]

After the ordeal was over Lily betook herself to the studio of

American photographer Harry Vander Weyde, who documented the occasion with the traditional presentation photograph as crowds gathered around the Marlborough carriage, emblazoned with the duke's coat of arms, to await her reappearance.[33] She must have given few of the resulting images to family and friends, for none seem to have survived.

Despite the uncertainties surrounding her delayed court presentation, Lily busied herself in London during the 1889 Season with the kind of benevolent activities expected of aristocratic ladies. Only a few upper-class women took an active role in organized charities at this time, but all of them were constantly solicited for donations and subscriptions to worthy causes, particularly medical charities and those connected with the relief of women and children. They were also called upon to staff booths as saleswomen and waitresses at the many charity bazaars and fairs that took place during the Season. The visible support of a member of the royal family was considered a guarantee to swelling attendance at such events among the elite and those who wished to rub shoulders with them, but "failing the Queen any distinguished lady, preferably with a title, ensured an increase in sales."[34] Well-bred women responded to the importuning and accepted the time they put in selling trinkets and serving tea at these venues as occasions to visit with friends and extend social contacts as well as opportunities for personal display.[35] They could also be counted on to be liberal buyers of fair goods—which were likely to be recycled at future charity bazaars.[36] Lily, along with another American woman, Lady Mandeville, presided over the United States stall at a mid-March fair to benefit the Hospital for the Treatment of Joint Diseases. She was on call again in May at the "Al Fresco Fete and Village Fayre" at Albert Hall in support of the Grosvenor Hospital for Women and Children. There, in the company of her sister-in-law Jennie Churchill, she manned the refreshment booth, and wearing a white apron, served customers with tea, coffee, and ices.[37]

There were a few occasions when Lily's anticipated presence as hostess at a bazaar was announced with much fanfare in the newspapers but the duchess failed to appear, later claiming indisposition or that she had never had any intention of being on hand. It is likely that in these instances Lily had bowed to circumstances—the Marchioness of Blandford having expressed a wish to participate in the event, thereby forcing Lily to absent herself. Indeed, the Hamiltons put a great deal of effort into insuring that Bertha would not come into contact with the woman they viewed as her enemy during the course of the Season. "You can have little idea of the complications that have arisen," commented one observer. "The most astute diplomacy has been exercised in order to avert the consequences of carelessness on the part of certain hostesses. On one occasion there was a very narrow escape from a meeting that only the most self-controlled could have prevented from resulting in a scene."[38]

Queen Victoria may have succumbed to political necessity in allowing Lily's presentation at a drawing room, but she felt no obligation to extend her welcome further. Why, asked naïve lookers-on, now that the Duchess of Marlborough had been formally introduced at court, was she not to be seen at the state ball or the state garden party or the state concert that counted as key events of the Season? The answer was simple enough. One might be *permitted* to attend a drawing room, but one had to be *invited* to other state social proceedings. Neither Lily nor her husband was about to receive any royal invitations.

A sardonic newspaperman caught Lily's first visit to the House of Lords that spring. The duke had not been much in evidence in the House since his marriage, but Lily was on hand when the Land Transfer Bill, a measure in which he took an interest, came up. "A peeress dressed all in white silk surveyed the scene from one of the side galleries," noted the journalist:

> Her dress was charming, so was her carriage, her bearing, her pale, interested, and somewhat coquettish-looking face. . . . She was in the center of the gallery, and was the cynosure of all eyes. I detected the Lord Chancellor having a glance at her amid the distresses of the Land Transfer Bill, and many other grave and reverend seigneurs scrutinized her in the interludes of the debate. . . . No one had ever seen the peeress in the House, but she was perfectly at home. She cast her eyes hither and thither with curiosity and without flinching, and bore the

scrutiny of more than two-hundred peers with the composure of a monumental statue. At last she gracefully rises, and, like a heroine of a romance, sweeps out of the House with all the dignity of an Eastern princess. Who was the little lady? Evidently many of their lordships did not know. Inquiry was made. It was the Duchess of Marlborough. Fresh from Manhattan island.[39]

Despite the powers of exclusion wielded by both the royal family and the Hamiltons, the duke and his duchess did not lack for social opportunities. Marlborough had a wide circle of loyal friends, many of whom, like him, cared little for the social spotlight. According to T. H. S. Escott, one-time editor of the prestigious *Fortnightly Review* and a long-time acquaintance of the duke's, "the Marlborough house never knew a head who . . . was more widely eclectic in the choice of his company."[40] Some hosts and hostesses of high standing refused to be bullied by those who claimed the right to impose social sanctions and entertained the Marlboroughs when the couple's professed opponents were not expected to be on hand. It can hardly be said, however, that the duchess triumphed during her first Season. It was clear that she had underestimated the degree of aversion felt by many toward her husband.

Lily nevertheless continued to have expectations about a role in society. She employed the public relations technique learned in New York to alert the press to her doings in order to maintain social visibility, and threw herself into the seasonal fray for a second time in 1890. Everyone in London of consequence was expected to appear in court once a year, and a spoon-fed announcement appeared in *Vanity Fair* in early May to the effect that Lily would "be present at the [next] Drawing Room, and the Duke and Duchess will be in town during the greater part of the Season."[41] But her effort had little positive result, and despite her stated intent, Lily did not turn up at another drawing room. In theory, women who were "on the list" of those already presented at court were allowed to attend later drawing rooms and were required to put in an appearance at least once every two years in order to keep up their court "privileges." But the queen must have made an exception in this case, deciding that she had done enough in the way of conciliation when it came to Lily's family, and crossed her name off the list of prospective drawing room attendees.

Compounding Lily's embarrassment at her social failure was a public snub to the duke that spring by the Prince of Wales during a chance hotel encounter in Paris. The import of the slight was well understood by everyone, and the Paris edition of the *New York Herald* assumed its readers would catch the allusion when it reported flatly of this occasion, "The Duke of Marlborough paid his respects yesterday evening to the Prince of Wales."[42] How the duke, it intimated, must have squirmed. Lily covered her defeat by retreating to Aix-les-Bains, a popular spa town in southeastern France, where, it was leaked to the press, she had been "since Whitsuntide for the benefit of her health, which has been uncertain for sometime past."[43]

It would take a while for Lily to overcome her disappointment at being excluded from a societal role, but she could console herself with the fact that there were plenty of "men and women with the bluest blood in their veins who cannot be said to be 'in Society' at all" and who preferred not to be. "They afford," it was observed, "little material for the society paragraphist, and they not unnaturally resent being identified with, as one of their number is said to have expressed it . . . those odious people whose names one sees in the newspapers."[44] Lily had not expected to find herself among such inconspicuous, albeit highbred, company, but she got used to it.

CHAPTER 13

Homecomings

ও

Lily made her first trip to the United States as the Duchess of Marlborough in late March 1890. She came, as she put it, to see "old friends and perhaps do a little business."[1] This initial homecoming set the pattern for what became near-annual visits to the country of her birth, each lasting no longer than two or three weeks and passed largely in New York City.

Lily's anticipated arrival elicited "no small curiosity among lookers-on as to the nature of the reception with which she will meet."[2] How had she changed since joining the English aristocracy? Would she be lionized by the full complement of New York's social elite, or would those who had in the past expressed disapproval of her husband and his moral lapses cut her? How would the hostility of the enemies she had acquired as a result of the Hamersley will case affect her welcome?

Press coverage of Lily's visit began when her steamship, which had occasioned considerable consternation by arriving two days later than expected, made fast at its Hudson River pier in a blinding rainstorm. Lily chatted affably with the journalists who crowded on board to question her about the crossing and her New York plans. "Much to the surprise of some of her British fellow-passengers," it was reported, "the Duchess mingled freely with the saloon passengers" during the voyage. She dined with them, having been assigned to the seat of honor on the captain's right, and often sang and played the piano in the evenings. Her favorite songs, she disclosed, were "Home Sweet Home," "Who's Dat a Calling," and "Suwanee River." "I must have been a success," Lily added playfully, "as all my efforts were encored."[3] Lily's democratic spirit and lack of haughtiness became leitmotifs in journalistic coverage of her visit: how "in most democratic fashion she walked right up to the desk and registered" at her hotel; how her following an evening at the opera with an evening at the theater proved "that her vaunted democracy is an honest portion of her temperament."[4] "Her Grace was never more American," pronounced the *New York Mail and Express* with pride and relief.[5]

Nell Nelson, a woman journalist, brashly knocked on the door of Lily's hotel the morning after she landed to ask for an interview. To her surprise, the hotel lackey who relayed her request to the duchess told her that she would be received. It was, no doubt, the journalist's name that gained her access, for Nelson was known as a crusading investigative reporter as well as a successful society writer in a profession that denied respect, recognition, and equal pay to the few women who tried to earn a living at it. She had made her reputation by going undercover as a poor working girl for the *Chicago Times* to write a sensational series of articles on women's labor conditions, but had recently moved to New York and the *New York World*, a daily paper with a wide immigrant and other lower-class readership that was perhaps the best known of all local newspapers for its provocative interviews. One of the *World*'s specialties was "pen-portraits" of female celebrities: artists, cabinet wives, and socialites. It was partial to articles comparing New York women with women from other countries, "always to the benefit of the domestic specimen," and could be counted on to point out the "fact that the British aristocracy shows a marked tendency to improve its stock and manners by marrying American girls."[6]

The hardheaded journalist could not have been more sycophantic when it came to interviewing Lily. She paid tribute to Lily's youth, beauty, melodious voice, air of repose, and "that gracious, gentle way of saying and doing things that women envy and men adore."[7] Lily let the reporter know at once that she was a practiced interviewee. "You are the first female representative of the press I have seen since I left London," she declared.

Personally I am glad to see you, but I do not like to be interviewed. I would not mind if I was quoted, but I don't like the way I am made to talk. The interviewers mean well enough, but somehow they succeed in hurting my feelings very often. . . . In type words get a dignity of importance that does not belong to them when uttered, and you know of all the paragraphs written only the harsh parts are remembered.[8]

Women journalists, she went on, were more to be feared than men. "Don't you know—you as a woman," she asked Nelson,

that we women are not true to one another? It is a fact. We are not loyal; we don't play the shield, and we are not as staunch in standing by our sex as the men are in upholding one another. A newspaper man may ridicule a woman in print, but a newspaper woman will rail; and so it is in society—the stabs that are deepest and sorest are dealt by the smaller, whiter, softer hands.[9]

The duchess spoke without bitterness, but from experience. She had no trouble in controlling the interview, lightly turning aside personal questions that she chose not to answer, such as what it felt like to be a duchess and to live at Blenheim "Castle." There was some discussion of English women's beauty, which Lily attributed to the English climate—a quality "in the air and in the fogs" that made them "moist"—and to their habit of indefatigable walking. "And do you walk?" she was asked. "Certainly I do—by the hour," was Lily's response.

I have become very fond of country life and I almost live in the open air. . . . In a cloth suit and . . . half boots we walk miles and miles in all sorts of weather."
What is the English woman's fad?
Politics I should say.
Have you adopted it?
Yes, I had to. It is obligatory. You couldn't live in an English community a week without catching the political fever.[10]

After a few other bland exchanges about the education and reading tastes of English women, as well as Lily's *de rigueur* proclamation that there was "no beauty on earth superior to that of our countrywomen," a guest was announced and Nelson shown out. "Take her all in all," concluded the interviewer, "the Duchess of Marlborough is a lady who will shine in any circle, company or country."[11]

New York's "regular entertainers," declared *Town Topics*, "do love a duchess,"[12] so it was not surprising that the social elite of New York warmly welcomed Lily in her new role. Journalists outdid themselves in reporting on the most trivial aspects of her visit. They had plenty to say about the compelling topic of her weight. "The Duchess is a much handsomer woman than was Mrs. Louis Hamersley," noted one. "The tendency which showed itself at one time as a redundancy of health has subsided."[13] Another reporter glibly characterized Lily as "perhaps the handsomest woman in New York society. . . . Her eyes are bright, her complexion is as clear and smooth as a school girl's, and she has the carriage of a cadet and the health of a child of nature."[14]

"The dinners of the week have been many in number," noted the *New York Times* on 13 April, "but seem to have been chiefly given in honor of the Duchess of Marlborough, several of them, an observer well remarks, by the very people who most persistently snubbed the Duke of Marlborough at Newport two [*sic*] years ago."[15] "I have no doubt," observed *Town Topics*, "that the handsome Duchess recalls the days, not yet long dead, when she was pretty Mrs. Hamersley, and her house . . . was not so heavily besieged by fond friends." While the titled guest was noted as "having it in her power to take revenge upon the suspicious and haughty gentry that were wont to question her rights to recognition" as a young widow, "she has refrained with most commendable magnanimity, and has smiled on all alike as they came madly flocking to her presence."[16]

The social significance of Lily's title was manifested in a press report providing details of the chief event of the post-Lenten social season: a ball given by society leader Mrs. William C. Whitney. The floral arrangements, favors, and menu of the affair were fulsomely praised in a write-up that concluded with a listing of many of the ball's 300 guests. First cited in accordance with New York's loose rules of social precedence was the Duchess of Marlborough, followed in descending order by a prince, a count, the German and Turkish ministers, members of the English legation, and most of the cream of the city's social elite.[17] Mr. and Mrs. Cornelius Vanderbilt's dinner for the duchess also welcomed, "among others,"[18] President Grover Cleveland (then out of office between his two non-consecutive presidential terms) and his wife. If Lily had gone into her ducal marriage with the hope of achieving social recognition, she certainly found it on her return to the United States, where she was proclaimed "the sensation of the hour and the most conspicuously brilliant feature of the waning social season. Such," sighed one reporter, "is tuft-hunting nowadays in New York society."[19]

Two questions preoccupied the press. Why was Lily here, and why was she here alone? The general consensus was that she had come to extract funds from the Hamersley estate, a not unreasonable surmise given the heavy expenses recorded in her name in connection with the restoration of Blenheim. It was thought that she wanted, in particular, to divest the estate of vacant Fifth Avenue real estate parcels that constituted a significant portion of the estate's worth but incurred heavy taxes and brought in no income. It was impossible, however, to sell these properties, as clear title could not be provided until the will case was settled. There was thus a story abroad in society to the effect that the duchess "had come over here to induce the trustees to borrow money on the property, but it is not at all sure how this could be done."[20] Lily traveled alone, it was surmised, because she believed that, "to use the French phrase, as a *femme seule* she will be able to do more than if those opposing her felt that they were really fencing and fighting with the English duke who has married her."[21] She applied pressure as best she could, but no information about results appeared in the press before Lily's mid-April departure for England.

Much to the astonishment of her compatriots, Lily returned again to New York in the fall, arriving on 8 October with the duke in tow for what would be a stay of some two months duration. A few friends met the couple at the dock, as did an errant journalist. The duke relayed the information that he and his wife had "come over for a pleasure trip" and that their schedule was as yet unsettled. "In fact," he added, "I am here without any definite plans at all. That is all I can say."[22]

Despite Marlborough's stress in this interview that *he* had no settled plans, one motive for the couple's transatlantic voyage so recently after Lily's spring visit was tied to maneuvers in connection with the Hamersley estate. Startling news about Lily's finances became public not long after her arrival, when the press announced that judgments to the tune of $676,122 for unpaid loans had been taken out in England against her and the estate in favor of the Bank of Birmingham and two Birmingham individuals.[23] These debts, it was understood, had been incurred in Lily's purchase and equipping of her London home and the refurbishment of Blenheim, and it puzzled many that "those Englishmen, who are usually so careful in financial matters, came to let the Duchess have so much money without knowing how they were going to be paid."[24] The judgments turned out to be part of a strategy devised by Lily's advisors after she failed on her previous trip to secure a loan against the estate. While, by law, she could not mortgage her estate income, a portion of the surplus above what was provided to her directly could be applied to payment of debts contracted by the estate. Thus the judgments were, in effect, a legal fiction perpetrated to bring about such a disbursement, and the Surrogate's Court quickly approved a settlement allowing for annual payments of $50,000 to the creditors until the debt was discharged.[25]

The Marlboroughs were seen together at the horse show, at a society wedding, at the opera (where they were guests in the box of Mrs. Paran Stevens), and at the theater. Lily was, as she had been during her earlier stay, much in demand; among her visitors were some, like Jennie Churchill's cousin Eva Purdy Thomson, who did not know her, but convinced themselves that it would be "polite" to call on the duchess (and then, perhaps, like Eva, slipped a subsequent note from her into a diary as a keepsake).[26] Lily again charmed everyone with her vivacious manner and "her appearance, if possible, is more girlish than ever."[27]

Marlborough, while his wife was otherwise occupied, wandered "about town with the air of an amiably amused sight-seer,"[28] and made an early trip out to New Jersey to spend another day with Thomas

Edison. "As the door of the library closed after the Duke said good-bye to Edison and me," recalled the inventor's secretary, Alfred Tate, "Edison turned to me and said: 'Tate, there's the only man in the world I'm afraid to talk to.'" His associate, assuming that Edison was referring in some way to ducal pomposity, started "to make a facetious and quite obvious retort when Edison anticipated me with a laugh and said: 'No! No! I know what you're going to say. It's not that. It's because he's the most accomplished scientist I've ever known.'" Tate considered this high praise from Edison, who, he noted, "knew all the scientists of that era, personally, through correspondence, or by their works."[29]

The duke passed another day in Jersey City, where he arrived early in the morning and

> spent the whole day among the grain elevators. No one knew who he was, and he went without guides or letters of introduction. He wore a sack suit, a pair of not particularly new gloves, and he studied the machinery of the big elevators carefully and examined all the details of their construction. The engineers, foremen and superintendents with whom he talked easily discovered that he knew all about machinery, and they showed him a degree of respect as a mechanician which they never would have thought of offering his title.[30]

The most newsworthy aspect of the Marlboroughs' visit was their two-week expedition in November to the industrializing "New South." This region, then emerging from its post-Civil War slough, seemed to offer investment promise through the exploitation of its rich mineral resources and undeveloped land. Indeed, speculative enthusiasm for American real estate had driven British investors for over a generation, and English ownership of immense tracts of property in the American West had created something of a nativist backlash, leading to the passage of laws by a concerned national Congress and a number of states and territories that restricted foreigners' land ownership in various ways. But the South still welcomed international investment, and Marlborough, wearing multiple hats as entrepreneur, journalist, and tourist, took his wife and one of her women friends with him to see the region for himself. Abram Hewitt, now a close personal friend of the duke and regarded in the South "as one of the most helpful of Northern businessmen," was of active assistance in organizing the Marlboroughs' expedition and facilitating contacts.[31] The duke took voluminous notes, providing raw material for two pieces published the following year in the influential English journal *Fortnightly Review*: one on "Farms and Trotting Horses of Kentucky," and a long, two-part article on "Virginia Mines and American Rails."[32] New York's *Town Topics* begrudgingly praised the latter in reporting, "Whatever men may say about the Duke's morals, no one has ever accused him of mental dullness, he makes an interesting article of it, with comparatively few errors."[33]

In deference to Lily's Kentucky heritage, and because of Marlborough's interest in horse farming, the itinerary began with an exploration of the Kentucky Bluegrass Country, birthplace of Lily's father and center of American thoroughbred horse breeding. The duke and duchess left New York by night train, traveling in an elegantly appointed private Pullman car, the "Mariquita" ("ladybug"). By the following evening they were in Cincinnati, and the next morning found them in Lexington, Kentucky. The region around Lexington entranced Marlborough; it was, he reported, "the one place in America where one would desire to live." Several days were spent in making the rounds of thoroughbred stud farms, where Marlborough admired the quality of Kentucky-bred trotting and saddle horses—even mules, which he judged to be the finest he had ever seen.[34] (His purchase of six highly bred trotting mares in foal from Woodburn, a famous stud outside Lexington, made national headlines in March 1891.)[35] Lily accompanied Marlborough on most of his jaunts, and was admired by one journalist as "the sort of woman the Bluegrass would be proud to boast."[36]

John Proctor, the Kentucky state geologist, joined the party for its tour of the highlands of southeastern Kentucky, eastern Tennessee, and western Virginia. The terrain here, with its long ranges of heavily timbered mountains, foothills, and deep valleys, was altogether unlike that of the gently rolling Kentucky Bluegrass region. The area was reputedly home to the "congenital feudist and the incurable moonshinist" of Appalachian lore,[37] and Marlborough recounted for his readers some of the "blood-curdling stories of their shooting and blood feuds told all about the South."[38]

The Marlborough excursion coincided with a peak of frenzy in speculative real estate activity in the central Appalachian region. Land improvement companies had sprung up like weeds, each with its own promotional campaign promising to recreate the phenomenal success of recently launched industrial centers with a new town or city built on an underpinning of iron, coal, steam, and railroads. The model for many imitators was Middlesborough, Kentucky, the marketing brainstorm of a transplanted Scot, Alexander Arthur, who was general manager and chief American representative of an English development company, the American Association, Ltd. What was projected to be a great metropolis had already begun to rise in the center of an 80,000-acre tract. Streets had been laid out, house lots sold, a dam built, and a twelve-mile railroad bed laid. By the end of 1889, some 5,000 people were living in Middlesborough, now home to sawmills, factories, and business houses. Two blast furnaces and an electric plant were in the works, and fourteen coal-mining enterprises were under contract in the surrounding hills.[39] Arthur, who understood the value of public relations, ostentatiously entertained Marlborough and his party during the two days they spent in the emergent city. Half of the first floor of the town's new hotel, still under construction, was turned over to the duke and duchess for their use.

Arthur's secretary later described the duke as "a man of short stature, with Roman nose and rather rotund figure," dressed in riding clothes. He recalled with amusement that Arthur addressed the duke as "Your Grace," whereas a prominent real estate dealer, "of large form and stentorian voice," simply took off his hat when introduced and said "with great vigor and good fellowship: 'Duke, howdy sir! I'm glad to meet you.'"[40] Lily, during the course of a lavish dinner held in the visitors' honor, "gave a neat little speech" in which "she graciously permitted the Town Company to name one of the streets of the city after her, and complimented Mr. Arthur by christening him the 'Duke of Middlesborough.'"[41]

"The country is in some way crazed," noted Marlborough of the boom and bustle he observed in passing through the southern countryside. "The enterprising land agent and speculator is to be found all over the country. Leaflets, advertisements, and such literature of all sorts are thrust at you at every station you stop at." Their train, he continued, "must have passed fifteen different towns in progress of one sort or another," each with its "blast furnace in course of building," its latticework plan staked out on still vacant farmland, its main street, and its large hotel "in the rambling wooden villa style dear to the American eye." Every town was doing its best to project "an illusion of irrepressible progress."[42]

What Marlborough did not recount was that he and Lily caught the speculative fever themselves, participating in a well-advertised auction of building lots in the "new city" of Glasgow, Virginia. General Fitzhugh Lee, a nephew of General Robert E. Lee and the president of the Anglo-American enterprise that was developing the acreage, served as the auctioneer at the sale, held in a drenching rainstorm under a tent pitched in the middle of the hypothetical city.[43] "I am bound to say the sale went off well," wrote Marlborough in the *Fortnightly Review*. "The lots sold from £400 to £500 a lot in good streets, and you had to go and locate your lot after the sale with a sale map on the ground."[44] The duke and duchess each purchased two lots, for which they paid one-third down and were expected to give notes for the remainder. But they, like other buyers, never undertook to build the stipulated "handsome three-story brick building" to be begun within ninety days on each lot, nor, presumably, did they make the required deferred payments.[45] For Glasgow, like most of the region's town-planning schemes, folded shortly thereafter.

Trouble began in Middlesborough within a few days of the Marlboroughs' visit, when Baring Brothers, the London bank that had provided much of the funding for the enterprise, failed; investment capital ceased flowing in; and the value of shares in the project plummeted.[46] The Glasgow boom "turned out to be a mere pop. No manufacturing plants were obtained . . . and the field crows were never disturbed." By 1892 investment had ceased altogether, and the palatial Glasgow hotel, opened for a single gala event, fell into ruin.[47] The phantom city's population stood at 992 in 2009.

Newspaper coverage of the Marlboroughs' trip included assertions that the duke had cabled London and made a "heavy investment" in whatever new town he had most recently toured—$50,000 in the case of Glasgow.[48] The duke was quick to announce through the New York press that this was a misrepresentation. *Town Topics* found all of the hoopla amusing. That the duke was not, in fact, making a great southern investment, it surmised, was "because the duchess does not look upon it with sufficient favor to encourage and further the scheme with any of her wealth."[49] But Lily had gamely entered into the venture, and the image of a well-dressed English duke and duchess standing in a rain-splashed tent and bidding on Virginian building plots in the middle of nowhere is appealing.

When the duke and duchess and their entourage weren't being squired about on tours of inspection, they entertained themselves like ordinary tourists. The trip's only mishap was the theft of Lily's jewelry when the train to which their private car was attached made a nocturnal stop for water. "A robber entered the ducal car and proceeded to slip several costly rings from the beautiful fingers of the Duchess while she slept soundly," reported a local newspaper. "After stripping one hand, his greed became so whetted at the sight of the glittering gems that he attempted to turn the Duchess over" in order to get at the other hand, at which point Lily "screamed from fright, and leaped from her berth, accoutred as she was in a vapory maze of laces."[50] In retelling the story at home, an Oxford journal noted that the duke had at first been "inclined to the theory that her Grace had had a very bad dream," a predictable result, it conjectured, of being forced to live on a southern American diet of "hominy, pumpkin pie, corn cakes, and dough, fetched up with molasses."[51] The thief was later apprehended and the jewels recovered.

Lily and Marlborough returned to New York, where they were entertained for a few more days, and left for England not long afterward. Jennie Churchill spotted her brother-in-law in London in late December. "Blandford & Lily have turned up," she wrote to her husband. "I saw him in the street. We talked for a few minutes. He looks very hale & trim—10 years older. They have gone to Blenheim."[52]

CHAPTER 14

Authentic Marriage

ॐ

Naysayers, including Churchill family biographers, have insisted that, given the duke's history and the bumpy first months of their life together, the Marlboroughs can have been nothing but unhappy as a married couple.[1] Yet, according to one longtime friend, this was hardly the case, and "the marriage became as genuine a love affair as between any two people in the humblest walk of life."[2] Unlikely as the pairing of Lily and Marlborough might have seemed, it worked.

American women writers with some experience of English men did not hesitate to contrast them to those of the homegrown variety. "Who would ever think," wrote Elizabeth O'Connor, Texas-born wife of a London-based newspaper publisher, "of describing the best mannered Englishman as deferential to women—and yet many foreign and American men are. The fact is, the point of view of an Englishman and an American is exactly opposite. The American man expects to make his wife happy—the Englishman expects his wife to make him happy. If he is happy he thinks she should be so too in the contemplation of his happiness."[3]

Californian novelist Gertrude Atherton, praised for her accuracy as a social historian, asserted in her 1898 *American Wives and English Husbands* that "an Englishman simply cannot adapt himself to anybody. It isn't in him." As the English father-in-law in her tale advised his son's American bride, "to live comfortably with an Englishman you've got to become his habit, and to be happy with him you've got to become his second self." This could be accomplished, he explained, by identifying herself with every one of her husband's "pleasures and pursuits," and furthermore, by learning to like them.[4] Lily did so, and found the technique to work.

In adapting to her English surroundings, and perhaps in response to Marlborough's early criticisms, Lily became skilled at tailoring her behavior to English expectations, eliciting admiration from a London society journalist in 1891 for her "peculiar charm of manner, voice, and inflection that render her so unlike other people, and so especially different from what we have wrongly come to accept as the typical American woman." To modify her style had been a conscious choice on Lily's part, for she was well aware of perceived cultural stereotypes, and as the same writer noted, her "exposition of the peculiarities and differences existing between the national characteristics of Englishmen and Americans is at once shrewd, witty, and original."[5]

The Duke of Marlborough weighed in on the topic of national differences in January 1892, authoring an article entitled "Merry England" for the *New Review* that compared aspects of social and domestic life in Great Britain with those of its former American colony. Much of his piece related to the fair sex, whose influence in the United States, he acknowledged, was "everywhere admitted." The American woman, he wrote,

> is perhaps the most different thing in America to anything in England. She has a natural quickness for appreciating the characters of the men around her, and she takes infinitely more trouble, and in some respects greater interest all round than the English woman displays. . . . The bright cheery girl remains the gay, carefully-dressed married woman who is always trying to show herself off quietly to the best advantage; and she understands the art perfectly, among all classes of the people. In middle age and even later in life she seems to preserve a perennial interest in everything around her; she does not grow old mentally as so many Englishwomen do.[6]

This praise from the duke, so often charged with cynicism, comes as a surprise. Marlborough knew only one American woman well, and had been married to her for nearly four years. Is it possible that in this article

Marlborough was offering an indirect compliment to Lily? Indeed, it seems hardly possible that he could have written with such enthusiasm about American womanhood in general had he not achieved some level of affection for, and domestic equilibrium with, his second wife.

Lily must have been relieved when, on 22 January 1891, the last Mason contestant's assault on Louis Hamersley's will was dismissed after nearly eight years of litigation. The judgment filed in the New York Surrogate's Court declaring that the "will now stands proved and confirmed" meant that Lily no longer had to submit requests for disbursements to the court for approval and her financial business ceased to be a matter of public record and conjecture.[7] The three individuals chosen by Louis to oversee his estate—George Williams, Jacob Lockman, and Lily—were able to relinquish their responsibilities as will executors and take up their roles as trustees. The declared value of Louis's estate at the time of transfer in May of that year was $4,225,500.[8]

Great caution, according to New York State law, had to be exercised in the management of estate property under trustees' control. The only allowable categories for investment were government bonds of the United States and individual states as well as loans on real estate: i.e., bonds and mortgages. Speculation was forbidden, and trustees were liable for losses arising from financial ventures other than those stipulated.[9] Thus most of Louis's assets, including non-disputed real estate, insurance, and bank and railroad stocks had already been sold and converted into real estate bonds and mortgages. Even the Hamersley family pew in Grace Episcopal Church had been liquidated, yielding $1,750 to estate coffers.[10]

Louis's single most valuable asset—the vacant uptown Manhattan real estate parcels in which Mason family members had claimed an interest—could finally be disposed of. Two lots were sold for $500,000 to William Astor, Jr. on which was to rise a "double mansion" presented as a wedding gift to his son John Jacob Astor IV. Commodore Elbridge T. Gerry, grandson and namesake of a signer of the Declaration of Independence and vice president of the United States under James Madison, purchased six lots for $450,000 for his

Lily, from an 1892 photo session

family home. A third parcel of eight lots on the corner of Fifth Avenue and Sixtieth Street was bought by a group led by Cornelius Vanderbilt for what was labeled the new "millionaires club" by newspapers reporting the sale.[11] The Metropolitan Club went up on the site in 1894, designed by fashionable architect Stanford White. The estate took back a $380,000 mortgage on the $480,000 property that was repaid in full in 1893.

In the course of transferring Lily's status from estate executor to trustee, her co-executors, who were responsible for handling day-to-day transactions involving Louis's assets, solicited the court's opinion as to whether Lily might have disqualified herself from participation in the management of the estate by "becoming a resident and subject of the United Kingdom."[12] At the time the will was first submitted for probate in 1883 this might have been the case, as an executor by law could only be someone who was "not an alien—that is a resident of a foreign country." Legal interpretation had, however, become more flexible in this area. Courts increasingly construed their role as acting with "due regard to the wishes of the maker of the trust if they can be discovered," and by the early twentieth century a designated trustee who lived permanently outside a court's jurisdiction was allowed to serve provided he agreed to abide by the regulations set forth within it.[13] Lily disagreed in any case with her representation as a subject of the United Kingdom. According to the argument set forth by her attorney, she "has never abjured her citizenship in the United States of America, and has never become a naturalized citizen or subject of the Queen of Great Britain and Ireland." Nor did she. She remained an American citizen and a trustee of Louis's estate for the rest of her life, but to facilitate her role in estate transactions, assigned power of attorney in New York to her friend Walter Gillette.[14]

Lily's role as trustee was passive rather than active. She had no involvement in routine estate management, but "consulted and advised with these executors and their counsel from time to time, and joined in the sale and conveyance of the testator's real estate, and in the transfer of securities."[15] She never had any public quarrel with her co-trustees and regularly collected the trustee compensation due her. This was set by law at 1 percent of all sums of money received and paid out by the estate in a given period.[16] Lily's commission for the weeks between 6 July 1893 and 3 April 1894 came to $2,639.53. This payout, which was in addition to the $180,300 income she received from the estate during the same period, was identical to that received by Louis's other trustees.[17]

In 1891 two legal disputes further damaged the already shaky relationship between the Duke of Marlborough and his son. The first was similar to earlier lawsuits brought on the minor's behalf against the duke by a trustee—in this instance, an objection to the intended use of capital derived from the sale of some agricultural land to develop other holdings (a case decided, once again, in Marlborough's favor). The second had directly to do with money, and was raised in Divorce Court by the Marchioness of Blandford, who petitioned for a supplemental allowance for her nineteen-year-old son's maintenance. She was then in receipt of an annual sum of £2,500 from the duke for her own and her children's support. Sunny was, in addition, the beneficiary of the income from £7,000 settled on him by his father at the time of the divorce.[18]

The duke, it was said, "did not wish to deal unfairly in the matter" but questioned the validity of the Divorce Court as the venue for settling the issue. His solicitor contended "that no order could be made by the Court after the age of sixteen, that the father was under no legal responsibility for the maintenance of his son, and that the Court should not make any order." The Attorney General appeared on Marlborough's behalf, during the course of which he remarked that he thought the £380 a year Sunny was then receiving annually from the earlier settlement quite sufficient for a young man's maintenance; the presiding judge determined that the court had no jurisdiction.[19] The press took great interest in the affair but garbled the legal details and showered the duke with bad publicity. "Lady Blandford," commented *Vanity Fair*, "has had much sympathy from her many friends, and practical help from members of the family."[20] Some journalists went so far as to suggest that the duke had cut Sunny off completely because his wife was jealous of Lady Blandford.[21] Lily stayed clear of the legal squabbles, and although Sunny was henceforth something of a persona non grata at Blenheim, she remained on good terms with her stepson. She was known as a "warm champion" of his interests who "never shared in the bitter feeling which the duke felt toward his son"; the attachment was said to be "returned in kind."[22]

The Prince of Wales's on-going refusal to "meet" the duke continued to cause problems for Marlborough's mother and siblings as they struggled to balance family loyalty with their own positions at court. The conflict could not have been more palpable than it was on the occasion of the 1891 marriage of the duke's youngest sister, Sarah, to Lieutenant Gordon Wilson, son of a Portsmouth parliamentarian with a fortune derived from Australian sheep-farming. The Wilsons were disdained as "grasping toadies in the social world, and thorough-going and heedless snobs in connection therewith,"[23] but the Churchills were pleased that Sarah would be, as Randolph phrased it, "settled down & well off,"[24] and the wedding was expected to be a very smart affair. "So many people are invited," announced *Vanity Fair* in advance of the event, "that it seems simpler to mention the few who are omitted. Amongst these are the reigning Duke of Marlborough and his Duchess."[25]

Sarah's brother and his wife were excluded from the wedding because it was fervently hoped that royalty would be on hand to mark the ceremony. "If nothing prevents the Prince of Wales and the Duke of Cambridge [Queen Victoria's cousin] being present," confided *Vanity Fair*, "they will enter by the vestry door." In the extensive press coverage of the wedding it was noted that the assembled crowd was made up of "our highest and haughtiest," among them "Churchills to the third and fourth generation."[26] The duke and duchess's absence provoked little comment beyond one reporter's casual statement that Marlborough "was otherwise engaged that afternoon."[27] Randolph was in South Africa, and it was one of Sarah's brothers-in-law who gave away the bride. "An electrical feeling of relief passed over the church when the Prince of Wales arrived," noted the *London World*, for his presence was taken as a sign that Sarah's husband would be accepted within the royal circle. The prince compounded the honor he bestowed in attending the ceremony by escorting the mother of the bride up the aisle when the service ended.[28] The Churchills were able to come to terms with their awkward social situation, and Lily was godmother to Sarah's only child, born two years after her marriage.

The Marchioness of Blandford, whose eighteen-year-old daughter, Lillian, was one of her aunt Sarah's bridesmaids, was also absent from the wedding and subsequent festivities. It would have been impossible for the Churchill family to break openly with the Hamiltons, who had long been political and social allies, and Bertha was accorded the deference due to her as Sunny's mother. But mutual relations were no more than superficially cordial. Bertha's collusion in the on-going Hamilton effort to exclude her former husband and his wife from society rankled, and she was not invited to mix with her son's paternal aunts and uncles. "Always smart, well-dressed, and very young-looking," the marchioness reportedly "loved Society" and attracted favorable press attention. She rarely maintained a home of her own, but was usually to be found staying with members of her extended family. Her life revolved around the chaperonage of her three unmarried daughters.[29]

There was said to be "no more delightful host" than Marlborough, and Lily was known as a charming hostess, so Blenheim saw a good deal of entertaining under their social administration.[30] A sprinkling of titles, liberal and conservative parliamentarians, and foreign worthies were usually on hand for weekend house parties. One 1891 Blenheim guest list included Count Hatzfeldt, German ambassador to the Court of St. James, and his American wife; the Marquis de Santurce, London-based Spanish banker and art collector; Plunkett Greene, celebrated Irish baritone and author of a classic book on fly-fishing; and composer Arthur Sullivan, best known for his operatic collaborations with librettist W. S. Gilbert.[31] Country-house sports such as shooting, in which the duke took no personal interest, were revived for the benefit of visitors, and previously rented-out coverts in which birds and small animals could find shelter were reclaimed as leases fell due.[32]

"We opine," commented *Modern Society* in June 1890, "that if all the Americans now in England who say they will spend a few days at Blenheim Castle with the Duke and Duchess of Marlborough are really going there, the ancient pile will soon resemble a huge hotel. . . . The prospective arrivals . . . according to telegrams and private letters up to date, number 713!"[33] This figure was certainly a gross exaggeration, but Lily and her husband welcomed American friends, and Lily's countrymen and -women considered an invitation to Blenheim a mark of distinction to be honored if at all possible. One story was told of a social-climbing New York youth just returned from a trip abroad who received a cable from Lily, "inviting him to spend the week-end a fortnight hence. Whereupon he booked an immediate return passage, arrived at Blenheim in time and had the supreme joy of writing fifty letters to his friends on stationery bearing the magic name of this wonderful ducal estate."[34]

Marlborough's business commitments took up more and more of his time in the early 1890s. A particular interest now was the telephone, which reached only 45,000 English subscribers in 1890, or 0.12 percent of the population.[35] The duke had spoken in favor of a government-owned telephone system in the House of Lords in 1889 and wrote an article on telephony for the *New Review* in 1891; the *London Times* published five letters from him between mid-1891 and mid-1892 that detailed the existing English system, compared its inefficiency and prohibitive expense with the better schemes of other countries, and outlined concrete ways in which the English technology could be improved.[36] He "made himself master of every detail in regard to telephony," noted *Truth*, "alike in its scientific and practical aspect, and, if we do get in London a good system, this will be mainly due to his exertions and energy."[37] Marlborough served at this time as chairman of the New Telephone Company, the Electric and General Investment Company, and the Brush Electric Company, and was a director of the City of London Electric Lighting Company.[38]

Lily and her husband continued to improve Blenheim. In 1891 they replaced an organ installed during the early months of their marriage with a magnificent instrument that surpassed many a cathedral organ in its size and tone. It was centered in a bay on a long wall in the Long Library and its case was adorned on behalf of the duke and duchess with the inscription, "In memory of happy days as a tribute to this glorious home, we leave thy voice to speak within these walls in years to come when ours is still." The instrument was "opened" at a festive 18 May assemblage of guests with an organ work especially commissioned for the occasion.[39]

One of the more surprising of Lily and Marlborough's mutual enthusiasms in these years was angling. Lily, despite her youthful flair for croquet and her recently proclaimed passion for walking, had no reputation as a sportswoman and knew nothing about sport-fishing when she arrived in England. It was Marlborough, an ardent fisherman, who introduced her to salmon fishing at a time when women were showing more than passive interest in sports that until then had been largely male bastions. The duke, according to *Fishing Gazette*, gave the same attention to the sport as he did to his scientific studies and other hobbies. He had his own idea of what a perfect salmon rod should be, and specified its details "with a minuteness as to build, weight, balance, mounting, and finish as if it were a national monument he was designing."[40] He had often explored the salmon-fishing rivers of Scotland, but in the summers of 1891 and 1892 he took Lily with him on long trips to the fishing grounds of Norway.[41] Even today, serious anglers do not necessarily invite spouses along in their pursuit of what can be one of the most physically uncomfortable of outdoor sports, so this gesture must be interpreted as another testament to Marlborough's fondness for his wife as well as to Lily's willingness to share his pastimes.

The couple returned from Norway, where they had been since late June, at the end of August 1892 in time to put in an appearance at the various agricultural shows in the villages surrounding Blenheim. Lily continued to participate in this aspect of rural life, winning prizes for her Blenheim spaniels and expanding her repertory to include the competitive raising and showing of poultry. The annual Woodstock Agricultural, Horticultural, Poultry, Pigeon, Rabbit, Cat and Dog Show was held at Blenheim as usual in late September, when Lily won awards and honorable mentions for her spaniels and poultry, and the duke took prizes in the categories of "best half-barrel of barley," "best twelve Mangels" (beets cultivated as cattle-feed), and "best ornamentally-arranged 2-lb. of Butter." Of special interest was an unusual competition for Shire foals open to breeders residing within ten miles of Woodstock. Marlborough had clearly had some success in moving the neighborhood into the breeding of these horses, as the event attracted thirty-nine entries. He provided one of a number of money prizes for the contest, personally presented several winners with their awards, and mounted a parade of his own Shire mares and foals after the judging was completed. The duke, noted *Jackson's Oxford Journal* in reporting the show, "is to be congratulated and deserves the praise of the agriculturalists of the district for persevering in the line he has adopted" in a region well-adapted to this type of animal husbandry in soil and climate.[42]

At the close of the program, Lily awarded prizes with "suavity and kindness" to cottagers for their produce, among which were 1,300 specimens of potato. The fair's president closed out the festivities with a proposal of "three cheers for her Grace the Duchess of Marlborough. The large number of persons assembled around the ring responded to the call very heartily. . . . Shortly afterwards rain began to fall, and quickly increasing in volume the ground was soon cleared of visitors."[43]

Commissioning portraits of oneself and one's spouse and children were inescapable responsibilities of titled life. Marlborough decided in mid-1892 that it was time to add his own portrait to the gallery of family likenesses adorning the walls of Blenheim. Lily was to be painted at the same time. The duke had a specific portraitist in mind for the project: James Whistler, the American-born painter who, after years of struggling for recognition and financial success, was finally achieving status in London as "a minor cultural hero."[44] The duke had written enthusiastically about Whistler two years earlier, praising his delicacy and merit "when the English Pharisees of art laughed at him," but his choice was considered a courageous one, for the artist's personal exploits as well as his egocentrism and "stagy personality" had made him many enemies.[45] Whistler accepted the commission for a large, full-length portrait of the duke at a price of £2,100, "or, if Whistler would also paint the duchess, £3,000 for the two portraits"—suggesting that Lily's likeness was to be on a smaller scale. The artist made a beginning on his representation of the duke, roughly sketching a figure in dress robes. Lily rescheduled a planned sitting that conflicted with one of the duke's rare appearances in the House of Lords, and the duke wrote to Whistler in the autumn, inviting him and his wife to Blenheim for a visit that would include a series of sittings.[46] The undertaking went no further.

CHAPTER 15

Death of the Duke of Marlborough

Ꝗ

The eighth Duke of Marlborough passed away at Blenheim Palace during the early morning hours of 9 November 1892. Death came without warning, the duke having spent much of the previous day working in his office with John William Palmer, his estate agent, who reported him as "apparently in splendid health and spirits." After dinner with Lily and an American houseguest, he retired to work on a newspaper article about modern railway cars composed in response to a recent railroad accident; the piece was left unfinished on his desk. Lily's maid last saw him in his dressing gown at four o'clock in the morning outside his wife's bedroom, she recounted later. He gave her some instructions regarding her mistress, who was suffering from painful neuralgia and whom he had been nursing, and then went into his own bedroom next door.[1]

The duke's valet discovered him shortly after eight o'clock. He had made several trips into his bedroom—to arrange his clothes and to bring him his morning cocoa and milk—and was surprised that the duke did not awaken. Finally, he recounted, "I banged the door. Even then I could see no movement and all of a sudden it struck me that he was dead." The valet, who had been "some years" in Marlborough's service and declared himself "much attached" to his master, summoned Lily, who, he reported, "hurried into the bedroom, and when she realized the terrible truth she caught hold of my hand and exclaimed in an awe-struck tone of voice: 'Dead, dead!' She seemed stunned and uttered neither cry nor sob, but sent me out of the room and remained with the body of her dead husband."[2]

Sunny and Randolph arrived later in the day. A post-mortem determined that the duke's death had been caused by heart failure, or "calcereous degeneration of one of the large vessels of the heart,"[3] the same disease that had carried off his father nine years earlier. Marlborough was forty-eight.

Lily was reported as "prostrate with grief" over Marlborough's passing,[4] but she handled her personal tragedy with dignity. She notified the Marchioness of Blandford of her former husband's death, and, at her invitation, Bertha and her three daughters arrived to say their farewells the following day. Randolph, who chronicled the details of the twenty-four-hour period immediately following his arrival at Blenheim in a letter to his wife, reported Bertha as being "very quiet and nice" during her stay. "A short visit to the room where he was lying & conversation with Sunny & with me occupied the time till she returned to Oxford. Poor thing," he added, "I could not help feeling for her but at any rate her long period of acute trouble is over." Despite the efforts Marlborough's two wives had made to avoid one another during the previous four years, there was some talk of their meeting for the first time while Bertha was at Blenheim. Randolph discouraged the idea as "going a little too far," and the encounter did not take place.[5]

Randolph pronounced himself "much vexed" at rumors already in circulation to the effect that his brother "could never bear the idea of [Bertha] coming back here. Of course she must come back here," he insisted, "& live here with her daughters while Sunny is unmarried and desires the arrangement. In fact it is the only natural & proper arrangement and I cannot understand people carping at it."[6] As Lord Lansdowne, Bertha's brother-in-law (and the other groom in the 1869 double ceremony that united the ill-fated Blandford couple), wrote to Queen Victoria, he believed that Lady Blandford would "feel the Duke's death a great deal."[7]

Randolph assumed the role of head of the family, a position he could claim until his nephew attained his majority on 13 November, four days after his father's death. "I think I am of much use to Sunny," he confided to Jennie, "& many things arise from day to day on which he likes to be advised." In regard to Lily, the sister-in-law he had so often disparaged, he could only write, "You were really quite right about her and I quite wrong. Nothing could exceed her goodness & kindness of disposition, & my belief is that she means to do nothing but what is right liberal & generous by the heir."[8]

In concluding his letter to his wife, Randolph displayed a surprising degree of enmity toward his older brother. "It is certainly a sad and anxious business," he wrote, "but I cannot help the feeling from all I know and from all I have heard that perhaps everything has happened for the best."[9] Randolph's own life had little focus at this time; he seems to have begrudged his brother the grounded and productive existence he was leading before his death.

There was one family difference of opinion to be resolved regarding the duke. Marlborough had explicitly stated in his will, dated July 1889, that he wished not to be buried in the family vault in Blenheim Chapel, "but in any suitable place that may be convenient in which others of my own generation and surroundings are equally able with myself to find a resting-place together."[10] He was understood to have softened somewhat on this position after executing his will, but Lily and the Marlboroughs' solicitor, Spencer Whitehead, felt that his written request should be honored and proposed that he be interred in the Bladon churchyard just outside of Blenheim. Randolph argued on behalf of his mother and himself that, in deference to family tradition, his brother's last resting place should be with his father in the palace chapel. Lily and Whitehead acceded to their wishes.[11]

The interment took place five days after Marlborough's death. The day before, a Sunday, his body lay in state in a glass-lidded coffin at Blenheim, and nearly 2,500 former neighbors, tenants, and employees passed by to pay their final respects. Among the wreaths bedecking the coffin was one from the Marchioness of Blandford. Most of the shops in Woodstock were closed on Monday and blinds were drawn in private homes during the afternoon as an outward sign of respect. The only other indication that anything unusual was taking place that day was the flying over Blenheim Palace of the flag bearing the family coat of arms that was reserved for special occasions.[12]

Three saloon cars brought family and friends from London for the obsequies in the Blenheim chapel. They were received by Sunny, who had been chastised by the press for having, during the course of the post-mortem examination, "had the late Duke's favorite hunter brought out of the stables and rode all over the place in a suit of tweed, yellow leather boots, and a cricketing cap, rather a curious mourning costume for the yet unburied father."[13] Now suitably attired, Sunny was assisted in his duties as host at his father's funeral by his paternal uncle by marriage Lord Richard Curzon—and not, as the papers insisted on pointing out, by Randolph.[14] Having quietly commemorated his twenty-first birthday the previous day, Sunny was the chief mourner. Supporting him were Randolph, four of his father's six Churchill brothers-in-law, and Lady Blandford's oldest brother, the Duke of Abercorn. The Woodstock parish church bell tolled at half-minute intervals during the chapel service, which the widowed duchess observed from the privacy of the chapel balcony in the company of two of her sisters-in-law. It was rare for aristocratic women to attend funeral services, as they were considered too emotional to handle themselves gracefully at such events. Lily proved the logic of the ban by fainting, and had to be carried out of the chapel.[15]

Writers looking back on the duke's life offered conflicting assessments of his legacy. Lord Lansdowne expressed his opinion in writing to Queen Victoria that Marlborough's "sudden death forms a tragical ending to a very sad and unsatisfactory career. He had great abilities but there was an element of hopeless perversity in his character."[16] *The London Times*, known for its detailed and beautifully written death notices, dismissed Marlborough as "his own worst enemy," who "by the scandals of his private life . . . threw away the certainty of attaining to a position of great influence in the country."[17] At the other end of the spectrum, Henry Labouchere of *Truth* articulated his belief that not only had Marlborough been "an exceptionally able man," but, "indeed, it might be said of him, without any exaggeration, that he was one of the very ablest men of his generation."[18]

Others tendered variously nuanced reflections on the man and his past. Noted an obituary writer for *Vanity Fair*, "I am not wholly in sympathy with those good people who are always so prone to cackle about a wasted life when it is ended, . . . but it is none the less certain that the Duke might have accomplished much that he did not— possibly he would have accomplished much, had he lived; for he has died in the very prime of life." Too modest to make the most of his "brilliant intelligence," he continued, Marlborough was

> broad-minded, vivacious, witty . . . always fascinating, even since he desisted, as he long ago did, from playing the courtier. . . . [I]t is within my knowledge that his sins were often magnified till he was painted blacker by far than many a worse man; and, after all, the Duke was an honest gentleman who never sought to whitewash himself. It is no doubt owing in part to his rather cynical contempt for the respectable meddler with other people's characters, which prevented his ever posing as a better man than he was, or even as so good a man.[19]

It was to be expected that comparisons would be made between Marlborough and Randolph in summing up the duke's life, and the duke, as he had before, came off as the abler and "more widely cultured" of the brothers.[20] Some writers chose to pass over "the regrettable incidents of his early manhood," focusing instead on what he achieved "after he settled down seriously in life."[21] He had, recalled one who had known him, "in spite of the philosophic ennui that he affected, so many aims in life that it is hard to believe that the different things in which he was deeply interested must succeed or fail without him."[22]

Oxfordshire newspapers reviewed the duke's farming operations "conducted upon scientific lines," and acclaimed him "a perfect landlord"; no farm on his estate was to let and the waiting list should any become available ran to twenty names.[23] An aged tenant of property adjoining Blenheim was quoted as saying that "he had known four Dukes of Marlborough, and that he had not known one who was of such great benefit to the estate."[24] The duke, it was said, left his domain in "excellent order . . . and, thanks to him, Blenheim Palace, which was in rather a neglected condition when he inherited it, has become the perfection of an abode for a millionaire." More than one obituary mentioned the role of Lily's fortune in this achievement.[25]

Marlborough's sudden death could not help but remind those familiar with Lily's history of the similarly unanticipated demise of her first husband. Malicious gossips were quick to draw comparisons, and Lily was still susceptible to being hurt by them. Years later one memoirist recalled an instance of her sensitivity that would "have been comic except for its tragic associations." After Marlborough died, he wrote, "the old Duchess Pozzo di Borgo said—of course in fun—'Probably that American wife of his killed him!' And this idiotic remark having made its way to [Lily] made the poor widowed Duchess so unhappy that she actually contemplated denying the allegation in the newspapers!"[26] The innuendos Lily had borne after Louis Hamersley's death had not hardened her to the more insidious forms of human cruelty.

Marlborough showed, as had Louis Hamersley before him, his confidence in his wife's judgment and administrative abilities by naming her an executor of his will, a responsibility she shared with the couple's solicitor, Spencer Whitehead. The will document and its ramifications were communicated to all of England by assiduous journalists. "It seems that the late Duke behaved more handsomely to his children than it was thought he was willing or able to do," commented one. "In his will he left £20,000 a year to his heir, and to his daughters also a comfortable competency." This legacy, £10,000 to each, assured the girls of future incomes in the range of £400 to £500 a year, "a very nice little dowry," and thanks to the welcome alteration in her financial circumstances Marlborough's eldest daughter, Fanny, was able to announce her engagement within six weeks of her father's death.[27]

An unusual provision of the will was a bequest to the executors of £5,000, "to invest the same and accumulate the income for twenty-one years, and then to apply the trust fund in repairing, renovating, and improving the roof and outside of Blenheim Palace." Marlborough had recognized it as unlikely that another Lily-like benefactor could be found to voluntarily put money into such thankless building projects. "All the residue of the real and personal estate to which at his death, he might be beneficially entitled, or over which he might have power of disposition beneficially," Marlborough bequeathed to his wife. A dollar figure was never put on this legacy, but it came to very little.

Each of the duke's domestic servants, every clerk in his estate office, his head gardener, and his clerk of the works (responsible for building erection and maintenance) was left £100 according to the duke's will if in service for five years, £150 if in service for ten years. This amounted to generous bequests to those staff members who met the criteria, but many were left out. In connection with the duke's last testament, revealed the *Oxfordshire News*, an interesting ceremony took place in the Blenheim Palace saloon after the duke's funeral. "By direction of the Duchess of Marlborough, after the departure of the friends and relations of the late Duke, the whole of the domestic servants at Blenheim, and from 3, Carlton House Terrace, with as many of the men engaged upon the estate as could be rounded up," were assembled in the presence of Lily and Whitehead.

The solicitor, before reading out the particulars of the will that affected them, had an announcement to make. "When the will was made," he stated, "the establishment was not on the present scale, and he was directed by her Grace to say that she felt sure if the Duke had made the will more recently others would have been remembered, and it would be her pleasure to supplement the will by paying from her own purse gratuities to those whom she thought his Grace would have considered." Names were read out, and each additional beneficiary received a monetary gift of up to £50 (or more than a year's salary).[28]

One disconcerting bequest left by the duke was the sum of "£20,000 absolutely" to Lady Colin Campbell "as a mark of my friendship and esteem." Lily would surely have wished this legacy expunged, as it raised again the question of whether or not Marlborough continued his love affair with Lady Colin after he settled into his second marriage. It is possible that he did, for it has been suggested that in the spring of 1891 the duke leased an apartment in

Venice on Lady Colin's behalf. An allusion to an on-going relationship survives in a letter written by Lady Colin to a friend on 18 December 1892, when she was in Venice selling off furniture and ornaments recently purchased for her apartment—which, if its expenses had been underwritten by Marlborough, she was no longer in a position to keep. "It was sad work," she penned, without mentioning any man by name, "putting the prices on all the things I had chosen with such loving care thinking He would enjoy the majority of them with me! For we had looked forward so much to being there each autumn together, & exploring the lagoons and mainland. . . . All life is one great yawning grave of memories & blasted hopes to me now."[29]

If the romance between the duke and Lady Colin did persist, the couple can have had little extended time together, for Marlborough and Lily lived largely in one another's company and never the hint of an on-going connection appeared in the press. Marlborough may have finally mastered absolute discretion; Lily may have learned to put up with the wandering ways of the English aristocracy. She had, after all, the unconventional lifestyle of her sister-in-law Jennie Churchill always before her.

Randolph, who had been warned about the possibility of a bequest to Lady Colin by Whitehead immediately after his brother's death, confided his uneasiness about the matter to Jennie. It would, he wrote, "be a great scandal,"[30] but there was nothing he could do to keep the information private. The duke's monetary bequest to Lady Colin was not the only postmortem humiliation Lily had to suffer as a result of Marlborough's old love affair. She was immediately forced into taking on a mission to suppress an unpublished article her husband had written for the *Fortnightly Review*—a piece that she not only found tasteless but felt would be damaging to her husband's memory. The circumstances leading to its composition were discussed in some detail by Frank Harris in his 1925 autobiography, *My Life and Loves*.

Harris, editor of the *Fortnightly Review* from 1886 to 1894, was a prominent public figure in London and knew everyone of importance in politics, the arts, and society. He was remembered as "a generous and indulgent friend to most men, devoid of meanness and pettiness, though he had hurt many persons through his crudity and indiscretion."[31] He is best known today, thanks to the sexual explicitness of its content, for *My Life and Loves*. This was to some degree a creative work, as its author was renowned for his lively inventiveness, especially when it came to his own life. Although many of Harris's recollections have been subject to historical correction, they represented their author's version of facts as he recalled them.

Marlborough became a friend, wrote Harris, "through sheer similarity of nature. He too wanted to touch life on many sides. He liked a good dinner and noble wine whether of Burgundy or Moselle, but above all, he loved women and believed with de Maupassant that the pursuit of them was the only entrancing adventure in a man's life." The genesis of Marlborough's article, according to Harris, had been an agreement made "some years" before his marriage to Lily, "when the Duke asked me to dinner and soon told me, without unnecessarily beating about the bush, that he was in love with Lady Colin and had promised her that I would publish her next paper." Harris, who knew and disliked Lady Colin's writing, claimed to have already rejected one or two of her pieces and told Marlborough that he "couldn't do it." But Marlborough, he went on, "pressed me so earnestly that at length I said, 'If you will write me an absolutely frank article, setting forth the sensuous view of life you have often preached to me, I'll accept Lady Colin's contribution blindfold; but I want absolute frankness from you.'" Marlborough "broke in, laughing. 'It's a bargain and I am greatly obliged to you; I'll write the article at once and let you have it this week.'"[32]

Marlborough kept his promise, recounted Harris, and Lady Colin's "paper" was duly published. The duke's article, described by Harris as "frank to indecency," was put "away for some real need" with the certainty that its eventual appearance "was sure to cause a large stir." Harris, known for his prodigious memory, claimed to remember a few of its lines, and his narration is likely to have captured the tenor if not the exact wording of Marlborough's piece. "'There are persons,'" he recited, "'who will object to my frank sensuality. I have been asked in astonishment whether I really could see anything to admire in the beautiful knees of a woman. I have no doubt there are little birds who sip a drop or two of clear water at a lake-side and wonder what a healthy frog can find in the succulent ooze that delights his soul,'"[33] etc., etc. It is not difficult to imagine that Lily would have found these trifling effusions offensive.

The duke's death struck the market-savvy journal editor as the opportune moment to bring Marlborough's piece to light. "At once," wrote Harris, "I announced that I was going to publish in the *Fortnightly Review* an article on 'The Art of Living' by the late Duke. I showed phrases of it to reporters, and as everyone knew the brains and frankness of the Duke, it was easy to work up a tremendous sensation, for indeed the article was almost too outspoken to be published."[34] Lily learned of Harris's intention and undertook to quash publication of the piece. "I am anxious to get it back," she wrote to her brother-in-law Randolph. "I could not have it appear in print. See Mr. Frank Harris, and get this article from him at any price."[35]

Harris chronicled a long, colorful interview with Lord Randolph on the subject of the provocative article, but it is just as likely that Churchill's appeal to Harris was made in writing, as a fragment from a germane letter surfaced in a rare-book and autograph dealer's catalog many years after the appearance of *My Life and Loves*. "For reasons you will readily imagine," wrote Lily's envoy to Harris, "I should be very greatly obliged to you and so would others of [more] importance than I, if you would refrain from inserting in the *Fortnightly Review*, an article written for that review by my poor brother."[36] No matter by what means Randolph's commission was carried out, it was successful. The offending piece, which had already been set in type, was magnanimously handed over to Lily through Marlborough's solicitor, accompanied by a brief letter from Harris, and what Lily had anticipated as yet another scandal linked to her late husband's name was averted. The duke's final published literary effort was an innocuous article on American trotting horses written for the *Live Stock Journal Almanac*, the revised proofs of which arrived at the publisher's offices on the morning of his death.[37]

It is impossible to accurately date the composition of Marlborough's article for Harris, as nothing by Lady Colin was issued under her name or a known pseudonym in the *Fortnightly Review* during his tenure, and the editor may have been embroidering—or indeed, fabricating—part or all of his story. But Marlborough certainly wrote the tongue-in-cheek piece attributed to him, probably in 1887. Lily's reference to the duke's "last article" in a note to Harris thanking him for its suppression suggests that she knew nothing about its genesis.[38] Thus its contents are likely to have been doubly shocking to a woman who thought she had achieved a degree of essential rapport with her husband.

Rumor linked one more incident concerning Lady Colin to Marlborough's death. Popular histories of the Churchill family have repeated it as gospel that a nude portrait of Lady Colin by James Whistler "hung, in plain view, permanently" over the duke's bed during the course of his marriage to Lily—a portrait that Lily maliciously destroyed after her husband's death.[39] There did at one time exist a partially executed portrait of Lady Colin by Whistler in which the sitter posed, not naked, but fully clothed in a bouffant white satin gown. Entitled "Harmony in White and Ivory," the painting was exhibited in a London gallery at the time of the Campbell vs. Campbell divorce case, a circumstance thought to have been contrived by Whistler to capitalize on the notoriety of its subject. George Bernard Shaw, who covered the exhibition as art reviewer for the *London World*, dismissed the work as one that "being unfinished, has no business in the gallery," and it has been suggested that the artist, frustrated by his inability to complete the portrait because Lady Colin did not again sit for him after the legal proceeding, disposed of it as an unfinished work.[40] Followers of the salacious court hearing who could not gain admittance to the courtroom were said to have done "the next best thing. They went off to Piccadilly, to look at Whistler's new portrait of Lady Colin," where "a crowd ten deep hung round it all day long."[41]

CHAPTER 16

Alone Again

ৡ

" A s for Lily Marlborough, we cannot find it in our heart to pity
 her very deeply," observed *Modern Society* some ten days after
Marlborough's death.[1] This reaction was fairly general, for after Lily's
abortive attempt to enter London society she had largely disappeared
from view and the English public lost its emotional investment in
her. But with her husband dead, Lily once more became an object
of interest and conjecture. Her allure lay in her unusual position as
an American widow of high title without deep roots in England,
known mostly for having spent a sizeable chunk of her fortune on the
enhancement of Blenheim. What would she do now?

Henry Clews immediately scotched American rumors to the
effect that the widow's finances were in dire disarray as a result of
her husband's death and that she would soon resettle in the United
States. "The Duchess of Marlborough is not likely to return to
this country to live," he announced to the New York press in mid-
November, "and there is no truth in the reports that her income has
been sadly reduced." He went on to explain that, while it was true that
she had invested heavily in the restoration of Blenheim, the "bric-a-
brac, paintings and movables that she purchased for the castle she will
keep. The duke was a very honorable man," he added, "and when these
purchases were made they were all recorded in his wife's name." Of
course, he concluded, she owned her London house, "and the duchess
will make it her home."[2]

Whether or not the Carlton House Terrace residence belonged to
Lily turned out to be not such an open and shut question as Clews
made out. She had, it seems, assigned the house to her husband during

their marriage "so that he could raise money on it," and it had not yet been legally returned to her at the time of his death. This gave rise to a lawsuit claiming the house as part of the Marlborough estate. *Town Topics* referred to the "outspoken or rather outwritten affidavit" submitted by the duchess to the court in connection with a hearing on the issue. She and her husband, it averred, had informed their solicitor of the step she was taking in advance, as they "knew from previous experience that friends and the trustees would ask questions."[3] It was eventually determined that the house was Lily's, and that it was only the unexpectedness of the duke's death that had delayed its return to her.[4] Lily was too astute about money matters to have made the gesture of assigning her home to her husband without fully understanding what she was doing. The incident illustrates how familiar she had been with the duke's financial concerns as well as her level of confidence in him. "In England," it was said, "the wife is the partner of her husband at home only." She rarely shared his hardships or his pleasures and was seldom consulted on important matters.[5] The Marlborough alliance had been a far-reaching collaboration.

With his father gone, the public spotlight shone for the first time on Lily's stepson, Sunny, the ninth Duke of Marlborough, and on the nature of the relationship between the two people most affected by the eighth duke's passing. The heir had just entered his final year as a student at Trinity College, Cambridge, where he was reading for honors in history and was known as an "able student . . . a clever polo and cricket player, and bold rider to hounds."[6] "I know one or two Trinity men," reported a Londoner some years later, "who profess to having been impressed with a certain magic something in him while he was there, but I suspect that what they unsuspectingly discerned was his capacity for inheriting a dukedom." For the most part, it was agreed that Sunny "excited no personal enthusiasm" at Cambridge or elsewhere. "In all that is said of him you get an effect of scrupulous decorum, a trifle chilly and priggish if anything."[7] One critic chided Sunny for resembling a bit too closely the foppish, avant-garde, young illustrator Aubrey Beardsley.[8] "By excess of courtier-like zeal," intimated another, "he shows himself, perhaps, over-anxious to efface the memory of his father's indifference to the royal as well as to the smart."[9]

In the weeks following her husband's death Lily began to take on a more public persona, its broad outline founded in her warm championship of Sunny's interests. "Everybody is speaking of the Duchess of Marlborough in the highest terms," it was noted by the press in early December. "She is behaving with great generosity and kindness to the new Duke, and smoothing many difficulties in his path."[10] "Even his mother," declared the *New York Times*, "admits the delicacy and generosity of the American Duchess, and while the peculiar relations of the two women scarcely permit of friendship there is between them a strong mutual respect."[11]

Lily stayed on at Blenheim after the funeral and was said to be "managing the estate for the Duke,"[12] who it had been decided would finish his education before taking up his estate responsibilities. Despite the cut and dried laws of inheritance by which Sunny was entitled to immediate occupancy of his property, rumors were floated that Lily might remain at the palace indefinitely or, at least, that having spent so much money on the estate, would have some compensation.[13] One newspaper not singing Lily's praises huffily attributed what it considered untoward suggestions regarding the possibility of Lily's extended Blenheim occupancy to Americans, who "show a great amount of public spirit in desiring to arrange for the future of the duchess at the expense of the Marchioness of Blandford and her son. They even go so far as to suggest an expression of public opinion—as if the public had any right to offer one—that the widowed duchess should be given over Blenheim for her life."[14]

Lily had no intention of lingering at Blenheim. That she was once again laying long-range plans became clear a month after her husband's death when John Palmer, the estate agent who for the past three-and-a-half years had been in charge of the management of both Blenheim and the Carlton House Terrace establishment, placed his resignation in the hands of the newly anointed Duke of Marlborough and accepted the appointment of agent to the duchess.[15]

The English estate agent was the chief operating officer of a landed estate, functioning as the proprietor's alter ego and deputizing for him in his absence. He handled all aspects of property management, was responsible for agricultural practice and improvements, "cultivated the expected reciprocation of respect between the landlord and the community," and according to social historian Eric Richards, "was often regarded as the respected, knowledgeable and even impartial conductor of the rural scene." Most agents were drawn from the "middling" ranks of society—younger sons of country gentlemen, farmers, lawyers, and clergy—and rose in their vocation without formal training but through a process of apprenticeship. "Their extreme diligence, loyalty and identification with their masters," observed Richards, "certainly sustained the old aristocratic order and permitted many landowners to follow careers of extraordinary leisure or of political and social leadership."[16]

Able agents were hard to find, and Palmer had achieved a position of preeminent status at Blenheim. He was barely forty when he pledged himself to his new employer, less than two years older than Lily. He had a young family and a wife then eight months pregnant with her third child. Palmer took a chance in quitting the employ of the new duke to follow the star of a recent widow who was not then able to offer him a comparable situation. But he had confidence in his employer and must have been aware of her plans for the future when he accepted his new position. Lily knew what she was about when she hired Palmer; he was to be her most trusted and valued employee for the rest of her life.

Sunny spent the 1892 Christmas season with his mother as a guest at the great country estate of Longleat. Lily passed the holiday quietly alone at Blenheim.[17] With Mr. Palmer's assistance, she saw to it that estate employees received the usual gifts of beef and that the frozen pond in the park was opened for public skating. She sent poultry to the sick inmates at the Union Workhouse in Woodstock and doled out funds in the villages surrounding Blenheim. The vicar of nearby Combe received through Palmer a grant of ten pounds "for distribution among the poor of your parish in such a manner as you may yourself determine," although it was stipulated that the duchess wanted the gifts made on or before Christmas day. Lily's bounty provided more than eighty families in the parish with cash and tickets that could be spent with local tradesmen for meat, groceries, or coal. Needy families at the other end of the village were given presents of clothing and groceries directly from the estate.[18]

In early January Lily went to Brighton for a few days. "She vacates Blenheim Palace almost at once," it was announced in mid-month, "having hurried her departure, against the young Duke's wish, as she needs a change of air and scene. Lady Blandford will keep house for her son until he marries."[19] Lily returned to Blenheim later in January, packed her personal belongings—leaving behind all of the artwork and furniture purchased with her money for the palace, and moved to a rented house in Brighton. On 18 February the ninth Duke of Marlborough, accompanied by his mother and three sisters, arrived at Blenheim to settle into his new home.[20]

As one Woodstock resident said simply after the departure of the town's former benefactor, "We were all so sorry when Lily Duchess went away, because we loved her."[21] Blenheim employees presented her with a farewell testimonial in the form of an illuminated address inscribed by the 200 members of the indoor and outdoor staff. "The knowledge that your Grace is about to depart from our midst has filled us with deep regret," it proclaimed, "as by the influence of your active and never failing sympathy you have won the hearts of all on the estate." In her letter of thanks Lily wrote that it would be "a solace" to her to look at the testimonial "often, and I think there is not one name among all those inscribed that I did not know personally. It was my dear husband's dearest wish to make those about us happy and contented, and it was my great happiness to aid him in this by every means in my power."[22] Lily had made a success of her role as chatelaine.

While she was setting her own life in order, the duchess performed her duties as executor of her husband's estate. This entailed making, in conjunction with solicitor Whitehead, decisions necessary to implement her husband's bequests, to dispose of items that were not entailed in order to meet death taxes, and to put the estate on a footing that could be maintained on the income of and met the personal requirements of the heir. The first thing to go was the orchid collection, some 25,000 specimens selling well at a five-day auction in late December. "Every one who knows anything of the growth and cultivation of orchids," noted the *London Times*, "is, of course, aware that the Blenheim collection is probably one of the largest and finest ever got together," one that it was doubtful would again be found in any amateur's possession. Among the many private and trade buyers was the Prince of Wales's gardener.[23] The greenhouse plants were sold in early January. The herds of Shorthorn and Jersey cattle, comprising about one hundred head, were auctioned off in March, as was the stud of Shire horses. The cattle sale attracted purchasers from all over England and from Ireland, and there was keen competition for some of the "plums" in the lot. The Shires went for high prices as well. The prizewinning stallion *Hydrometer*, "a great favorite amongst the farmers in the neighborhood," was awarded to the Warwickshire Cart Horse Society for the impressive sum of more than £600. The success of the duke's Shire auction, observed *Truth*, "afforded conclusive proof of the sound judgment with which the animals had been selected."[24]

There was, too, the question of what to do about Marlborough's laboratory of scientific instruments. A thoughtful choice was made in the donation to Oxford University of what a university historian called "a magnificent collection of expensive, and in several cases ostentatiously large," pieces of equipment appropriate for research on electricity, spectroscopy, and chemical physics. The gift enabled Oxford to add practical instruction in physical chemistry to what had until then been no more than a course of lectures. A number of the instruments are now on display in the university's Museum of the History of Science.[25]

Lily, who had sequestered herself so rigorously from social interaction for more than two years during her first widowhood, did not do so during her second. The rules of mourning were continuing to evolve, and although the "orthodox period of seclusion" for a widow was reckoned as one year during the 1890s, one advisor on etiquette reported in 1898 that "modern widows" were choosing to reenter society after only six months. Female members of society's "smart set," she added, and professional women (journalists, actresses, and businesswomen) were, like their male counterparts, apt to shorten their formal observation of mourning even further. There was also more latitude when it came to rules for dress. In the old days, our etiquette specialist reminded her readers, it could seem as if one spent the better part of one's life in mourning, and "the buying of colored clothes was looked upon in the light of a bad omen, which might draw down on us the speedy death of some near relations." Now, she continued, "nobody goes into mourning if they can possibly avoid it, and the one idea seems to be to get out of it again as soon as possible."[26] Lily, who donned traditional black crepe once more in honor of her second husband, was nevertheless remembered years later for having worn "white mourning" during the summer after Marlborough's death.[27] Such a convention was the subject of no discussion among etiquette authorities, so may have been an invention of Lily's own.

The widow spent the first months of her bereavement living quietly in Brighton. During that time, she struck up a friendship with Marlborough's nephew Winston Churchill. A fall down a ravine at an aunt's Bournemouth estate in January had left the seventeen-year-old boy unconscious for three days and in pain for two months thereafter. (Although not recognized in these days before the invention of the x-ray, it was discovered seventy years later that Winston had fractured a thigh in this fall.)[28] He spent some of his weeks of recuperation at Lily's Brighton home, where his aunt, Winston reported to his father in early February, was "kindness personified. The care that was taken of me would I am sure astonish you 'muchly.'"[29] In writing to update Randolph about his son's condition, Lily reported that the doctor pronounced "Winston as doing very well: not quite 'fit' yet but going on nicely." She added that she had done a little medical prescribing of her own. "I discovered the right shoulder wasn't quite right," she explained, "so I have had my masseuse rub it for him—and it is already better." She hoped that Randolph would let Winston stay longer. "I will be so pleased to keep him another week—after wh[ich] I 'believe' he will have nothing left of that nasty fall but its memory. . . . I don't quite like to discharge my patient until he is *cured!*"[30]

Winston, who was preparing with a "crammer" for his third try at passing the entrance examination to Sandhurst, the prestigious army training college for infantry and cavalry officers, went down to Lily's house again during the Easter holidays. "I got here all right on Friday," he wrote to his mother on his first typewriter (given to him by his aunt), "and have not so far injured Myself in any way. Aunt

Lily put me up in a very comfortable room & I have enjoyed myself immensely; the weather is delightful and the town is crowded with people. . . . I have just returned from the Swimming Baths, whither I go every morning."[31] As Lily wrote to Randolph, "I am *very* glad to have Winston with me—for I have grown really fond of the boy. He has lots of good in him—and only needs sometimes to be corrected, which he always takes so smartly and well. . . . I made him send for his books and I will see he does a good bit of work while he is here."[32]

Lily's dinner guests during her nephew's visit included Arthur Balfour, a future Conservative prime minister (and highly eligible bachelor), and Winston's mother worried about her son's social skills in such distinguished company. "I don't want to preach dear boy," she wrote, "but mind you are quiet & don't talk too much & don't drink too much."[33] Lily had no complaints, and when Winston felt the need for some salt-sea air thereafter he went down and stayed with Lily at her Brighton residence.

Just what accounted for Winston's partiality to this relatively recent addition to his large, extended family? Lily was good-natured and maternal by nature, had no offspring of her own on whom to lavish affection, and is likely to have made a particular effort at this time to charm the lively youngster as a way of reaffirming her Churchill family ties and gaining the good will of her hostile brother-in-law, Randolph. She was also disposed to dispense financial largesse to a self-indulgent young man always beset by money worries, one who would in future be "often in debt and beholden to those much richer than himself."[34] Lily was generous to her nephew, but recognized Winston's shortsightedness in pecuniary matters early on and gently teased him about it. Reminding him in a mid-1893 letter of a gift of ten pounds she had promised him, she added, "only I fear you are a wee bit extravagant and I do not mean you to have it until you begin your Army work!"[35] Despite the mutual self-interest that propelled their friendship, Lily and Winston's fondness for one another was sincere. It must have been soothing to Winston to be a little overindulged at this time, when both his mother and father were leaning on him heavily.

Winston's parents were irritated at his having twice failed to pass the Sandhurst entrance exam in 1892, since Randolph had categorically determined that his son was to pursue a career in the army.[36] In July 1893 Winston took the examination again and passed, but his marks were high enough only to qualify him for the cavalry, not the infantry as his father had intended. He jubilantly notified his family of his examination success, but his father was furious at his having failed to meet the requirements for the infantry. "I am rather surprised," he wrote, "at your tone of exultation over your inclusion in the Sandhurst list." In achieving only middling exam results, he continued, you have

> demonstrated beyond refutation your slovenly happy-go-lucky harum scarum style of work for which you have always been distinguished at your various schools. . . . Your own conscience will enable you to recall & enumerate all the efforts that have been made to give you the best of chances which you were entitled to by your position, & how you have practically neglected them all.[37]

Randolph was, he intimated in this letter, essentially washing his hands of his useless son.

Winston's mother's letter on the same subject was tender enough, but reflected his father's mood. "We have just received your letters," she wrote,

> "and are very pleased to think you are enjoying yourself—I am glad of course that you have got into Sandhurst but papa is not very pleased at yr getting in by the skin of your teeth & missing the Infantry by 18 marks. We are not as pleased over your exploits as you seem to be!"[38]

His aunt expressed nothing but enthusiasm for Winston's accomplishment. "I was *so* pleased to get your wire today," wrote Lily in response to his news, "and to know you had 'got in'!! Never mind about the Infantry: you will *love* the Cavalry, and when Papa comes back we will get the charger. . . . Truly, my dear Boy I am very glad for you."[39] Her reference to a "charger" (a large, strong cavalry horse) indicates that she and her nephew had discussed the possibility of his entering the cavalry, and although Winston was eventually offered an infantry cadetship, he opted to join the cavalry. He did so not only because of his love of horses and riding, but because he believed the cavalry offered more opportunities for rapid advancement,[40] and, perhaps, because this branch of the army was considered more aristocratic than the infantry.

Lily understood Randolph's alarm at his son's original placement as being in part economic. To Winston she wrote, "I thought your Father would be disappointed at your not getting into the Infantry—for the Cavalry is so much more expensive."[41] In making a gift to her nephew of a horse, Lily eased the financial burden of fixed costs in cavalry service, one of which was the expense of procuring one's own mounts. Winston knew that Lily was a soft touch in this matter and was not disinclined to take advantage of it. In summarizing for his mother his anticipated outlay when preparing to join his unit, he reminded her that it was his "personal charms" that had "induced the Duchess Lily to give me a charger," thereby decreasing his necessary outlay by £100 or £120.[42] The veteran horseman assigned to act as agent in purchasing the mount was to be dispatched to see the duchess about it personally. "I fear he will be very grasping," Winston confided to Jennie, "but she will not mind paying a good deal—if he is diplomatic and tactful—as I am sure he will be."[43] Historian David Cannadine noted of Winston that, as "a member of Britain's charmed, inner circle . . . he early on learned how to pull its strings to his own advantage."[44]

The unremittingly bitter tone of Randolph's letter on the subject of Winston's Sandhurst entry results reflected the icy attitude he maintained toward his son throughout much of his life. There were, however, extenuating circumstances in this instance. For, although Winston was as yet unaware of it, his father was gradually succumbing to a disease, diagnosed by his doctors as syphilis, which was undermining both his physical and mental health. The anger Randolph expressed in the summer of 1893 was an alarming manifestation of the virulence that had already begun to show itself and would burst forth with increasing frequency as his mind failed and his nervous system deteriorated.

Randolph's acrimony extended to Lily, against whom, as we have seen, he had taken from the beginning. His appreciation of her kindheartedness on the death of his brother was now forgotten, and he tried to discourage the relationship she and Winston shared. As he confided to his mother, "I don't agree with you about the Duchess Lily being a useful friend to him. I think her very silly & gushing and I should be horrified if he got money from her."[45] He tried again to elicit his mother's support on the subject a month later. Winston wanted, he reported, "to go & stay with D[uche]ss Lily but I told him he had seen nothing of his mother & ought to devote himself to her. For some reason or other also I do not care about his being with the Duchess Lily. A dinner or lunch '*ça se passe*' but staying in her house is not very good for him."[46] Randolph no doubt recognized that Lily spoiled Winston and felt that her attentions only encouraged what he perceived to be his son's indolence.

Winston was, in any case, an independent young man and simply ignored his father. He and his aunt continued to be the best of friends and he visited her on a regular basis. Nor was Winston above dissimulating about the connection. Separate letters to his parents on 20 November 1893 reported somewhat contradictory news. To his father he wrote, "I went on Sunday to see Grandmama—who was staying with the Duchess Lily. I stayed there all day—as I had not seen grandmama for more than 3 months."[47] His letter to his mother read simply, "Sunday I went to see the Duchess Lily and found Grandmama there."[48]

The several brief letters written by Lily to Winston and to his father during 1893 comprise the only cache of her personal correspondence known to have been preserved. This makes them of particular interest as providing a window, not only into Lily's emotional state after Marlborough's death, but also into her personality through an examination of her style of writing and composition. The letters' absence of self-pity was remarkable, although the earliest among them were written less than three months after the duchess had been widowed and unexpectedly exiled from Blenheim. Their focus was on their intended recipient and rarely on herself. Nearly all were addressed to Winston, a young man just passing from childhood to adulthood, rather than to a friend with whom she could share confidences, but they brimmed with personality. Lily's easy, bantering style, her frequent use of dashes and exclamation marks, even double exclamation marks, suggest openness, warmth, and informality. So does her penmanship—a graceful script so large and free that often no more than three or four words could be forced into a single line. Lily, it appears on the basis of these letters, was coping with what life had thrown at her.

In July 1893 news surfaced that Lily was actively looking about for a rich American bride for her stepson. As the most recent chatelaine of Blenheim, as well as an executor of her late husband's estate, she knew better than did twenty-one-year-old Sunny that his income as the Duke of Marlborough was insufficient to meet the expenses of keeping up the palace and maintaining a ducal way of life. Proud of her own contribution to the refurbishment of Blenheim, she was eager to see Sunny marry an American fortune as a means of insuring that the palace and its recent enhancements would be preserved.

Lily chose as her successor Gertrude Vanderbilt, the eighteen-year-old daughter of her New York friends Cornelius and Alice. Gertrude and her sixteen-year old cousin Consuelo Vanderbilt were offspring of the wealthiest family in the United States. The 1885 death of their grandfather, William H. Vanderbilt, had meant the distribution of his $200 million railway fortune, and the girls' fathers, who had the most expertise in managing the family business, were the primary beneficiaries of his estate, each inheriting around $50 million. The brothers could not have been less alike. Cornelius, Gertrude's father, was stolid and methodical, and while he had no need to work, chose to involve himself in the family business and serve on a number of charitable boards. He and his wife, Alice, lived conventionally, avoided newspaper notoriety, and were much admired as models of civic duty. Consuelo's father, William Kissam, on the other hand, was a "gentle hedonist"—a convivial, easy-going sportsman with a "melancholic, passive streak" who devoted his time to horseracing, yachting, and world travel. His wife, Alva, a mercurial woman with boundless social ambition, ruled their household with a firm hand and the expectation of absolute obedience from everyone around her.[49]

Gertrude and Consuelo grew up not far from one another in New York City but led very dissimilar lives. Gertrude, despite the fact that her parents were both conservative and strict, was given considerable independence as a child and an adolescent; was free, for the most part, to choose her own friends; and attended private school. Consuelo, whose mother managed every aspect of her life, was allowed few outside contacts and was tutored at home. It is not surprising, given the disparate personalities and lifestyles of their parents, that the girls did not see one another very often.[50] Nor is it surprising that Lily favored Gertrude over her cousin as a potential bride for her stepson. Not only was Gertrude two years older than Consuelo, but more importantly, the duchess and the Cornelius Vanderbilts were friends of long standing. Her box had adjoined theirs at New York's Metropolitan Opera and they had hosted a dinner in her honor on her first visit back to the United States. Lily's personal style was, moreover, closer in manner to that of Gertrude's mother and father than to that of Alva and her husband.

The press found it impossible not to compare the two heiresses as they neared marriageable age. Physically, Gertrude was described as "quite effective in appearance, though scarcely pretty." Consuelo, "while not exactly a handsome girl," was of a "piquante and unusual type. Her face is almost Japanese, and while her figure is too slight and her neck too thin and long, when she matures she will undoubtedly be a handsome woman." Both girls were credited with having sweet manners, but Consuelo possessed an "unconscious timidity" and charming "half-shy expression and manner" that drew people to her. Gertrude was said to have "a more positive, if not stronger, character."[51] Although industrious and charitable like her parents, she was passionate and restless; unlike her tractable younger cousin, she often clashed with her mother.

Lily's rumored ambition to capture Gertrude as a stepdaughter-in-law caused a minor flurry of interest that quickly died down. "Unless Miss Vanderbilt is thoroughly in accord with the plan herself," it was reported, "it is sure to fall through, as Cornelius Vanderbilt is not the man to barter his daughter for any such bauble as a title."[52] The question of the duke's matrimonial future was laid aside for the time being, but Lily's early pronouncement in favor of Gertrude as a bride for her stepson would have repercussions later on.

Lily's Churchill sisters-in-law, who appreciated the graceful way she was handling her widowhood as well as her kindnesses to Sunny and Winston, continued to support her, and their solicitude intensified the level of public enthusiasm beginning to be expressed for the American duchess. It was her "marked generosity" and her goodwill, according to press reports issued little more than two years after Marlborough's death, that

> completely won the friendship, not only of her relatives by marriage, but of sections of society which some years ago were disposed to give her a none-too-cordial welcome. . . . Goodness of heart and open-handed generosity are, indeed, not the least of her attractions, and it may truly be said that there are few more popular society leaders than the present Duchess. . . . Personally, she is a handsome woman, with a height and bearing befitting a ducal station, and with manners that are winsomely courteous to people of all degrees.[53]

Lily may not have succeeded in her attempt to plot a future for her stepson during the year following the loss of her husband, but she was successful in arranging one for herself. It was announced in December 1893 that she had signed a twenty-one-year lease on Deepdene (sometimes called "The Deepene"), an elegant but faded 4,000-acre property on the edge of the old-fashioned town of Dorking, Surrey, some twenty-two miles southeast of London. Deepdene took its name from the amphitheater-like dell or "dene" that was a prominent feature of its undulating landscape. Set in a valley at the foot of the North Downs and surrounded by some of the most pleasing countryside in England, the estate had been justly famous for more than two centuries and housed an imposing residence in the Victorian Italianate style. The new proprietor took up residence in mid-February. By early May she had begun to stock the estate with pedigreed cattle, the earliest of which to arrive were the remnants of the Shorthorn herd from Blenheim.[54] Lily's intentions in hiring away the Blenheim estate agent after Marlborough's death now became clear. She was on her way to creating a little Blenheim of her own.

A less restrictive role for women was widely, sometimes stridently, promoted in the late nineteenth century. Ibsen's *Doll's House* was first produced in England in 1889, and Hardy's controversial novel *Jude the Obscure* shocked readers in 1895 with its apparent criticism of marriage and frank treatment of female sexuality. Lily was no doubt as scandalized as most of her aristocratic contemporaries by these and other fictionalized attacks on social conventions and traditional gender roles, but she was not beyond being influenced by the new ideology. A woman of the world who had been twice married, Lily knew at what loose ends she had found herself in the years following her first husband's death. There were plenty of ways—many of them trivial—in which she could have spent her time and her money as an unattached widow. But Lily was not at heart a frivolous woman. The one-time chatelaine of Blenheim recognized that not only had she delighted in the social prestige that had come to her through her connection with that famous home, but that she had found pleasure in the business and associational aspects of running a large estate. In taking on Deepdene she chose a "career" for herself, one that would enable her to make use of her accumulated know-how in a meaningful way. At the same time, she provided herself with a recognized prerequisite for a uniquely upper-class British mode of existence as well as an aristocratic underpinning befitting her noble title.

Lily enthusiastically set about to enhance her property, using criteria she had absorbed at her last home. "A considerable number of new cottages are likely to be built," noted a local newspaper shortly after she took on her project, and "orchid-growing on a large scale is contemplated." Electric lighting and the telephone were immediately introduced, and Dorking shopkeepers soon knew Deepdene's mistress as "a most generous patron."[55] She held her first Deepdene house party in June 1894 in connection with the Derby horseracing week at nearby Epsom; among her guests were her stepson, Sunny, and two of her Churchill sisters-in-law and their husbands.[56] Later that month she made a trip to Norway. Her earlier visits to that country with Marlborough had evidently meant more to her than the willingness of a dutiful wife to accompany a sporting husband. Now referred to as a lover of Norse scenery, Lily was considered a skillful and enthusiastic salmon-fisher in her own right.[57] She was away until early August.

Randolph Churchill, meanwhile, was rapidly descending into madness. In order to protect his reputation by removing him from a social milieu in which his disabilities were becoming too marked, it was decided that he and his loyal wife, Jennie, would embark on a yearlong world tour. Nothing was said to their sons about their father's condition, and the boys, now nineteen and fourteen, saw their parents off on 27 June 1894. The journey was a trying, often heartbreaking, ordeal for their mother. Randolph's physical and mental health worsened in Japan, and the doctor who traveled with them tried to convince him to abandon the trip in October, but Randolph insisted on going on as planned.

Randolph had previously given up the family's leased London household as a cost-cutting measure, and during their parents' absence Winston and Jack were handed into the keeping of their grandmother who, like them, was told little about her son's illness. This custodial arrangement created a strain on all parties, and Lily, who was frequently updated about her brother-in-law's decline, made a special effort to look after the three of them during Randolph and Jennie's absence. The Duchess Fanny was a guest at Deepdene for the first time in mid-September. "This is a lovely place in a lovely country," she wrote to Randolph,

> & it's most comfortable in every way. You are "nourri et chauffé" first rate & do just as you please for as you know she has her own ways & does not come down till near luncheon. It suits me *very* well & I really think I shall spend Xmas here with her for she invites the Boys & is only anxious to do what she can for them & me in your absence. I do not know where else I can pass Xmas equally well so I hope you & Jennie will approve and I have accepted.[58]

As for Lily, she added, she "sends you all sorts of kind messages. She seems well only she gets rather stout but is active & certainly very kind & devoted to the family."[59]

As the Duchess Fanny's Christmas plans for her grandsons went unacknowledged, she brought them up again in a letter to Randolph at the end of November. "You must wire your wishes about the Boys," she insisted. "Duchess Lily will be glad to take charge of them at Deepdene & I think this will be the best place for them & cost nothing. She is most kind & will do her best to make them happy & give them shooting."[60]

It was arranged, wrote Winston to his mother from Deepdene in mid-December, that Jack would spend "all his holidays at this beautiful place—a prospect which fills him with pleasure." As for himself, he had turned twenty the previous month and was quite capable of organizing his own social life during the break between his finishing at Sandhurst and obtaining the commission that would launch his military career. Between visits to other country houses, he planned to use Deepdene as a home base and was, he reported, "sorry to have to hustle away to Blenheim tomorrow as the shooting is very fair. We killed 132 pheasants this morning, of which I was responsible for 20."[61] As Winston was leaving Deepdene, Jack arrived. "I am alone here with Aunt Lily, who is not very well," he wrote to his father four days before Christmas. "She has had a nasty cold and headache. She stays in bed and after dinner we sit up and play bezique." He had been riding that morning, he reported, and "I think I am going out to a meet tomorrow of some hounds close by. I wish I could follow them but my Gee will not jump. I should like to see a meet."[62]

Jack's halcyon holiday was cut short on Christmas Eve when his parents returned unexpectedly to London. Winston, who had called on Randolph's physician in late November and now understood the gravity of his father's illness, noted that Randolph was now "as weak and helpless in mind and body as a little child."[63] After a painful month of dying at his mother's London home, he passed away on 25 January 1895. The boys stayed at Deepdene during their father's final weeks and visited their mother in town when they were allowed to do so.

Jennie Churchill, unwilling to go on living with her mother-in-law and emotionally and physically depleted by the strain of the last difficult months, gratefully retreated to the quiet of Deepdene after

Randolph's death. She didn't stay long, however. Hardly one to pursue mourning convention, she decamped in mid-February to Paris. There, according to Ralph Martin, one of her biographers, "it was perfectly permissible for a beautiful young widow wearing long black bloomers to bicycle in the Bois de Boulogne."[64]

CHAPTER 17

Lord William Beresford

ஃ

In October 1894 veiled announcements began to appear in the press about a possible April 1895 marriage between "a charming and popular widow" and a gentleman who was "a very general favorite wherever he goes."[1] The charming widow was, of course, Lily, and the purported groom-to-be was Lord William Leslie de la Poer Beresford, a forty-seven-year-old Anglo-Irish bachelor recently returned from government service in India. Lily had met Beresford at her Deepdene house party in June, to which she had invited him at the suggestion of her Churchill sister-in-law Lady Sarah Wilson, who appreciated the many kindnesses she had received at his hands on a recent visit to India.[2]

"Bill" Beresford was one of a trio of larger-than-life brothers said to glow "with some of the popularity of modern film stars" during the last quarter of the nineteenth century.[3] The brothers were often spoken of as a single phenomenon, and, it was alleged, "those who know all three will dispute with you which of the three is the cleverest, or quickest, or most amusing."[4] English actress Lillie Langtry recalled them as "probably the most entertaining of the Prince's set" in their early manhood. "They were all as handsome as paint. . . . Full of native wit, charm, and *bonhomie*, they positively radiated high spirits, their ready *bons mots* and amusing doings causing constant mirth."[5]

Charles, William, and Marcus (born in 1846, 1847, and 1848) were the middle three of five sons born to the Anglican Reverend Lord John de La Poer Beresford, a "wild Irish Rector" and "savage kind of Christian" who was remembered for knocking about his wife and boys. (As Lord William declared in later years, "he would rather meet

— *209* —

an army of Zulus than his reverend father in a bad temper.")[6] Lord John gained aristocratic precedence in 1859 when his older brother, Henry, the third Marquess of Waterford, died in a horseback-riding accident and John succeeded to the Irish title. This had been created in 1789 for the Earl of Tyrone, an ancestor who merged the ancient pedigrees of the English Beresfords and the Breton de la Poers, a family name that first appeared in Ireland in 1179. A marquess stands just below a duke in noble ranking, and Waterford was and is the senior marquessate in Ireland. The change in John's status took the family to Curraghmore, the Waterford seat and one of the more princely estates in Ireland. Its great house and surrounding acreage became the home and playground of the Beresford children.

The three brothers had an early reputation for rowdiness, and their lifelong propensity for outrageous wagers, storytelling, and practical joking (an aristocratic British pursuit with no American counterpart) was attributed to their upbringing in "the days when Irish wit and humor had lost none of their gloss."[7] These characteristics were certainly inherited: the boys' uncle Henry, the third marquess, was immortalized as "Lord Waterford, reckless and rollicky," in *Patience*, Gilbert and Sullivan's light opera of 1881. Although Henry may have jumped his horse over tollgates by lantern light, although he may have trussed a London police officer and painted him pea green, although he may have slit the mouths of portraits at Curraghmore and inserted cigars into them,[8] he was posthumously remembered as "one of the best landlords and most improving cultivators in Ireland, and universally popular and respected."[9]

The de la Poer Beresford name was associated with horses, hunting, and above all, hard riding. Many people recalled an Irish steeplechase or obstacle horse race in which the three brothers took part during which all three, along with two others of the six competitors, broke their collarbones in negotiating a particularly difficult jump.[10] Their older brother, John Henry, who was born in 1844 and inherited the Waterford title in 1866, was an equally audacious rider. He was permanently crippled in a hunting accident in the 1880s, and after a decade of living in unendurable pain would take his own life in

October 1895. A much younger brother, Delaval, born in 1862, emigrated to Mexico as a young man.

Beresford was educated at Eton, where he was "the leader in everything, afraid of nothing, generous, loyal, ungovernable."[11] He was "chiefly conspicuous for his love of sport and fighting" and pursued an early passion for the racetrack by slipping off from school to the Ascot races, taking "his subsequent caning as part of the lark."[12] As an adult he was known for a breezy manliness of character that enabled him to shine "just as much in the society salon as he does in the tented field," and for his ebullient temper, one that "pleasantly affected every gathering of which he was a member."[13]

It was decided when he finished his schooling that Lord Waterford's third son was to make his way in the army, and in 1867, at the age of twenty, Beresford joined a popular cavalry regiment, the Ninth Lancers. Little of a military nature was required of the unit, and the next several years were spent in the British Isles in a round of social hi-jinks, horse and pony racing, and polo. In 1875 Lord William was dispatched as a subaltern to India, where he served as extra aide-de-camp to Lord Northbrook, the retiring viceroy. Northbrook's successor, Lord Lytton, kept him on as aide-de-camp in charge of the stables. In connection with these duties, Beresford was present at the 1877 official durbar or reception at which Queen Victoria was proclaimed Empress of India.[14]

Beresford took to India, and apart from home leaves and time spent in military campaigns in Afghanistan, South Africa, and Burma, he chose to remain there for nearly twenty years. For gallant service in the Zulu War of 1879 he was awarded the Victoria Cross, bestowed for personal bravery in face of the enemy and recognized as the highest and most prestigious military honor in Britain. It was conferred upon him, reported the *London Times*, "for halting, when closely pursued by the enemy, to take a wounded non-commissioned officer on his horse. When the soldier at first declined to risk the officer's life by giving the latter's horse a double burden, Beresford is understood to have hotly declared that unless the man immediately got up on the saddle he would himself dismount and 'punch his head.'"[15] (Archibald Forbes, a celebrated war correspondent, called this feat "the bravest deed I ever saw.")[16] When summoned to Windsor to accept his decoration, Lord William informed Queen Victoria that he could not do so unless the sergeant who assisted him in the rescue were similarly honored, which he was.

The viceroy's establishment in India, staffed by more than 500 servants, was run as a miniature court in keeping with the British government's strategy of projecting an imperial, "oriental" image that it thought native inhabitants—particularly India's princes—would understand and appreciate.[17] Lord Ripon, who replaced Lytton in 1880, appointed Beresford as his military secretary, a post assumed to represent a combination of ruling aide-de-camp and "master of horse," but in reality carrying a broad range of administrative responsibilities. Not only was Beresford, described as "a prince of an organizer,"[18] now closely involved with the headquarters supervision of the many corps not belonging to the great Indian military commands,[19] but he was also responsible for the steady day-to-day hum of the viceregal household and the bravura display of pomp and hospitality that gave it status. The viceroy's popularity rested to some degree in the hands of his military secretary, noted Beresford's biographer, "hence the importance of having a man who understands, and is in touch, with the native princes and people, who has the table of precedence at his finger-ends, and is pleasing and courteous to all. Lord William excelled in all of this."[20] "His talent for dealing with natives and acquiring influence over them," according to the *London Times*, "was especially remarkable."[21] Beresford was so capable in his role as military secretary that he was asked to stay on by Ripon's two successors, lords Dufferin and Lansdowne. This meant that over the course of his India career Beresford adapted to the styles of five viceregal employers.

Beresford was remembered in India for his ability "to keep the ball of amusement rolling in all phases of society,"[22] but his chief impact during his Eastern career was on the world of sport. No one, it was said, did more to "encourage and promote sport of all kinds in India, and no one was keener after jackal or pig, or more devoted to horse racing and steeplechasing than 'Bill Beresford.'"[23] His first love was racing, and by late 1877 he had collected a number of promising mounts and was running them in competition under his own name. In 1880 he entered into the first of what would be three Indian racing partnerships, two of them with wealthy, young, horse-loving maharajahs whom he infected with his own enthusiasm. Thanks to their financial backing, Beresford was able to build up a stable with a string of good horses and send them to races all over the country. His entries won six Viceroy's Cups—the pinnacle of ambition among racing men in India—as well as a number of other nationally important contests, and Lord William's name became perhaps the most celebrated on the Indian turf. By 1890 he had been dubbed, "originally in jest, and finally in earnest," the "Jockey Club of India," as he took on all of Indian racing's official roles: steward, starter, judge, and handicapper.[24] Lord Bill continued to ride himself, piloting five winners in the Grand Military steeplechase races. After a number of accidents and injuries (including breaking his collarbone another five times) he was forced to cut back on racing and give up polo. He did not, however, give up gambling on horseracing, and was known to "do a good deal of buying and selling over the horses' chances" during his Indian career.[25]

Beresford's big personality caught people's attention, and during the 1870s and 1880s he served as the basis for a character in at least three works of fiction. He first turned up in 1872 as "Soldier Bill" in *Satanella: A Story of Punchestown* by Scottish author G. J. Whyte-Melville, a prolific writer of fashionable novels about military and sporting life. The fictional Bill was the "younger son of a great nobleman" known for "his kindness of heart, combined with that tenacious courage Englishmen call 'pluck,'" who acted in every aspect of his life in accordance with his expressed moral creed: "If you've got to do a thing, catch hold and do it! Keep square, run straight, and ride the shortest way."[26]

American author Francis Marion Crawford drew upon Beresford for aspects of Lord Steepleton Kildare in his 1883 novel, *Mr. Isaacs*, a sketch of Anglo-Indian life that anticipated Rudyard Kipling in introducing India to a non-Indian audience. Kildare, "a fine specimen of a young Englishman of Irish descent," was a "frank and honest" army officer, a gentleman and athlete who owned a string of thoroughbreds, and a keen and capable organizer of sporting entertainments from polo matches to tiger hunts.[27]

Indian-born Kipling was inspired by Beresford too, using him as the basis for a fictional character of a less flattering cast in an early short story, "A Germ-Destroyer," published in 1887 in the *Civil and Military Gazette* and the following year in *Plain Tales from the Hills*. His John Fennil Wonder, a viceroy's "turbulent" private secretary, was "a hard man with a soft manner and a morbid passion for work." He had a propensity "to draw matters which were entirely outside his province into his own hands," wrote Kipling, in an administration in which "all Simla agreed that there was 'too much Wonder, and too little Viceroy.'"[28]

While Lord Bill was building his reputation as an Indian military secretary and racing personality, his brothers Charles and Marcus made names for themselves at home. Lord Charles was a flamboyant figure who spent a full fifty years, from 1859 to 1909, in the navy, which he entered as a cadet at age thirteen. He achieved the rank of admiral and served three times as commander-in-chief of the fleet at sea. When not on active service, he pursued a parliamentary career and represented both Irish and English constituencies in the House of Commons. Charles was close to the Prince of Wales during his young manhood, but their intimate friendship was compromised by a dispute over a woman. "Their subsequent relationship," pronounced Charles's biographer, "was never much more than what is proper between an admiral and his Sovereign."[29]

Lord Marcus, another boon companion of the Prince of Wales, began his career as an army man, but his love of horses and racing diverted him from his original course. In 1890 he took charge of the racehorses and thoroughbred stud of the prince, later King Edward, winning the English Derby for him three times. He filled the same post under Edward's successor, King George V, until his own death in 1922.

One writer summed up the Anglo-India of Beresford's day as a world of "duty and red tape, picnics and adultery."[30] Duty, red tape, and picnics all fell within the sphere of Lord Bill's administrative responsibilities; nothing has been recorded about his amatory history during these years. He was called "the best dancer in the service and the worst flirt in Anglo-Indian society,"[31] but made no long-term commitments; indeed, from a romantic standpoint, he had the reputation of "a veritable butterfly, fluttering from flower to flower and sipping honey in the sunshine."[32]

Beresford was placed on the "unemployed active list" in January 1894 upon the retirement of Lord Lansdowne as viceroy and left India,[33] having passed into middle age in the country where he had spent, as he himself recalled, "the best years of his life."[34] No one anticipated that this carefree and supposedly confirmed bachelor would promptly succumb to marriage upon his return to the British Isles.

CHAPTER 18

Courtship and Marriage III

ॐ

Lily may not have known Lord William Beresford before her June house party, but she would certainly have known of him. He and his brother Charles were what one journalist called, "perhaps, the aristocratic idols of the man in the street,"[1] and their doings were closely tracked in the London press. Aspects of Beresford's Indian life were scrupulously chronicled: his riding exploits and injuries; the successes of his racing stable; the fancy dress ball he threw for children in 1893 to celebrate his forty-sixth birthday (a highlight of the Simla social season); the impressively attended farewell party held in his honor in Calcutta late that same year.

His return to London in the spring of 1894 was duly reported. "The man who was most warmly welcomed by his friends, as he flitted from one box to another and into the stalls, was Lord William Beresford," observed *Vanity Fair* in its coverage of the gala opening night opera performance at Covent Garden in late May. He was "just back from abroad, but looked as smart as though he had never left the neighborhood of Poole and Beale & Inman"[2] —Savile Row men's shops that dressed England's fashionable gentlemen. Given this flattering build-up, it is not to be wondered at that Lily responded enthusiastically to her sister-in-law's suggestion that she invite him to Deepdene.

Denials of an impending marriage appeared in the press after the October announcement of the couple's engagement. Lily's second husband had died, after all, less than two years earlier, and the widow was still wearing mourning garb in his memory. She had reasonable grounds, moreover, for deciding against a union with Lord William.

Despite his engaging personality and his impeccable social credentials, he was yet another suitor with little money; if she married him, Lily would again be in the unenviable position of controlling the family purse-strings and dispensing funds to a supplicant husband. She had, too, to consider the hard-won privileges now hers as a duchess that would be lost if she married an aristocratic third son with no noble status other than the right to use the non-heritable title of "lord." For one thing, she would be forced to cede her place of precedence in law and at court if she married below her current rank and would be officially received only as her husband's wife. For another, she would have to forego the prerogative of sitting on the coveted bench reserved for duchesses' use at state balls and other court entertainments.[3] Lily had never been to a court function other than the 1889 drawing room at which she had been presented, but could she relinquish such an entitlement?

She had plenty of time to reflect on her options, for Beresford returned to India in September to spend the winter of 1894–95 closing out his life there. It is telling that nothing about Lily's covert romance was mentioned in the spate of Churchill correspondence surviving from the period between September 1894 and January 1895 when the Duchess Fanny and her grandsons were visitors to Deepdene. This means that Lily did not discuss her thoughts with her in-laws. As usual, she kept her own counsel, proving that her ability to dissemble had not diminished since the days of her quiet New York courtship with the Duke of Marlborough.

But, as had been the earlier case, Lily made up her mind after a brief relationship, and shortly after Beresford's return to England in March 1895 it was officially announced that the pair would wed in April. Her decision was an expensive one. Lily settled £4,000 a year on her husband-to-be, and reassigned insurance policies totaling £100,000 taken out on her life during the course of her marriage to the Duke of Marlborough to a trust in Beresford's interest if she predeceased him.[4]

The British press was delighted with the match. *Vanity Fair* expressed its hope that Lord William, "who has always been so popular," and the "very clever, generous, exceedingly amusing, and pleasant" Lily, now "becoming one of the most popular women in London," would "be as happy as they deserve to be. . . . The lady and gentleman are so well matched that few can honestly avoid congratulating either of them."[5] The American press, too, wished them well. "When the Duke of Marlborough died," *Harper's Weekly* reminded its readers, the duchess

> neither complained nor repined, but went right on, and now adventures still another experiment in the same section of the matrimonial field. Lord Beresford [*sic*], her new choice, may be accurately described as a "dead-game sport." His impending bride seems fairly entitled to the same designation. He has proved himself to be a person of reckless courage. So has she. They will make a dauntless pair, and apparently they join hands with every prospect of mutual respect and satisfaction.[6]

The *New York Times* was succinct in expressing its position on Lily's marriage: "She has never injured any one, has been gracious, kind, and gentle. Long life and prosperity to Lady Beresford [*sic*]."[7]

Lily's third wedding was the social triumph she had been denied on her marriage to the Duke of Marlborough. It was reported as "the smartest event seen in London for a long time past,"[8] and took place on 30 April in fashionable St. George's Church in Hanover Square, where Lily's sister-in-law Sarah Churchill had been married four years earlier under such discomfiting circumstances for Lily. Some questioned the candor of an early announcement that the nuptials had been arranged to take place very quietly, as both the hour and the name of the church were well advertised.[9] Dense crowds filled the adjacent square hours before the scheduled one o'clock service, and the press of gawkers made it difficult for the police to clear a thoroughfare for the lines of carriages transporting those who held cards of admission to the ceremony.

Queen Victoria's cousin the venerable Duke of Cambridge represented the royal family at the service and was exhibited in a prime front row seat; United States Ambassador Thomas F. Bayard and his wife were similarly displayed.[10] Four of Lily's Churchill sisters-in-law were also on hand. Six months was now considered the proper length of time to grieve for a sibling,[11] yet here they were, celebrating a family marriage little more than three months after the death of their brother Randolph. Jennie Churchill remained sequestered in Paris, but both of her sons were present on the festive day. "Everyone was there," wrote Winston to his mother, "the Hamilton family—well to the fore."[12] Its members were present on this occasion, not to give their stamp of approval to Lily's matrimonial venture, but to convey their respects to her third husband, who was linked by family ties to the Hamilton tribe.

Lord Charles Beresford assisted in seating guests in their pews, and shortly before the appointed time the bridegroom and his brother Marcus arrived. The bride's carriage drew up promptly at one o'clock. "There was a vigorous pressing forward upon the part of the crowd, and a strong effort upon the part of the police to keep back the rush. This the policemen succeeded in doing," and Lily entered the church on the arm of her stepson, the Duke of Marlborough, looking "exceedingly handsome" in a coat and skirt of pearl grey brocade in a bold design of satin roses.[13] She took her place by the side of the bridegroom, who was noted to be much shorter than his bride and, "by the way, looks older than he really is." When the wedding ceremony was over, Lily's stepson "hugged her in very hearty style," and the invited guests repaired to the bride's home in Carlton House Terrace for the customary post-wedding breakfast.[14] "A most excellent breakfast which must have cost a great deal—and crowds to eat it—were the chief feature" of the day as far as twenty-year-old Winston was concerned,[15] and indeed the meal would have pleased any trencherman, as it was by tradition a great formal, sit-down feast. Late in the afternoon the Beresfords left for "the Duchess's seat in Surrey." Lily had politely demurred when the people of Dorking asked permission to greet the newlyweds with a public welcome, but local tradesmen saw to it that the couple was appropriately honored. They opened a subscription, gathered a "handsome sum," and presented the bride and groom with a pair of silver candelabra and "a beautiful illuminated address."[16]

Lily's still unfulfilled yearning to be a woman of social consequence justified the speed with which she was presented at a court drawing room for the second time—a necessary formality for remarried widows hoping to receive invitations to court functions. The rite took place less than three weeks after the wedding and raised eyebrows among those who felt that the bride should be quietly enjoying her honeymoon rather than showing herself at court. Beresford secured as Lily's sponsor his cousin Theresa, Marchioness of Londonderry. An eminent political wife, she had been Lily's first hostess in London as a family connection of the Duchess Fanny. Known for her staunch loyalty, the forceful if overbearing marchioness aptly referred to herself as "a good friend and a bad enemy" and was an excellent choice to launch Lily onto another wave of the social sea.[17] The invitations to royal parties that counted as highlights of the London Season but had eluded Lily as the wife of the Duke of Marlborough promptly followed her presentation.

There was some initial confusion as to how Lily was to be addressed henceforth. Before marrying Beresford she had been the Duchess of Marlborough, and as a widow would have remained so until the marriage of her stepson, Sunny, when the title would pass to his wife. The title of "Dowager Duchess" belonged to whoever had previously served as duchess, and Lily's Churchill mother-in-law was often referred to in this way. The custom was, however, said to be falling into disuse, as there was "a horrid growing-old and quite frumpy sound about the word 'Dowager,' which no young woman over forty could be reasonably or unreasonably expected to stand for a minute."[18] Many duchesses who had been forced to relinquish their place chose to precede their earlier title with their given name.

It was socially acceptable to retain one's earlier title as a "courtesy title" in a subsequent marriage, but not everyone thought that doing so showed consideration for the new husband. How would Lily handle this tricky point of etiquette? It appeared at first that she would go by the name of Lady William Beresford, a decision that pleased her democratic compatriots, for whom the *New York Times* spoke in declaring, "The Duchess of Marlborough displays good American taste in electing to drop the higher-sounding title of Duchess."[19] In the end, however, Lily was unable to relinquish what she had been so proud to attain and, to be fair, many individuals as well as the press continued to call her by the title she had thought to discard. It was eventually announced, to the dismay of some and the utter unconcern of others, that Lady William Beresford would henceforth be known as "Lily, Duchess of Marlborough." The British press followed its own protocol in continuing to assign Lily her lofty place among duchesses in the rigidly ranked order it followed when listing the attendees at social events.

The newlyweds forfeited some of the 1895 London Season to honeymoon and fish in Norway. As Lord Bill had never shown any interest in the comparatively tame sport of fishing, the trip can only have been an accession to Lily's wishes. From all accounts, the month-long excursion was not an angling success. The couple, it was reported, "paid $4,000 for a salmon stream in Norway and caught two fish. That was high for salmon, but Lady Beresford is too good a sportswoman to haggle over cost. She has angled for British dukes, and she knows that the fun of fishing is in the fishing, and bears no near relation to the value of what one lands."[20] The Norwegian excursion was not repeated, nor did Lily and her husband ever holiday in Beresford's beloved India, as there was "an idea that the climate might not suit the Duchess's health."[21] How the Indian setting might have undermined Lily's constitution is uncertain; perhaps she simply disliked heat.

Lily soon integrated her new husband and his possessions into their shared home. Beresford had brought some favorite horses and ponies back with him from India, and in the fall of 1895 it was reported that he had acquired some good hunters at the Dublin Horse Show and that Lily was enlarging the Deepdene stables to accommodate twenty-five more horses.[22] The house's interior spaces, praised by *Frank Leslie's Popular Monthly* as "beautiful and homelike with carved furniture, tapestries, palms and flowers,"[23] artfully absorbed Lord William's numerous Indian souvenirs, among them hunting trophies, regimental and racing cups, and a multitude of tiger skins. Mounted animal horns and crossed spears replaced the imposing bronze and marble statues that had come with the property and stood in lifelike poses about the entrance hall. Many of these, among them some colossal nudes, were relegated to underground chambers cut into the Deepdene hillside where, "damp and heavily draped," they were said to resemble "giants drying themselves in a Turkish Bath."[24]

Winston Churchill, now a second lieutenant with a cavalry unit, the Fourth Hussars, spent much of 1895 and 1896 stationed at Aldershot, not far from London, and was a frequent guest at Deepdene. He later recalled fondly of the trio of Beresford brothers that they "made one feel that the world and everyone in it were of fine consequence," and took "a strong liking" to Lily's third husband. His "Uncle Bill," he observed,

> seemed to have every quality which could fascinate a cavalry subaltern. He was a man of the world acquainted with every aspect of clubland and society. . . . There was nothing in sport or in gambling about sport which he had not tasted. . . . His opinions about public affairs, though tinged with an official hue, were deeply practical, and on matters of conduct and etiquette they were held by many to be decisive.[25]

Winston reported himself "never tired of listening to his wisdom or imparting my own."[26] Shane Leslie, cousin to both Winston and Beresford, counted Lily's husband among the earliest men who took Winston's "father's place and to a great extent interested and helped him" after Randolph Churchill's death, sustaining his passion for horses and kindling his interest in Indian army life.[27]

Beresford's niece Clodagh, younger sister of the recently elevated Marquess of Waterford and four years Winston's junior, was often at Deepdene during this period and later wrote about the effect her uncle had on Lily's nephew. Winston "was a soldier then," she recalled, "and very good company, but rather inclined to be bumptious and conceited about his brains," a trait that "did not make him popular." But, she continued, "I don't think that anyone could stay bumptious long with Uncle Bill. Though he was so charming and kind, he had a way of wittily picking the conceit out of anyone like the ribs out of an umbrella, and certainly he had a very good effect on Winston, who was always charming when staying there and most amusing."[28]

Lily's remarriage enabled her to lay claim at last to the ultimate English social triumph: the acquisition of the Prince of Wales as a weekend houseguest. She moved quickly after her court presentation to book the august visitor and long-time friend of her husband for an early October house party. This allowed adequate time for the hostess to fit out a royal suite, a necessary adjunct to homes in which the prince visited and by custom containing a sleeping apartment, dressing room, bathroom, breakfast-room, study, and reception room.[29] (Reupholstering the furniture and silver-plating the bathroom fixtures in the king's quarters at Deepdene was estimated to cost in the range of £30,000.)[30] Suitable lodging arrangements had to be made too for the prince's large staff, as he insisted on being "always surrounded by familiar faces" and the ministrations of his own servants at meals. There were many niceties of etiquette to be observed here, as some staff members took their meals apart from others, and those dining in the servants' hall were appointed set places at table in order of precedence or length of service.[31]

Lily once more implemented her New York training in self-advertisement to ensure that everyone knew of her royal conquest. In fact, the event was so widely announced that it took on the weight of a state visit in the press. One manifestation of Lily's promotional energy was her arranging for the publication of a tasteful, full-page jumble of pen-and-ink drawings in an issue of *Illustrated Sporting and Dramatic News*. Landscape scenes around Dorking were interspersed with front and rear views of Deepdene and an interior sketch of the residence's high, galleried entrance hall with, at its center, a typical Beresford touch added in honor of the prince's visit: a stuffed boar. The published title of this somewhat baffling collage? "The Prince of Wales at Deepdene."[32]

Compiling the guest list for the weekend presented a challenge, for the prince expected to be consulted on the matter of invitees to house parties at which he bestowed the privilege of his presence. He

152   THE ILLUSTRATED SPORTING AND DRAMATIC NEWS   October 5, 1895

Collage celebrating the Prince of Wales's weekend as a guest at Deepdene, October 1895

ILLUSTRATED DRAMATIC AND SPORTING NEWS, 5 OCT 1895

freely expressed his preferences and undesirables under consideration were ruthlessly crossed out. It was known that the prince, when not "impersonating Britannia," so to speak, liked to relax in an informal, "unfetteredly festive" atmosphere surrounded by "rich and simple" people who were attractive and witty but not malicious, who were not overawed by his position but knew how not to overstep the bounds of royal dignity, and who, preferably, played bridge. "A practical joke, in which somebody fell down, or found an egg in his pyjamas, or experienced other quaint happenings" was often among the highlights of a princely weekend, as were good shooting and novelties in food designed to tickle the royal palette.[33] Dorking hens, a celebrated five-toed species of poultry local to the region of Surrey in which Deepdene was located, announced one journal in advance of the prince's visit, were being specially fattened up for his degustation at the Beresfords' home.[34]

Winston Churchill was a Deepdene dinner guest on one evening of the historic weekend. He was, he later recalled, tardy, as was often the case, and arrived eighteen minutes late for the meal. This had been scheduled promptly for eight thirty in keeping with the prince's known preferences, and Winston expected to "slip in and take my place almost unnoticed at the table, and make my apologies afterward." To his chagrin, he entered the drawing room to find the entire company still assembled, as without him there would have been thirteen at the dinner table, and, noted Winston,

> the prejudice of the Royal Family of those days against sitting down thirteen is well known. . . . There, in this large room stood this select and distinguished company in the worst of tempers, and there on the other hand was I, a young boy asked as a special favour and compliment. . . . I stammered a few words of apology and advanced to make my bow. "Don't they teach you to be punctual in your regiment, Winston?" asked the Prince in his most severe tone.[35]

It was another fifteen minutes, concluded Winston, before the prince put him "at ease again by some gracious chaffing remark."[36] What his aunt Lily had to say about his bad manners went unrecorded.

That the Prince of Wales was unaccompanied by his wife on his Deepdene visit was not a mark of disrespect. Princess Alexandra was then perhaps the most popular personage in Great Britain, a reputation she held thanks to her genuine cordiality, her gracious bearing, and her still "most marvelous beauty."[37] But increasing deafness and painful rheumatism had led her to cut back on unnecessary private parties. The 1892 loss of her eldest son, the Duke of Clarence, to pneumonia at the age of twenty-eight was an irreversible blow, and in January 1894 Prince Edward announced his wife's decision to withdraw from society and to seldom again accompany him either on his country house visits or to London balls and parties.[38] The princess continued to punctiliously perform her public duties, but was henceforth most likely to be found at the royal couple's country estate of Sandringham, in her beloved homeland of Denmark (where she was on this occasion),[39] or in the Mediterranean on a yachting cruise. The prince's hectic social life, which provided him with the constant distraction he craved, continued merrily without her.

The Beresfords succeeded in showing the prince a good time despite the fact that "it rained cats and dogs" Saturday night and all day Sunday.[40] Thus the house party passed the greater part of the weekend in playing billiards and cards. Sunday evening was enlivened by music, another ritual of royal visits; among the selections requested by the prince of the seven-piece band hired for the occasion were "My Honey" and "Lazily, Drowsily."[41] As the honored guest wrote shortly after his visit to a friend, "From Saturday to Monday last, I spent at the Deepdene—& was delighted with the place. It is a fine & comfortable house—& the grounds are beautiful with such splendid vegetation & undulating ground. The marriage seems a very happy one & the D[uche]ss is a clever and sensible woman & seems to understand thoroughly English country life."[42] That it was the prince who had been the leading figure in ensuring Lily's exclusion from the London social round she craved as the Duchess of Marlborough did not seem to discomfit him in the least.

Lily and her husband entered enthusiastically into the doings of the town in which they lived. Dorking, with a population of less than

10,000, had its own weekly newspaper, and it was not long before the *Dorking Advertiser* was writing up the Beresfords' local endeavors in exhaustive, sometimes treacly, detail. Its reporters (or, perhaps, its sole correspondent) were much taken with the couple and their openhanded ways. It "would not be too much," concluded one article about them, "or be sycophantic, to say that in themselves they represent much that is best in our own aristocracy."[43]

The town was set atwitter in January 1896 by the news that the lord and lady of Deepdene were to hold a ball for Dorking tradesmen and other townspeople the following month. Over 250 invitations had been issued and accepted, it was announced in the *Advertiser* a few days before the event, and the floor of Deepdene's entrance hall had been temporarily laid with wooden blocks for dancing. "In a word," effused the writer of the two-column piece detailing the evening, "the Deepdene proved worthy of Dorking and Dorking proved worthy of the Deepdene, and all went merry as a marriage bell. . . . The 'fair' were pretty; and the men were pretty fair." Gowns were described with the dash, if not the technical accuracy, of London society columnists, and a complete list was provided of the music accompanying the evening's dances. It was rumored that the master of ceremonies on hand to call the dances had spent three hours at Deepdene the previous evening "when the Duchess and Lord William practiced the quadrilles, with whose movements they were not so familiar as with certain stately court dances; and that Lord William entered in the rehearsal with characteristic abandon." The Beresfords took an active part in the evening's sociability, a fact that was reiterated more than once in coverage of the event. It was perhaps rare for upper-class hosts to linger so long or mix so comfortably at gatherings of this sort. Lily's husband shared supervision of the evening with estate agent John Palmer (described as a "facile and spirited dancer"), and responded to the butler's toast and the crowd's obligatory "three cheers and one cheer more" with a little speech to the effect that he and his wife hoped to "live here for years to enjoy the pleasure of your society."[44]

Deepdene was in the local news again in July, attracting detailed press attention and fulsome praise for yet another party, this one for Dorking schoolchildren held in celebration of Lord William's birthday—an event that would become an annual Dorking occasion. From 1,500 to 1,600 youngsters marched in orderly array to Deepdene from local public and private elementary schools for an afternoon and early evening filled with swings, donkey rides, a steam roundabout, side-stall games, and "a capital series of sports." A band played during teatime, when tea, bread and butter, and cake were dispensed under an attractive marquee. Lily and her husband were on hand, and Lord William acknowledged the "lusty cheers" given in their honor and publicly thanked his wife for making him a present of this party— "just what she knew he most wanted as a birthday gift." Palmer was once more given credit for organizing the event, and it was he who saw to the distribution of a toy to each child.[45]

Having shown their willingness to commit themselves to the interests of the town, Lily and her husband were called upon to make frequent guest appearances at Dorking functions. They were especially receptive to invitations relating to children, and one or both of them often spoke or distributed prizes at local school events. They served together as vice presidents of the Dorking branch of the National Society for the Prevention of Cruelty to Children, and Lord William became a member of the governing committee of the Dorking Cottage Hospital. The couple could be counted on to turn up at a concert to raise funds for the Dorking Conservative Club or a county ball held in the public hall, often bringing houseguests along with them. As civic benefactors, their names became bywords in Dorking.

While Lily was busy with her own romance, wedding, and recharged life, others were maneuvering to marry off her Churchill stepson, Sunny, to whom she was still attached and on whose part she was said to have "acted the part of a fairy godmother, spending lavishly for his benefit" in the years after his father's death.[46] The latest prospective bride was Consuelo Vanderbilt, the younger cousin of Gertrude Vanderbilt whom Lily had sought as a marriage partner for Sunny in 1893. Consuelo had first been dangled before the duke as a seventeen-year-old, when she was seated next to him in the summer of 1894 at a London dinner party given by Minnie Paget, an old friend of

Consuelo's mother from New York. This was not a chance encounter. Minnie, like her mother, Mrs. Paran Stevens, had a reputation as a society matchmaker (and it was said that she accepted money for her services).[47] Alva Vanderbilt, reasoning that her daughter's marriage to the highest available English title would be just the feather she needed in her own social cap, had boldly set about to make it happen. The effort was hardly subtle, and after the young people's 1894 meeting the amazed Duchess Fanny wrote of her grandson to daughter-in-law Jennie, "Mrs. Paget has been very busy introducing him to Miss Vanderbilt and telling everybody she meant to arrange a marriage between them, but he has only met her once and does not seem to incline to pursue the acquaintance."[48]

Sunny did not follow up on the introduction and did not meet Consuelo again until she and her mother revisited London the following June, little more than a month after Sunny escorted his stepmother down the aisle on the occasion of her third marriage. From then on the romance progressed swiftly, thanks to the systematic prodding of Alva and her London friends and the promise of a marriage settlement of more than $5 million from Consuelo's father. The couple wed in an extravagant and much-publicized ceremony in New York on 6 November. Consuelo's cousin Gertrude married Harry Payne Whitney, son of Lily's New York friends the William C. Whitneys and the archetypal rich boy next door, the following summer. Gertrude later founded what became New York City's Whitney Museum of American Art.

Lily, who had Sunny's interests at heart, would certainly have encouraged him in his desultory pursuit of Consuelo as a means of assuring his financial future, and when he married she presented his bride with a wedding gift of "fabulous value": a girdle of rubies with bracelets and hair ornaments to match. (Only the duke and Consuelo's mother were believed to have given the bride more costly presents.)[49] It is unlikely, however, that Lily had any involvement in the negotiations leading up to Sunny's marriage, or even that she saw anything of Consuelo and her mother during their 1894 and 1895 visits to London. On the contrary, it is probable that Alva pointedly avoided Sunny's stepmother. It mattered to her, naturally, that Lily had little standing in the royal circle and was therefore a weak source of social favors. It mattered more that Lily was a friend of her brother- and sister-in-law the Cornelius Vanderbilts (and, incidentally, had earlier thought of their daughter as a possible bride for Sunny), for Alva was at odds with this couple as she was with the entire Vanderbilt clan.

After an increasingly disappointing marriage, and against the advice of her own lawyer, Alva had sued her husband for divorce before leaving for Europe with Consuelo in the spring of 1894. What's more, she had taken the socially unprecedented step of publicly citing her husband's adultery as a reason for the action. She broke off all relations with the Vanderbilts, who stood firmly by Consuelo's father and discouraged the divorce, and cut those whom she considered to be "against her."[50] The rift was lasting. Except for William Vanderbilt, whose responsibility it was to escort his daughter down the aisle on her wedding day and then slip unobtrusively away, not one member of the extended Vanderbilt family was present at Consuelo and Sunny's marriage; wedding presents from Vanderbilt relations were returned unopened.[51] Consuelo therefore arrived in England as a bride without knowing much about her predecessor at Blenheim, although she may have been aware of, even absorbed, her mother's casual hostility toward Lily as a friend of her in-laws. The absence of an early connection between the two Marlborough duchesses would not ease the situation as the relationship between the once fond stepmother and stepson deteriorated.

The seeds of trouble were planted during the late summer and autumn months of 1895 after Sunny arrived in America to woo, propose to, and wed Consuelo. He found little to like about the United States during what was his first and only trip to the country, and was embarrassed by the sycophancy and vulgar hoopla that attended his visit, the relentless and not always flattering press attention, and the awkward position in which he found himself as a central character in the most breathtaking of all Anglo-American exchanges of money for title to date. Public discussion of his father-in-law's financial largesse in connection with his marriage irritated him, as did published references to the role of his American stepmother and her money in the refurbishment of Blenheim. Indeed, Sunny became so touchy on these subjects that less than three weeks after his wedding he issued a statement through his lawyer stating that he had "declined to touch one shilling of his bride's money, all of which had been settled on her." Furthermore, he insisted, Blenheim had always been well maintained and it was untrue that his stepmother "had expended anything to improve the estate."[52]

Sunny's on-going aversion to the situation in which he found himself must have seemed sufficient justification to him for the release in early January 1896, while bride and groom were honeymooning in Italy, of a peculiarly detailed and strongly worded document on his behalf. "So many misstatements," quoted the *London Times* in dryly publishing its contents, "have appeared in the public Press with reference to Blenheim Palace, its condition, and the outlay made upon it during the ten years from 1883 to 1893, and the sources from which such outlay has been provided, that the Duke of Marlborough has caused an investigation to be made into the accounts by a chartered public accountant." The ensuing report enumerated the sums that had been added to the ducal purse as a result of his grandfather and father's house content sales. It then itemized, to the last pound, shilling, and pence, the cost of a long list of Blenheim repairs and enhancements that had taken place during the ten-year period. "The whole of the improvements," it emphatically concluded, "both to the palace and the gardens and to all the buildings and other portions of the settled estate, were, as a fact, paid for out of moneys the property of the present Duke of Marlborough and from no other source whatever."[53]

One wonders if Sunny really considered the consequences when he dropped this bombshell. His vexation with the American impression that it was Lily's money that had made Blenheim livable was one thing, but to disavow his stepmother's contributions altogether was another. It is likely that his unconscious motivation for issuing the ill-advised proclamation was to bear witness to his own significant means in the face of the humiliating public consensus concerning the avaricious motivation behind his marriage. The accounting also reflected the huge ego investment Sunny had already made in his ancestral connection with Blenheim, and the enduring meaning he found, as his cousin Winston wrote after Sunny's death, in the "particular task of keeping the palace and its treasures together which he had accepted as the main effort of his life."[54]

No matter what his intention, Sunny's callous pronouncement was a slap in the face to Lily, whose role in the restoration of the estate had been so publicly chronicled during the four years in which she reigned as Blenheim's mistress—a period when Sunny was still a schoolboy and university student and seldom at his father's home. Stunned and hurt, Lily couldn't help but take issue with her stepson's assertions, call him on them, and eventually threaten legal action.

The Churchill family was sucked into the fray, and Winston, writing from India in December 1896, promised his mother,

> I will write to Sunny if you think it would interest him to hear from me. I am sorry things are coming to a climax as regards his dispute with Duchess Lily. It is a great pity and I hope that even now the unedifying spectacle of a family wrangle may not be presented to the world. Sunny will certainly lose the respect of many—what ever the legal result may be—& will infallibly be charged with *ingratitude*—a charge which I do not think he will have deserved.[55]

Although the earlier bond between Lily and Sunny was severed by this dispute, Lily did not lose the friendship of her other Churchill relations.

It was inevitable that Lily would one day find herself within the same social orbit as Bertha, Marlborough's first wife and Sunny's mother. Lord William's sister-in-law the Dowager Marchioness of Waterford was a blood relation of the reigning Duchess of Abercorn, and when the marchioness died in early 1897, two years after her husband's suicide, it was the duchess who took on the guardianship of Beresford's nineteen- and seventeen-year-old nieces, Susan and Clodagh. The ties were reinforced in October of that year when the girls' brother, the sixth Marquess of Waterford, wed Lady Beatrice Fitzmaurice, daughter of Lord William's former India boss, the

Marquess of Lansdowne, then serving as Secretary of State for War, and his wife, Bertha's sister Maud. (The Beresfords may have had a hand in promoting this marriage, as Waterford and his sisters had been Deepdene guests for several days in June along with the Lansdownes and their daughter.)[56] Once introduced to one another, Lily and Bertha became, for a while at least, friends. Randolph Churchill, who had so objected to the idea of the two women meeting after his brother's death, would hardly have approved had he lived to hear that Lily was acting as chaperone for one of Bertha's Churchill daughters at an 1897 London cotillion.[57]

CHAPTER 19

New Roles for Lily

❧

Lily, to her surprise and delight, found herself in an "interesting condition," as pregnancy was euphemistically called, in the spring of 1896. It was a surprise, too, to those who knew her history. Jennie Churchill passed on the news to the Prince of Wales in late August. "What you tell me about D[uche]ss Lily is most interesting," responded the prince, "and I agree with you that a certain gallant Lord deserves a *clasp* to his V.C.!"[1] (A "clasp," in this instance, would have been a supplementary medal for getting Lily pregnant.) New York's *Town Topics* expressed astonishment on learning of Lily's pregnancy in November. "But, we shall see," gushed its London correspondent. "She is bonny enough and plucky enough for anything."[2]

It was accepted wisdom among aristocratic women that they were unusually delicate and less likely than women of lower classes to survive the rigors of childbirth. Later studies have proven this staunchly held conviction to have been a myth. After 1841, when comparable figures first became available, the death rate of upper-class women related to childbirth was found to be less than 5 percent—slightly lower than that of mothers in the general population. A woman was judged best fitted for childbearing between the ages of twenty-three and thirty-five, and older women were warned to expect considerable suffering during delivery. Lily, at forty-two, was nearly twice the twenty-two-year-old average age of first-time mothers, but she was statistically far less likely than teenagers to die in childbirth.[3] Such reassuring data was, alas, unavailable to this expectant mother, whose trepidation was augmented by personal concerns.

As the sister of a retarded sibling, Lily anxiously faced mounting evidence that the condition might have genetic roots. She had also experienced the recent loss of her only surviving sister, Lucy Price Renshaw, who died in childbirth in Troy, New York, at the age of thirty-eight a year earlier, leaving behind four young children. A maternity nurse settled in at Deepdene some six weeks before the anticipated date of confinement because of Lily's fears about her age and her health. She was said to have once again resorted to morphine for relief, "but of this habit Lord William has done much to cure her, so that she might live through the ordeal."[4]

The last thing Lily needed in her delicate condition was the riding accident that befell her husband at the end of December. His mount tripped or took off too late as it tried to jump a fence during a hunting outing with the Dorking staghounds, somersaulted its rider over the railings, and landed directly on top of him. Lord William, who had been in a smash-up earlier that week while out driving behind one of his trotters, was, according to his medical men, "badly squeezed" in this second incident. He fractured his pelvis, was unconscious for several hours, and hovered for some time between life and death. News of the mishap was kept from his wife until the doctors had done what they could to patch up the wounded man.[5]

Lily passed two nights at her husband's bedside and public concern for the popular sportsman and his wife was widespread. "So numerous have been the visits of kind inquirers," the press announced in early January, "that a man is placed at each of the lodges to take cards, and fresh bulletins are frequently posted."[6] Beresford's injuries were such that he was never again able to mount a horse, and later that month his entire stable of hunters—"one of the finest studs of horses that have come up for sale from any establishment for a long time past"—was sold at auction.[7] Lily must have been relieved, in some ways, that this phase of her husband's career was behind him.

A Dr. Allinson advised in his 1894 *Book for Married Women* that a pregnant woman should continue her household duties until the onset of labor; "if she belongs to the leisured classes, she must make it a rule to go out for a walk of an hour or more twice a day" until the

Lily, from cover of Country Life, *May 1898*

baby is born.[8] Lily was too unnerved to follow this sensible regimen. As Jennie Churchill, writing to Winston in January 1897, confided, "I hear anything but a good account of Lily Marlborough. It appears that she won't get out of bed which is very bad for her under the circumstances."[9] Despite her fears, Lily eagerly awaited the birth of her child. "All the household," reported a correspondent for the *New York World*, "sees how she longs for an heir."[10]

Lily's infant, William Warren de la Poer Beresford, arrived on 4 February 1897. It was an anxious time, as low birth weight meant that he spent the first weeks of his life in an incubator, but his father could joke about it later. "Uncle Bill," wrote seventeen-year-old Jack Churchill to his mother from Deepdene in mid-May, "says his baby got so strong, it broke its incubator."[11] His cousin Shane Leslie later remembered being much impressed that young William "was washed in a silver tub and spoon-fed with brandy."[12]

Those familiar with the old Hamersley will contest were well aware that the newborn had no legal rights in the estate of Lily's first husband that so amply provided for her and her family's maintenance. Yet the press couldn't help but speculate, and dragged the issue up again some fifteen years after it had been a subject of popular interest. "Babes May Fight for Millions" ran one headline, published in the *Philadelphia Inquirer* and other American papers shortly after little Bill's birth. Accompanying the article was a cartoon showing two children tugging in opposite directions on the ties of a sack labeled "$7,000,000."[13]

Lily now had a child to occupy as much time as she chose to devote to him. Her maternal ardor was often mentioned in news accounts of her doings henceforth, and she reportedly warned others "not to tempt her to talk about her boy, because he was such a duck that she wouldn't know when to stop once she began."[14] Lord William doted too. In October 1897 he and Lily were sighted in Brighton, where they could "usually be seen on the Front in devoted attendance on a very smart blue and white baby carriage." The parents' pride in its small occupant, noted one observer, was "pretty to watch."[15]

Beresford, despite his delight in the role of new father, had other ventures to pursue. He had told an interviewer not long after his wedding that he had little idea how he was going to occupy himself as a retired man of leisure or as a husband. Allowing that marriage was "a very big fence to get over," he added that he didn't "look forward to settling down to the ordinary humdrum life of a Duchess's husband," but offered no details.[16] Despite his bland dissimulation about his plans, Beresford knew exactly where his interests lay and what he hoped to do in England. Shortly before his wedding there arrived in London a valuable racehorse he had ordered from Australia, and it wasn't long before its owner was deeply immersed in horseracing, the diversion to which he had been passionately committed for most of his life.

The horse was the very symbol of English aristocratic power, wealth, and status. In a country in which sports were more obsessively pursued than anywhere else in the world, the breeding and racing of horses was the most quintessentially patrician of pastimes—a hobby made more prestigious by the Prince of Wales's enjoyment of the turf and his participation in the sport as an owner. In July 1896 it was announced that Lord William would enter into a racing partnership with American tobacco heir and Tuxedo Park developer Pierre Lorillard, whom Lily had known in New York, and was to share horses and a trainer with him in England.[17]

Lorillard had long been involved in American racing. He had also maintained a string of horses in England from 1879 through 1882, achieving distinction in 1881 as the first American to win the English Derby, one of the most prestigious flat thoroughbred races in the world. He was drawn back to England by corruption in American racing and consequent governmental tinkering with the sport,[18] and shipped twelve yearlings across the Atlantic in September, installing his American trainer, John Huggins, to oversee them.[19] The Beresford/Lorillard partnership became an immediate force in English racing. In 1898 Lorillard placed seventh and Beresford tenth in the annual ranking of English racehorse owners in terms of overall winnings; the Prince of Wales placed fourteenth.[20]

Beresford pursued an increasingly prominent role on the turf. His partnership with Lorillard identified him with what became known as the "American Invasion," a period of several years in which American owners, trainers, and jockeys made up a highly visible component of English racing activity.[21] When Lorillard, citing ill health, withdrew from the partnership in the autumn of 1898 and temporarily retired from the English racing scene, Beresford immediately took on another American partner, William C. Whitney, Lily's old New York society connection. Whitney purchased Lorillard's interest in the Beresford-

Lorillard operation, and the American trainer, Huggins, stayed on. He was credited with training the winners of 162 races for the combined Beresford partnerships during the years 1898 through 1900.[22]

Lord William went about the business of horseracing with the same thoroughness he had devoted to his career as military secretary in India. Race meetings of all kinds drew him, whether he had horses running in them or not, and he was said to be "the most ubiquitous of owners. . . . He appears one day in the North of England, at a Southern meeting on the next: always in the same equable temperament, and always ready to take or lay odds."[23]

Lily, despite the childhood years she had spent in the Washington home of her horse-breeding and racing great uncle Ogle Tayloe, neither knew nor cared much about the sport of horseracing when she married Beresford. As a prudent businesswoman she took exception to her husband's fondness for wagering on the horses, and early in the marriage this became a subject of marital contention. As Winston Churchill wrote to his mother from Bangalore in November 1896, "I am indeed sorry to hear Bill Beresford has had such a bad meeting. It will be very awkward for him—for though Lily will pay up—she will not forget to let him know about it."[24]

Lily learned, however, to put up with the expenses incurred by her husband in indulging his racing obsession. Furthermore, she came to take pleasure in her acknowledged position as the wife of one of the sport's most vibrant personalities, and was increasingly to be found at Beresford's side during race events to cheer on horses whose jockeys wore the traditional light blue with black cap of the house of Waterford. She soon found herself spending time with her husband at Newmarket, a bustling market center located some sixty-five miles north of London, where the springy turf of the broad, featureless heath just outside of town had been a favorite sporting ground since the early seventeenth century.

Newmarket had fewer physical attractions than its race-meet competitors, but it was the acknowledged headquarters of the technical or "horse" part of racing. A number of training enterprises had established themselves locally during the early 1800s, and racing was now a resident industry with a season lasting from April through

October. It took its flavor from the constant movement of horses piloted "by tiny, purposeful men in caps and boots" to, from, and across the heath, and rug-wearing racehorses were often seen to emerge from stable yards "to clip-clop amongst the shoppers" in town.[25]

In 1898 Beresford borrowed a venerable training establishment, Heath House, from the Duke of Portland for two October meetings. In early 1899 he leased the facility himself for a period of years and installed in it his fifty-odd racehorses and his trainer. "Lily, Duchess of Marlborough is one of several new faces to be seen now on the Heath," observed one Newmarket regular in May 1899, "and although she never bets, she takes the greatest interest in her husband's horses."[26] Later that year Beresford and Lily (by now referred to as "a well-known racing woman")[27] took a long-term lease on a residential Newmarket property, Stitchworth, for their use during the racing season. In doing so, they became members of a local social set that was so idiosyncratically focused on the sport and business of horseracing that Newmarket was designated as "perhaps the most exclusive place in England."[28]

The town's racing clique was an invigorating mix. The Prince of Wales could be counted on to appear at the most insignificant of races and on the coldest and gloomiest of days, which meant that the "upper ten" was well represented. Some male members of the group were merely rich, while women who were neither wellborn nor well bred might be "in the swim."[29] One of Lily's Newmarket connections was actress Lillie Langtry, a racing enthusiast who kept some twenty-five horses in a stud just outside of town and who partnered with Lily in 1899 to organize a theater benefit in Brighton for the local Asylum for the Blind.[30] It was a convention that women did not own horses (Langtry raced under the name of Mr. Jersey), but by the end of the century it was rumored that Lily was buying horses in silent partnership with her husband. Once again she had proved herself to be a quick learner and enthusiastic supporter of what most interested the man whose life she shared.

Lord William promoted his nephew Winston Churchill's fondness for horseracing by presenting him with a racing pony to enliven his military assignment when he was posted to India in 1896. Named "Lily of the Valley" in honor of the aunt who made the gift possible, the animal was a subject of some dispute between Winston and his mother. The Prince of Wales, Jennie wrote anxiously to her son, "begged me to tell you that you ought not to race, only because it is not a good business in India—they are not square & the best of reputations get spoiled over it. *You* don't know but everyone else does that it is next to impossible to race in India & keep clean hands."[31]

Winston responded with a host of arguments in favor of keeping his horse. His uncle, he pointed out, "would not be likely to have given it to me if it was certain to involve the unpleasant consequences you anticipate. Everyone out here possesses an animal of one sort of another which they race in the numerous local meetings." Furthermore, he added, Lord William had given him the pony "not in order that I might convert it into pounds and shillings—but to keep and use. He would be very disappointed as he has taken so much trouble about writing and sending it out, etc and would probably think very little of me for having screwed £125 out of the Duchess on such terms."[32]

Winston, needless to say, kept his pony. She raced for the first time in March 1897. "She is very fit," the proud owner wrote on the day of the race to his brother, Jack, but he did not expect her to win as she was up against strong competition. In fact, he added in a postscript, she "ran 4th—but did course in very good time—it will be a matter of months before she is properly trained. Then she may be a flyer."[33]

The four-legged Lily did not, however, show an early inclination to fly. "I am afraid she is not going to turn out anything good," Winston wrote forlornly to Beresford. "She cannot beat any ordinary ponies out here and though she eats well I cannot help thinking this warm climate has spoiled her courage."[34] Lily did eventually redeem herself, and by the end of the year had won two races. "Only £20 a piece unfortunately," Winston wrote to his mother. "Still—."[35]

When on home leave, Winston was a frequent guest at Deepdene, where he found the other visitors, many of them Beresford's friends, to be interesting and sometimes later to be useful to him. Among them was John Prescott Hewett, Home Secretary to the Government of India, who, Winston reported to his mother, was "most amiable and looked after us thoroughly" when he and a regimental friend visited Calcutta in 1896 for the races. Among his other attentions, Hewett contrived to have the young men made honorary members of Calcutta's Bengal Club ("a very good one," reported Winston smugly).[36]

Another of Winston's Deepdene contacts was Sir Bindon Blood, an experienced commander on the Indian frontier whom he met in 1896 and who promised him in a general way that if he were called upon to lead another Indian expedition he would let Churchill come along. Winston was staying at Deepdene in 1897 when he heard about an Indian frontier revolt. He immediately wired Sir Bindon, who was to command the troops assigned to oppose the uprising, and returned to India where Blood, having been urged to do so by Beresford,[37] took him on. He "was awfully good to me while I was with his force," wrote Winston to his uncle Bill in November 1897, "and I have never ceased congratulating myself upon having met him at Deepdene."[38] Winston's participation in Blood's military campaign was the basis for his first piece of professional writing: a well-received book entitled *The Story of the Malakand Field Force* published in 1898.

Jack Churchill was, like his brother, a regular guest at Deepdene. "Aunt Lily is in splendid form, better than I have ever seen her," he wrote to his mother at around the time of publication of *Malakand Field Force*. "Uncle Bill has still his fall to remember, & is not allowed to hunt. The house is empty and we have great fun. She is mad about Winston's book & has all sorts of schemes about it."[39]

Reminiscences of two very different sorts of Deepdene parties come down to us from memoirists who were children when the events they described took place. One of them was written for a niece by Dorothy Langdon, a children's book author who grew up as the daughter of a Dorking brewery agent. It must have been in 1897 or 1898, when Dorothy was nine or ten, that she and a cousin attended an afternoon gathering at Deepdene. This may have been one of the receptions Lily held from time to time for local members of the Mothers' Union, a 200,000-strong Anglican women's organization dedicated to upholding Christianity that effectively lobbied at the local and national levels for better conditions for mothers. The invitation to the event was issued to adults, but Dorothy's mother and aunt dressed their girls in their frilliest frocks, cautioned them to be on their best behavior, and took them along.[40]

The occasion, wrote Langdon, "was on par to an invitation to Windsor Castle to meet Queen Victoria!" The girls "had an idea too, that the Duchess would be wearing a crown." Langdon evoked for her young relative the lofty entrance hall at Deepdene, "lined on each side by uniformed flunkies," and a staircase, at the head of which "stood a very tall lady dressed in black velvet . . . and beside her stood a little man who spoke to every person as they shook hands." When the little girls reached their host and hostess, continued Langdon, "a deep contralto voice high up above Dorothy's head, said, 'TWO LITTLE GIRLS! I WONDER IF THEY HAVE A KISS FOR ME?'" Dorothy and her cousin "naturally lifted a cheek to be kissed. Very seriously, too, they shook hands with the Gentleman." They followed their mothers into a huge room "like a Fairy Palace," its "balcony hung with ferns and flowers." Tubs of flowering shrubs stood on the marble floor, "and best of all FOUNTAINS played!" After some "dull endless 'talking'" emanating from a raised platform at one end of the room, the company moved on to a huge drawing room, where "footmen with silver trays were passing sandwiches, and the maids came round with tea. . . . A tall footman served the two children as seriously as if they were 'grown-ups' which impressed them so much they could hardly nibble at their sandwich."[41]

> At this moment another voice, a hearty man's voice, came, saying, "I know what children like. You come with me," and before they realized it, the two cousins found themselves hand-in-hand with the short-statured gentleman who had stood at the head of the stairs of the hall. This time it was not a sandwich, but some delicious pink coconut cakes that they were handed, and after they had eaten these, even more delicious things were handed to them by their new-found friend. No shyness now, and at last, chattering gaily, they were led back to their respective Mamas. . . . It was not until they were going home that the children realized that not only had they been KISSED BY A DUCHESS but they had been "WAITED UPON BY A LORD."[42]

Langdon's breathless account conveys something of the Beresfords' gracious entertaining style as well as the awe in which the middle class—even its juvenile members—held titled aristocrats.

Lord William's cousin Shane Leslie provided another glimpse into Deepdene life in a published memoir that recalled the splendid family Christmas parties held by "this dear lady" Lily and her husband when he was a boy. "For children," he recalled, "Deepdene afforded the wildest excitement," for the Beresford brothers "encouraged every revolt against discipline. They once put up my brother and myself to fight each other until our noses ran blood. My brother was given a gold sovereign for winning and I was awarded another for taking it well." The holidays, he wrote, were filled with perpetual laughter, and "we began to suspect that life for grown-ups was one long uproarious party carried on from house to house and visit to visit. There was pheasant-shooting for the men and hockey for women and children, but always with some practical joke waiting in the background." The women, according to Leslie, were "slight and wasp-waisted, but too heavily skirted and veiled for outdoor sports."[43]

There was never any question in the Beresford marriage as to who owned Deepdene. It was Lily's, and she managed that part of the estate not directly connected with the residence or occupied by tenant farmers as an agricultural operation modeled on "scientific principles" of the sort she had learned from her second husband. In becoming a "practical farmer" she followed the example of Queen Victoria, who was said to take a deep interest in the farms attached to the royal estates at Windsor, on the Isle of Wight, and in Scotland.[44] Like the queen, Lily was not involved in day-to-day oversight of her agricultural venture. This responsibility belonged to her agent, John Palmer, who administered a commercial enterprise specializing in dairy cows, sheep, pigs, and poultry. Lily's cows produced some 650 quarts of milk and up to 75 pounds of butter a week for market. Her hens laid 16,000 eggs a year.[45]

Queen Victoria, according to the Prince of Wales, competed with "the whole of her dominions" in the competitive showing of farm animals.[46] Lily, too, exhibited the best examples of her livestock and won recognition for them. In 1896 she began showing Jerseys, and

Lord William Beresford and son, 1899

in 1899 entered both sheep and cattle in the annual show of the Oxfordshire Agricultural Society, held once again in Blenheim Park after a hiatus of ten years. She was no doubt quietly satisfied to win prizes at this fair for the best Southdown sheep and the best Jersey bull as well as two other awards for her cows.[47]

A large farm, "Golden Lands," was devoted to horses, for Beresford, despite having given up his hunters, still maintained stables at Deepdene and loved to chase around the local countryside behind a high-stepping trotter. "It used to be quite a joke amongst the people of Dorking," noted his biographer, "when they heard one of the trotters thundering down the road to shout out, 'Clear the way for his lordship.'" He was known for proceeding at such a terrific pace when driving a pair that his servants regarded it as no pleasant duty to be in the trap. If Lily was beside him on the driver's seat of their well-turned-out coach and he was making her nervous by going faster than she liked, he was apt to tease her by saying, "Oh, I thought you would be in a hurry to get back to the boy!"[48]

Thanks to Lily's free hand with money, Deepdene regained its one-time position as a horticultural showplace. As many as twenty-four employees were kept busy tending the extensive gardens, and journals such as *Country Life* and *Garden* raved about the plantings and sweeping landscape effects as well as the greenhouses, in which Lily was said to house the most complete collection of orchids in the country (including one variety named in honor of the Duke of Marlborough). Deepdene was at its most beautiful in June, when luxuriant banks of rhododendron and azalea bloomed in "a cloud of color" against a background of exotic conifers and forest. The park and the twelve miles of pleasure drives surrounding the residence were not open to the public, but their owner was generous in making the property available to advance the charitable causes of the Dorking neighborhood.[49]

Lily's name was mentioned in the press in connection with a number of popular pastimes during the mid- and late-1890s. In September 1897, no doubt to her amusement, she was featured as one of several "famous lady cyclists" in a news item that appeared in the midst of a brief English cycling craze, when chic society as a body took up the bicycle and could be found wobbling around Hyde Park in droves during the Season. The duchess, it was disclosed, "shuns the London parks, preferring to enjoy a quiet spin along the sequestered roads which surround her charming home of Deepdene."[50] She was a vice president that year of the Road and Path Cycling Association,[51] one of the many clubs that sprang up in response to the fad. The sport was short-lived as a society pursuit, as peddling was found to be tedious, and what was worse, it was becoming "common."[52] By 1900 it had been largely abandoned by the aristocracy.

In 1895 Lily was credited with a role in the brief revival of a particularly genteel hobby: lace-making. The collecting of fine handmade lace was already popular among well-to-do women, and the nearly identical black gowns in Queen Victoria's constantly renewed wardrobe were said to vary only in their rare old lace trimmings from

The Beresfords en route to the races, 1899. Lord and Lady Marcus Beresford on rear seat
FROM *TOD SLOAN, BY HIMSELF*, BY AMERICAN JOCKEY JAMES FORMAN SLOAN, 1915. COURTESY OF SCIENCE AND
ENGINEERING LIBRARY, STONY BROOK UNIVERSITY, STONY BROOK, NY

her important collection. Lily accumulated lace pieces herself, among them a three-yard "flounce" of Irish "Youghal point" that reportedly cost her $2,500. She furthered her lace-making knowledge by hiring a Belgian lace-maker to teach her the technique of "pillow lace," involving the winding of thread around bobbins on a padded cushion. "The Duchess's example," it was noted, "quickly found imitators among her titled equals . . . and now it is considered insufficient to merely pay big sums for scraps of fine old point; one should be able to discuss laces as a connoisseur and more or less successfully imitate their mesh and pattern."[53] The renaissance of lace work, like the bicycling craze, was fleeting, as it was found to be, noted a social commentator in 1897, "very trying to the eyes."[54]

Lily's sister-in law Lady Marcus Beresford piqued Lily's interest in the breeding and showing of cats during a period in which the propagation of domestic animals was in vogue with aristocratic women. The former Louisa Catherine Ridley, scandalously famous as a double-divorcée, had quietly wed Lord William's younger brother Marcus, like him a longtime bachelor, only four months after Lily's marriage. A celebrated beauty said to bear a striking resemblance to the Princess of Wales, Louisa's vocation as one of the foremost breeders of cats in England had "the effect of causing people interested in cats to pass a sponge over her former indiscretions."[55] Her Surrey "cattery" was home to some thirty cats living in pretty Cat Cottage and lovingly attended by a full-time "cat-girl"; among her prize felines were two Siamese beauties sent to her from Bangkok by Lord William in the early 1890s.[56] Lady Marcus established the popular Cat Club in 1898, which was judged to be a brilliant success thanks to "the untiring energy and generosity" of its founder.[57] Lily's cats were shown at Cat Club events, and she was one of the organization's first presidents, although it is likely that she leant the prestige of her name rather than her organizational talents to the enterprise; a rival club, the National Cat Club, proudly highlighted the Duchess of Bedford at the head of its officers' roster.

A nine-hole, private golf course was laid out on the grounds of Deepdene in 1897. Golf had been played in Britain since the fifteenth century, but reached huge new amateur audiences during the last decade of the nineteenth—the number of courses increasing from less than 100 in 1875 to 1,300 in 1900. John Palmer, Lily's estate agent and a golfer, took the lead in negotiating an agreement between the Dorking Golf Club and Lord William "on behalf of the Duchess" for a ground lease at the nominal rent of one shilling (five cents) per annum, in addition to which the club was asked to make an annual contribution of five pounds to the cottage hospital. There were eight women and three children of unrecorded age on the initial membership roster of fifty players, but whether or not Lily was a serious golfer is unknown. She was given keys to her own locker and to the clubhouse at the Deepdene course in 1902.[58]

John Palmer's responsibilities went well beyond acting as Lily's estate agent. His official title was "Secretary to the Duchess of Marlborough and Trustee to her Estate," which meant that he was involved in all aspects of her English business and financial affairs. He represented Lily in her dealings with the town of Dorking and was a respected local citizen in his own right, serving at one time as chairman of the Dorking Urban District Council.[59] Palmer and his wife often deputized as host and hostess at Deepdene charitable functions when the Beresfords were out of town, and Lord William relied on Palmer, an excellent shot, to arrange and manage Deepdene shooting parties for guests, as he cared little for the sport himself.[60] Another aspect of Palmer's job was to keep a rein on Beresford's impetuous generosity, for the lord of the manor was known to be a soft touch and "never had any ready money as he never could keep it."[61] Down-on-their-luck members (and purported members) of his old regiment, the Ninth Lancers, were said to methodically avoid Palmer when hitting Beresford up for a little financial assistance. They waited until he "had gone home, before going to ask for Lord William, knowing that if Mr. Palmer was there the case would be thoroughly enquired into, while if they saw his lordship they knew they could work upon his tender and kind heart."[62]

The Beresfords continued to go up to London every spring for at least a part of the Season, and Lily put in enough hours as hostess at charitable bazaars and fairs to keep her name in circulation. What she wore during these years attracted a good deal of press scrutiny, and Lily did her part to uphold the English stereotype of American women as better dressed than their British counterparts. The most systematic fashion coverage was given to the garments worn at court drawing rooms, and the gowns of Lily, who now made an annual drawing room appearance, were worth writing about. It is "absurd," noted the *Aberdeen Journal* in 1899, "to dream of going to Court unless you are well dressed, but it is the Americans to whom, apparently, money is no object. . . . Lily, Duchess of Marlborough has hardly ever been to the Drawing Room without wearing one of the most notably beautiful dresses at Court."[63]

It was announced in early July 1899 that Lily's Carlton House Terrace residence had been let for the remainder of the Season, as the duchess preferred to spend her summer at Deepdene, which she thought provided a healthier environment for her son than did London. From then on the Beresfords were little to be seen in town. Lily had made all the conquests necessary to satisfy her early social ambitions, was happy in the country life she and her husband had built together, and had nothing more to prove.

The prickly relationship between Lily and her stepson did not improve over the years. It annoyed Sunny that Lily continued to use her one-time title, and it no doubt disturbed Lily that Sunny persistently undercut his father's legacy while building up that of his uncle Randolph Churchill. Sunny's predilection for his late uncle was influenced, in part, by the close friendship he enjoyed with his cousin Winston, who was fascinated by his father and began in the 1890s to research what became a popular biography of this complicated man. Sunny wrote a brief but fulsome article about Randolph's youth at Blenheim for a Conservative party gazette in 1898, and underwrote, too, much of the cost of a life-size statue of his uncle that was installed in the Blenheim chapel in 1897.[64]

A new financial squabble erupted in early 1900 between Lily and Sunny over the matter of "jointure." A jointure was a contractual sum traditionally assigned to a wife at the time of her marriage by her husband and paid from family estate income after his decease for the support of his widow. Sunny was already paying the annual £2,500 jointure to the Marchioness of Blandford that had been settled on her by his father when the couple wed in 1869. According to legal documents executed in 1866, it was understood that the eighth Duke of Marlborough had the power of jointure as often as he married—so long as the total amount of such assignments did not exceed £4,000 per annum, and a £2,500 jointure was duly settled on Lily when she married Marlborough in 1888. She did not raise the issue of the estate's financial commitment to her immediately after her second husband's death, when she and her stepson were good friends. But she claimed her jointure after the death of Duchess Fanny in 1899 in a petition contested by her stepson. The legal question as to whether the eighth duke had had the right to create jointures in favor of more than one living wife was decided in Lily's favor, but her annual allocation was limited to £1,500 because Sunny's mother's claim preceded hers.[65]

This settlement was acceptable to Lily, but Sunny, who seemed unconcerned at this point about airing dirty family laundry when it came to his stepmother, appealed the decision. He was joined in his suit by his wife, Consuelo, and his mother. The argument pursued by the trio's legal representatives indicates how little changed since Lily's

1888 marriage was public perception when it came to the sanctity of wedding vows. Sunny's lawyers contended that the jointure to Lily as a second wife was unjustifiable because the right to marry after divorce was "contrary to public policy and illegal." Such a ruling as had just been handed down in Lily's favor, continued the legal argument, "might operate as an inducement to the husband to look forward to a divorce, because he would know that he might in that event be able to marry another woman, and to make a provision for her out of family estates." While the accuracy of this sentiment was acknowledged, the court determined that the words in the relevant documents allowing unlimited jointures to wives of the eighth duke "were express," and the appeal was dismissed.[66] Lily henceforth added £1,500 a year to the tidy fortune she was laying aside for her young son.

Sunny's dogged effort to deny Lily the jointure to which she was entitled infuriated her. To compound matters, it was mentioned in the press that his wife, Consuelo, had "on more than one occasion . . . snubbed her countrywoman . . . until the latter determined that she could not submit to such treatment any longer."[67] Lily once again threatened Sunny with a lawsuit in October 1900 to compel him to return to her the funds she had expended on Blenheim. Lily was not a litigious woman, but she refused to tolerate Sunny's public scorn.

The ninth Duke of Marlborough was not universally popular. He was known as an ill-tempered man, and was derided in 1898 as "undersized and puny, with a disagreeable expression and a self-satisfaction in himself and in his political ideas that would be amusing were it not so irritating."[68] As Consuelo wrote in her memoirs, her husband was "more inclined to criticize than to instruct" when it came to his wife's management of the Blenheim household, while at the same time begrudging any independent action on her part. When she gained maturity and confidence in her role as duchess, she came to resent both Sunny's high-handedness and his domineering streak— what she called his assumed "hectoring rights" over his wife.[69] There was gossip about marital dissension between the duke and duchess, and it was suggested that Sunny left for South Africa to join British forces fighting in the Boer War in January 1900 in order to escape his domestic troubles. He was back in England by late July (reportedly having been "sent home because he was such a failure" at his assignment, according to one acquaintance),[70] but relations between the couple did not improve. Sunny had political ambitions and the couple had two young children, so there was no talk of divorce.

In order to facilitate the stylish entertaining thought necessary to further Sunny's career, he and his wife decided that they needed a permanent London base. "I only had to mention our wish for my father to promise its fulfillment," later recorded Consuelo.[71] Exactly when the Marlboroughs' London real estate quest began is uncertain, but it is likely to have been sometime in late 1900, close in date to the appearance of a bizarre notice in the "Court and Society" column of *Lady's Pictorial,* a popular magazine that often documented the whereabouts of the duke and duchess as well as of Lily.

"The Duke of Marlborough," the journal announced in direct quotation from a received statement, "is naturally desirous that it should be known that reports to the effect that Mr. Vanderbilt has given the Duchess sums of money are quite untrue, and devoid of any foundation."[72] Sunny's public refutation of his father-in-law's financial largesse to his wife was an outrageous breach of good manners, but Consuelo's wealth, as other press outlets were fond of pointing out, was "rather a sore point" with the duke.[73] How similar in spirit was the duke's assertion on this occasion to his earlier dismissal of his stepmother's contributions to the refurbishment of Blenheim. Both pointed up Sunny's nearly pathological inability to accept that the financial wherewithal of women in his personal orbit might equal or outstrip his own. Her stepson's rant served to depersonalize the antagonism Sunny had so unexpectedly expressed toward Lily less than five years earlier. Her lingering rancor toward him, and her wish to extract some kind of remuneration from him to compensate for his cruelty to her, lost all importance in the following months.

CHAPTER 20

1901 and Beyond

ॐ

Lord William never wholly recovered from his 1896 hunting accident. He tired easily and felt less inclined to physical exertion than he had in the past. By 1900 he was suffering occasionally from an old malarial complaint, dysentery, and could be observed uncharacteristically resting in a chair before dinner. (A photograph signed that year for a friend bore the inscription, "W.B., 1900 . . . and feels it.")[1] In late December he contracted peritonitis and was confined to his bed. The annual Beresford family Christmas "Saturnalia" at Deepdene was cancelled because of his poor health,[2] and on 28 December 1900 Lily's third husband passed away at the age of fifty-three.

Beresford was widely mourned. The *London Times* allocated over a column to his obituary, the *Illustrated Sporting and Dramatic News* nearly two pages that glowingly recounted, in particular, his sporting past. Lord Charles Beresford observed in his memoirs that the *Times* intimated that his younger brother might have accomplished more than he did in life: "that he might have had a career in any profession; that he might have been a great soldier, a great diplomat, a great political officer, had not his passion for the turf diverted a part of his energies." That was possibly true, acknowledged Lord Charles, "but perhaps one may be allowed to say that one liked him for what he was and not for what he might have been; and also that he did not do so badly."[3] Lily was named the sole executor of his estate, which was valued at just under £34,000 and was left to his wife "absolutely."[4]

Because so much of Beresford's life had revolved around horseracing, his turf career and the amount of prize money he had won were frequently discussed in the following weeks. He had finished a good second behind the Prince of Wales and a long way ahead of other owners in his last racing season,[5] and his "enormous winnings" received respectful acknowledgment. But according to those who understood the sport, the real story was one of Beresford's "enormous losses." During a period when Beresford's "colors were considered invincible," it was explained, his horses became "hot favorites directly the numbers went up, and it was practically impossible for the owner to win any sum worth mentioning." By the same token, if one of his "outsiders" won a race at long odds, its owner was as likely to have bet on the favorite as on his own mount.[6] "If he had stuck to his own horses he would have won a fortune," observed English trainer George Lambton, "but he would bet on every race, which drove his trainer, Huggins, almost to despair."[7] Despite his reputation as a compulsive gambler on the turf, it was agreed that "there never was a better loser than Lord William . . . and he never blamed neither the trainer nor the jockey, who are usually the scapegoats when there is a tragical miscarriage of some good thing. . . . He thereby set an excellent example to other owners."[8]

A curious legal dispute arose immediately after Beresford's death in connection with *Volodyovski*, a horse Beresford had leased as a yearling and raced successfully as a two-year-old. The litigants? Lily, Duchess of Marlborough, and Valerie, Lady Meux, a former "actress," now the wife of a wealthy brewery tycoon and owner of the horse. Lily, on the advice, no doubt, of her brother-in-law Marcus, claimed the right to fill future engagements contracted by her late husband in connection with the promising mount; Lady Meux contended that the lease arrangement expired with the death of Lord William. The court ruled against Lily, who threatened to appeal but did not, and by mid-February the skirmish was over.[9] That Lily, in her early days of mourning, would initiate a lawsuit connected with horseracing was surprising. She was proven astute, moreover, in having wanted to retain Lord William's interest in the horse, for William Whitney leased *Volodyovski* in his own name and with him won the English Derby in 1901—the first American after Beresford's earlier partner

Pierre Lorillard to do so. Whitney donated his Derby winnings to the English Jockey Club for the creation of the Beresford Trust to provide support for improvident individuals connected with the turf, a trust he later increased to a considerable degree.[10] Lily retained a mild interest in horseracing and was sometimes, but not often, to be seen at Newmarket in later years.

Once again it proved difficult for onlookers to avoid comparing Lord William's early passing with the sudden deaths of Lily's previous husbands. As Winston Churchill wrote in early January to his mother from Ottawa, Canada, where he was on a lecture tour, "I was very sorry to see the death of poor Bill Beresford chronicled in the paper and I telegraphed to Lily. What a remarkable thing it is that when a woman begins killing husbands she goes on. I prophesy she will marry again. I think it very sad because they got on very well together lately and as you know I had a very great affection for him."[11] New York's *Town Topics* was callously blunt in reporting on Lord William's death. Its only allusion to the event, on 3 January 1901, was, "Poor 'Bill' Beresford! Next!"[12]

Two weeks later the same journal offered up the name of the individual it thought likely to supplant Beresford in his widow's affections. "They are already saying," it proclaimed, "that within the next eighteen months the sorrowing widow will find consolation in the arms of 'Reggie' Ward, the brother of the Earl of Dudley, if he is not killed by the Boers before then. He is a nice young fellow of twenty-six, and is an officer of the Worcestershire Regiment. He has long been devoted to Lily, Duchess of Marlborough."[13] English press outlets, reluctant to spread hearsay because of the country's strict libel laws, did no more than hint in the following weeks that Lily was expected to take a fourth husband, adding obliquely that the anticipated bridegroom would be considerably Lily's junior, "the prevailing fashion of the hour."[14] This allusion was to Jennie Churchill's July 1900 marriage to George Cornwallis-West, an army lieutenant nearly twenty-one years younger than his bride (and two weeks younger than her son Winston). Jennie's family and friends had not been enthusiastic about her marriage to Cornwallis-West, described by a fellow officer in the Scots Guards as "a good-looking fellow, bit short on brains."[15] The connection ended in divorce in 1913.

Lily never gave any sign that she had an interest in marrying Captain the Honorable Reginald Ward. She may have known the young man through Beresford's racing connections or, as likely, through her Churchill relatives, as Ward was the best man at the 1903 wedding of the Duke of Roxburghe, a Churchill nephew. The putative suitor (who was the same age as Cornwallis-West) was distinguished mostly as "a gentleman rider," good at polo and steeplechasing and "well-known and very popular in sporting circles."[16] Unfortunately, the oblique linkage of his name with Lily's seems to have brought him ill luck, for Ward died in early 1904 following an operation for appendicitis. Rumors that Lily would remarry continued to circulate. "There is, of course," noted one newspaper later that year, "the inevitable report that she intends to wed again, but no foundation can be found for it, though it is stated that a rich American has proposed to her."[17] Despite such predictions, the widow succumbed to no further offers of marriage.

Lily grieved for Beresford, but as *Lady's Pictorial* pointed out in 1902, the duchess was "a brave woman with a singularly healthy, cheerful mind,"[18] and she took up the strands of her life with, if not the fervor of former years, the same good nature and kindliness of spirit. She busied herself, as she had done since first settling in Surrey, with her Deepdene property, with the needs of estate dependants, and with the philanthropic concerns of the town of Dorking. Deepdene's park and its elegant home hosted many entertainments to benefit local organizations, and Lily could be counted on to pass out prizes, open bazaars, and be on hand in schoolrooms to compliment Dorking girls on their stitchery in needlework classes. She served as president of the Dorking Choral Society and attended its concerts; was a generous patron of the Albany Home that worked with poor girls, as well as of the Literary Institute and the Rifle Club (an enthusiasm of her agent's); actively supported the local Anglican church; and headed up the subscription list for new instruments for the Town Band.[19] She continued to entertain local elementary school children with an annual summer outing at Deepdene in honor of Lord William's birthday. On these days, noted the *Dorking Advertiser*, "needless to say, the Duchess was about the park during the whole of the afternoon, seeing to the enjoyment of her youthful guests."[20] Another event still celebrated "in the usual happy manner" was little Bill's birthday. The Deepdene employees, with their wives and families, were entertained in 1904 at tea, and at dusk there was a magnificent display of fireworks to which choir boys of the parish and cemetery churches and the child residents of St. Joseph's Convent were invited. The evening concluded with a traditional servants' dance.[21]

Lily expressed her on-going commitment to the Dorking Cottage Hospital, her husband's charity, by seeding an endowment fund in his name shortly after his death. She also made an occasional special gift to the facility, such as a new dentist's chair or fresh linoleum for the floors, and at Christmastime saw to it that it was well supplied with treats. Lord William's brothers Charles and Marcus often joined their sister-in-law in visiting the hospital on Christmas Day, when Lily personally presented each patient with a gift accompanied "by a few cheery words."[22]

Lily was seldom seen in London after Beresford's death, and her name was rarely mentioned in connection with the city's social life. She never attended another drawing room (called a "court" under the regime of King Edward VII, who inherited the throne in 1901) or worried about keeping up her court privileges. "Of all the grand dames in London," observed a journalist in 1904, "none has ever so quickly dropped out of prominence as has the duchess. She avoids all the gayeties of London society, and is seldom seen at any big, important gathering, where she would be warmly welcomed."[23] She had withdrawn, it was surmised, not because of heartache over the loss of her husband, but out of devotion to her young son, who was still considered delicate and from whom she was not often separated.

"I don't believe very young mothers ever get wrapped up in their babies," hypothesized Nancy Mitford in her novel *Pursuit of Love*. "It's when women are older that they so adore their children, and maybe it's better for the children to have young unadoring mothers and to lead more detached lives."[24] There is no gainsaying the fact that Lily was besotted with little Bill. His health was a subject of zealous concern to her; indeed, when he was ill in 1903 "with childish ailments, so intense was her anxiety about him that she never left his bedside until compelled to do so by medical advice."[25] The boy was reported to share "the sporting tastes of the family, and is never happier than when in the saddle. He rides to all the local meets, attended by a groom, and in his tiny dog-cart he often drives his nurse or governess along the coast roads from Brighton."[26]

Since Bill was seldom allowed to visit London, Lily sold her home in Carlton House Terrace in 1903, preferring to motor up to town as necessary rather than maintain a city household. She replaced her London establishment that year with a house near Brighton, England's favorite seaside resort for over a hundred years. Lily had long been a devotee of this "little London by the sea" and had been a regular visitor from the time of her marriage to the Duke of Marlborough. Only fifty-one miles from London, Brighton was easily accessible by train and was popular with all classes—its "complicated informal systems of internal local zoning" in time and space enabling all comers to enjoy themselves. Working-class excursionists owned the town from June through August, but it was home to the "fashionable set" from October through February and again for a short season around Easter.[27]

Lily's second home was in sedate Hove, a town directly to the west of Brighton that was smaller than its sometimes rackety neighbor. Known for its opulence, Hove was said to offer "nothing but air and aristocracy" and had a higher number of domestic servants as a percentage of separate households than any seaside resort in Britain.[28] Lily's attached house at 35 Adelaide Crescent was in one of two wings of a never-completed crescent that faced one another across an open lawn and directly abutted the seafront esplanade. The building facades remain among the architectural highlights of the town.

The Brighton-Hove hub appealed to Lily for two reasons. The first was its "stimulating and restorative climate"—attributed to a combination of bracing sea air, a greater number of sunny days per year than other English locales, and temperatures that were seven degrees warmer in winter and ten degrees cooler in summer than those of London. The second was its primacy as an educational center, and some 125 schools were then listed in Brighton town directories.[29] Climate and easy accessibility to London accounted for the academic abundance, and Bill started his boarding school life in Brighton (as had Winston Churchill—considered, like Bill, a delicate child). Lily was driven over to watch her son on the nearby school playing fields every day when she was in residence.[30]

Lily's name appeared most often in press accounts from 1901 on in connection with the opera. The Royal Opera House at Covent Garden had undergone various organizational modifications during the decades since its 1847 opening as the Royal Italian Opera, when all operas, including the early works of Wagner, were sung in Italian. Restored and revitalized in 1888, the house (which dropped "Italian" from its name in 1892) was enthusiastically supported by the Prince and Princess of Wales. Its spring and early summer schedule coincided with the London Season and presented well-publicized occasions for at least figuratively rubbing shoulders with the royal family. It was also a venue for parading wealth and status, although its four tiers of "dull-looking, pen-like boxes" were said to offer less glittering brasswork and more privacy than those of its New York counterpart, the Metropolitan Opera, thereby discouraging the vulgar personal display manifest in New York.[31]

As the Duchess of Marlborough Lily had occasionally attended the opera with her second husband, but Beresford had no interest in the art form, so she leased a box at Covent Garden in her own name next to the royal box for the spring seasons of 1897 and 1898. The following year she subscribed, again in her own name, to a new organization, the Grand Opera Syndicate, "composed of some of the most powerful and socially important members of Society" and launched to underwrite the theater's activities.[32] Aristocratic wives with a fondness for opera and its setting had long pushed their husbands into participating in operatic support societies, but it was traditionally the men who financed their wives' enthusiasms whose names appeared on membership rosters. Lily and the well-known opera singer Adelina

Patti were the only women listed among thirty-two syndicate members in 1899.[33] Money made available through the organization enabled the house to embark on a physical overhaul of Covent Garden, and the enhanced venue became one of the most important opera houses in the world. Subscriptions were highly prized and their acquisition from the syndicate considered a symbol of social acceptance; "much heart-burning," it was said, "resulted among those who found themselves 'left out.'" Lily had a prize box located directly next to the stage in the pit tier, and she was referred to in 1904 as "perhaps the most faithful patron of Grand Opera" among "the musical Duchesses."[34]

Lily may have expressed an interest in British politics in an 1890 New York interview when she was the Duchess of Marlborough, but she did not take up this popular feminine pastime until after the death of Lord William. The turn of the twentieth century was marked by heightened political tension over the "Irish question" and a British effort to reconcile liberal political values with a perceived need for "firmness" in Ireland, which had a history of violent outbursts related to what it considered repressive government policies. The 1906 electoral triumph of the Liberal Party raised the possibility of more independence for Ireland, and political tensions over the issue ran so high that members of society with conflicting Irish views avoided one another.

The Beresford family, having experienced the Irish temper firsthand as aristocratic landlords in Ulster, Ireland's northernmost, heavily Protestant, province, adhered to the tenets of Unionism, a party in the Conservative camp intent on keeping Ireland within the United Kingdom. Lily became caught up in political activity on Unionism's behalf and aligned herself with like-minded patrician women who, although ineligible to vote, exerted considerable influence through their use of social functions and personal contacts to lobby key politicians. Deepdene became the scene of mass meetings, and Lily the president of the Divisional Women's Unionist Association of Surrey. Thanks, in part, "to her strong personality, to say nothing of her hearty enthusiasm," Surrey's was reported to be the largest and most active women's Unionist organization in the country at that time.

Lily presided in 1908 at the annual spring meeting of the Women's Unionists and extended her lavish hospitality to members of the Dorking and neighboring branches at a summer fete in the Deepdene gardens.[35]

While occupied with her local projects, Lily also succeeded in amassing a comfortable fortune thanks to the generous income stream provided by the Hamersley estate, her reliance on good financial advisors, and her own acumen and experience. Most of her personal investments were in the same kinds of ventures that had so steadily increased the wealth of Louis Hamersley's family: real estate and real estate mortgages. She held mortgages on properties in both England and the United States and invested directly in commercial real estate; a five-story apartment building or "flathouse" on West 134th Street in New York was recorded as sold in Lily's name in April 1904.[36] It is possible that she made the occasional more speculative real estate investment, although without further proof one has to question the accuracy of an American newspaper report in 1895 that both Lily and Jennie Churchill were participants in Sir Edward Reid's English syndicate that owned two million acres of undeveloped Florida land.[37]

In 1902 Lily undertook a commercial real estate venture in Dorking, financing a well-designed, three-story building on the high street that offered accommodation on long leases to the Urban District Council and post office as well as retail and residential rental units. The endeavor won her both the grateful thanks of the community and praise as a financial wizard. "There is no question," commented the Dorking paper several years later, "that it has proved a profitable investment on the part of her Grace, an investment made, there is little doubt, in the interests of her son."[38]

The tradition of brief annual trips to the United States in connection with matters related to the Hamersley estate continued, and in 1904 Lily made an American real estate purchase for her own use: a shingled house in the tiny hamlet of Fort Salonga, some fifty miles from New York City on the north shore of Long Island. "Beresford Lodge" was, according to a local journal, "no show place but a comfortable home." Surrounded by forty acres of land, it was located directly across the road from the waterside weekend home

Lily and her son, from cover of Bystander, *1906*

of Dr. Walter Gillette. The property was bought to provide Lily with a stateside address through which to establish her United States residency in connection with estate planning. She spent little time there—perhaps three weeks in the course of three years; gave one house party; and made one Sunday appearance at the local Episcopal church, causing "a great flutter." She did not return to Fort Salonga after 1906.[39]

American visits never exceeded two weeks and varied little from year to year. Lily came alone, accompanied by one or two servants; made a short visit to her mother in Troy; and passed several days in New York City. She kept the business that brought her overseas quiet and accepted few invitations. Her most frequent hosts, arranging both luncheons and dinners in her honor, were her old friends Henry and Lucy Clews, still ensconced at the peak of New York's society pyramid. Despite the attentions of these social lions, Lily's New York excursions no longer attracted much notice. "Fifteen years [*sic*] make a great change in New York," lamented *Town Topics* in 1905, and who, it queried, remembered the celebrated City Hall wedding of Lily and the Duke of Marlborough?[40] American oblivion didn't much bother the one-time duchess.

Among the rare press notices devoted to Lily after 1900 were a photograph of her and her son that graced an early 1906 cover of the *Bystander*, a popular English weekly magazine, and a 1908 article in the *Tatler* about Deepdene.[41] Such pieces represented no more than opportunities for publishers to highlight the activities of social luminaries, so these attentions to Lily suggest that she was still an object of interest.

Her avoidance of the limelight did not mean that Lily became a recluse. While she presided over no balls or ostentatious parties, she socialized quietly with members of the Surrey gentry and with a steady stream of houseguests. Beresford's brother Marcus and his wife, Louisa, were her most frequent companions, and she remained surprisingly close to her Churchill sisters-in-law. Two of the eighth duke's sisters died in the early 1900s (Fanny in 1904 and Georgiana in 1906) but Anne, Cornelia, Sarah, and Jennie continued to be close friends. Lily's most intimate companion in this group was perhaps

Anne, Duchess of Roxburghe, who, like Lily, had been unexpectedly widowed in 1892. Described as "rather duchessy but . . . kind and good at heart," Anne lived a life of "unostentatious decency" and resumed her former position as a Lady in Waiting to Queen Victoria after her husband's death.[42] She and her two unmarried daughters were regular Deepdene guests. Her oldest daughter, Lady Margaret Orr Ewing, who had honeymooned at Deepdene in 1898 and whose husband was killed during the Boer War, often made her home at Deepdene with her young daughter.

Lily maintained an association with the aristocratic element of the American expatriate community, and made 1905 news in connection with the leasing and makeover of Dorchester House as a residence for Whitelaw Reid, the newly appointed United States Ambassador to the Court of St. James. "House hunting," it was reported, "which most folk regard as an unmitigated nuisance, the American Dowager Duchess really enjoys." Her services were said to be always at the disposal of her friends, particularly those from the United States. "She knows Mayfair and Belgravia as few women know these fashionable quarters," it was noted, "and not the most wily of house agents or landlords can impose upon her. When she appears on the scene it is no use holding out for fancy prices." Lily was considered something of an expert in plumbing and ventilation, knew all the London County Council's by-laws and regulations with respect to construction and drainage, "and where she discovers that they have been disregarded insists that they shall be conformed with under penalty of lodging information against the delinquent." The impression given by agents who disliked Lily's methods that she charged a commission for her investigations was dismissed. "This is not true," it was emphatically stated. "She spends her time and money freely on her fad."[43]

Lily experienced the first symptoms of the illness that was to kill her in the closing months of 1906. The disease was probably cancer (the cause, too, of the earlier death of at least one of her two Churchill sisters-in-law), but the press was circumspect in never openly referring to this malady; death "after a long illness" was the euphemism usually employed. "The various phases of her illness," reported the *Dorking Advertiser*, were "watched with keen and melancholy interest; its nature was such as to cause some anxiety from the first, but the intermittent improvement from time to time reported gave reasonable hope of a satisfactory issue, and that her life might be prolonged for some considerable time."[44]

A late letter written by Lily was the 29 August 1908 note to accompany a check made out to her nephew Winston Churchill shortly before his marriage to Clementine Hozier. "As I do not know in the least what you would like," she wrote fondly, "and I tremble to think of the avalanche of gifts that will descend upon you, I am sending my little offering in a form that I hope will best please you. With all my heart, I wish you every joy, and I will be with you in thought on your wedding day." Two Louis XVI wardrobes were credited to Lily in the list of Churchill wedding presents proffered by newspapers.[45]

Lily's illness intensified in October, and "sudden and alarming symptoms" presented themselves two months later. A bulletin posted at nine o'clock in the morning on 11 January 1909 outside the Deepdene carriage entrance gate read, "During the night her Grace had a sudden attack of heart failure, and is now in an unconscious state. Her condition is hopeless." She died forty-five minutes later, at the age of fifty-four. With Lily during the final stages of her illness and when she passed away was her Churchill niece Lady Margaret Orr Ewing.[46]

Lily's remains were cremated by her order—an unusual choice for a woman of her strict Episcopal upbringing. The burning of corpses had only become legal in England with passage of the Cremation Act in 1902, and the pace of what was promoted as a sanitary and medical reform was slow, given Christian faith in the resurrection of the body and emotional distaste for the procedure. Lily's insistence on a ritual that was "very reluctantly tolerated and still generally regarded as heathen and unnatural"[47] pointed up, for the last time, her autonomy when it came to making decisions for herself.

A number of farewell obsequies were held for Lily as her remains made their way to the little churchyard on the Curraghmore estate in

Waterford, Ireland, where she had requested that her ashes be placed beside the grave of her third husband. A short religious service, attended by Lady Margaret "as representing the family," the household staff, and all of the estate employees was held on 14 January in the hall of Deepdene. Afterward, her body, "enclosed in a shell covered with violet velvet, and an outer coffin of polished oak with brass fittings in medieval design," was borne to the station, where an array of town officials, tradespeople, parish churchwardens, Unionist Association members, and the town bandmaster assembled to say their farewells.[48]

Another service was held at the crematory at Golders Green; among those present were Lily's Churchill relatives Jennie (now Mrs. George Cornwallis-West) and Lady Sarah Wilson. The Marquess of Waterford and John Palmer, Lily's estate agent, accompanied Lily's ashes, enclosed in the coffin that had delivered her body to Golders Green, to Paddington Station and on to Ireland. Among the chief mourners at the Curraghmore graveside besides the marquess, his wife, and his sister Susan, was the Marquess of Lansdowne, whose life had been so long intertwined with those of both the Duke of Marlborough and Lord William Beresford.[49]

Waterford's sister Clodagh, with the Beresford propensity to find humor in any situation, remembered "Aunt Lily Marlborough's" interment as perhaps the "most extraordinary funeral" in her experience of such family events. The coffin in which Lily's ashes reposed, she recalled, was "enormous," for "Aunt Lily was a very large woman . . . and when the men who were going to carry it to the grave prepared to pick it up, you could see that they expected it to be very heavy, so when the signal was given to lift it up they put forth all their strength and the empty coffin shot up into the air in the most disconcerting way."[50]

One mourner at the Irish funeral brought the saga of Lily's long and varied experience of married life full circle in an astonishing manner. Lawrence Timpson, a cousin by marriage of Louis Hamersley,[51] was, wrote Clodagh, "over in England at that time, and he thought he ought to attend the funeral. He stayed at Curraghmore for it, and they showed him round, persuading him to stay on another day as he seemed to appreciate it all so much." As the Hamersley relation was not, she dryly noted, "actuated by any personal sorrow," he "forgot the sad occasion of his coming and kept on assuring my brother that he never had enjoyed any visit so much in his life."[52] What would Lily have thought of the appearance at her last rites of this cheerful shadow from her long-ago past?

Her Surrey neighbors mourned Lily's passing. We "could say of her," observed the chairman of the Dorking Town Council, "that she was a true, a great and a noble-hearted woman, ever ready and anxious to do good, and that she tried faithfully to discharge the duties in that station of life in which it had pleased God to place her."[53] Among local tributes to Lily were a stone mosaic memorial in St. Martin's Anglican Church and a street named in her honor. Addressing its large and cosmopolitan readership, the *London Telegraph* eulogized her as "an American lady who had won for herself a secure place in the affections of the British people. . . . Of handsome and dignified presence, she was always a remarkable figure in society. Kind-natured, hospitable, and generous, she had crowds of friends."[54]

CHAPTER 21

After Lily

ॐ

L ily left behind two wills: one English and one American. Both were executed in May 1908 on behalf of "Lily Warren Beresford, Duchess of Marlborough, a citizen of the State of New York and the United States of America sojourning in the Kingdom of Great Britain and Ireland." As her English executors and trustees, she named Lord William's nephew Henry, the Marquess of Waterford; her London solicitor; and John Palmer, the one-time Blenheim estate agent who had served her so loyally for the past sixteen years. Their American counterparts, whose task was to wind up her American affairs and remit the proceeds to the English trustees, were the husband of her late sister Lucy and her New York attorney.[1] The Marquess of Waterford and Lord Marcus Beresford were named as her son's guardians, and it was decided shortly after his mother's death that William was to make Curraghmore his home when he was not at school. Lily left an annuity of £200 a year to John Palmer (who would also collect fees as an estate trustee), and two annuities of £80 pounds each to the maid who had been with her since her 1888 arrival in England and her clerk. Her butler received a bequest of £1,000; her head gardener £500; her under-gardener and second coachman each £300. A few other outdoor servants received individual bequests, and every indoor servant who had been in Lily's employ for five or more years was given one year's wages.[2]

Because of her experience as estate executor for three husbands and her personal involvement in the extraordinary contest over Louis Hamersley's will, Lily tried her best to ensure that her own testamentary documents anticipated all possible eventualities. Her intention was naturally to pass her personal fortune on to her young son and any wife and children he might one day have. During William's minority it was to provide for his maintenance, and at the age of twenty-one he was to have access to all of the income from the estate after the payment of annuities. Lily placed some restrictions on her son's right to this income. If ever he faced personal bankruptcy or was subject to mental instability, she stipulated, her trustees were to act "as they shall think best in the interest of my son . . . in their sole discretion without being liable to account for the exercise of such discretion." Upon his death, William had the right to assign up to one half of the estate income to a wife, but the whole of the estate was to be held in trust "for all his children who being sons or a son attain the age of twenty-one years or being daughters or a daughter attain that age or marry." If William died childless, he had absolute power to dispose of the whole of his mother's residuary estate.[3] No reference to Louis Hamersley's estate was made in either of Lily's testamentary documents.

Her death served, nevertheless, as the signal to rekindle the old Hamersley will dispute, which had remained dormant since it was settled in Lily's favor in 1891. Louis's estate had lately provided its sole beneficiary with an income of $300,000 a year, and Lily was reported to have told her executors shortly before dying that she had no desire that there be any new will contest after her death.[4] But, as expected, suit was brought in 1910. It was precipitated by the seemingly innocent request of Lily's executors to have an accounting made of the Hamersley trust in reference to "certain interests" possibly due to Lily's son thanks to his mother's clever handling of Louis's assets and the estate's subsequent substantial increase in value.[5] This action bestirred former claimants and their descendants (as many thought Lily had known it would) to question not only the final disposition of what was now a $7 million estate, but also to once again raise the underlying issue of the will's legitimacy.

Any change in the interpretation of Louis's 1883 will at this point could only benefit young William Beresford. He had no claim to any portion of the Hamersley estate under the decision that gave his mother the lifelong right to its income, but if the will were declared to have been invalid, he would be entitled to a settlement based on Lily's share by dower right of her first husband's fortune. Eighteen-year-old Louis Gordon Hamersley, Hooker Hamersley's only son, stood, on the other hand, to inherit the entire estate under the existing interpretation of the will, but would have a great deal to lose if the will were overturned and other family members were allowed to share in will proceeds. Thus young Hamersley—both of whose parents were now dead—was one of seventy-one claimants to enter into the latest round of legal haggling over Louis's will (as was Lawrence Timpson, the Hamersley family mourner at Lily's funeral). Louis's extended family, some of whose members had been contesting wills disposed to benefit Louis Hamersley for over seventy years, had by now expanded through generations of intermarriage within their social set to constitute a virtual "who's who" of New York's elite, and their interests were represented in the court proceeding by no less that twenty-three leading New York law firms. This "legal array," it was noted, "will be the largest and strongest ever seen at a single trial. In fact, it is said that but one prominent law firm in this city has no participation in the reopening of the will case."[6]

The family's attempt to extract entitlements from the Hamersley estate met with the same fate as had the challenge of 1884. The case went all the way to the New York State Court of Appeals, but the validity of the 1883 will was once again upheld in 1913.[7] Louis's estate passed to his nephew, whose responsibility it became to perpetuate the Hamersley family name as his uncle had desired if he had no children of his own. Young Louis was already a wealthy man through inheritance from his own parents; thanks to the windfall provided by his uncle's will he had no need to earn a living. After graduating from Harvard University, he served in the First World War and made his name as a sportsman—racing his schooner and winning several records as a speedboat pilot. He was a generous philanthropist and supported a number of worthy causes. At his death, at the age of forty-nine in 1942, he left behind three sons and a daughter.[8]

Lily's mother, Elizabeth Price, passed away in her Troy, New York, home in 1910. She was eighty-two years old and had outlived all three of her daughters. Three hundred shares of Rensselaer and Saratoga Railroad stock were set aside by her will to provide income for the support of her son, Willie, still a resident at the Elm Hill School. The school closed in 1946, and Willie, who had spent sixty-nine years in its sheltering atmosphere, was transferred to the Marshal Sanitarium in Troy, New York, where he died two years later at the age of seventy-eight.[9] He lies buried with his parents, two of his three sisters, his great aunt and uncle Phebe and Ogle Tayloe, and other members of the extended Warren family in the Warren Mortuary Chapel at Oakwood Cemetery in Troy.

The reconciliation of Lily and her mother had never been wholehearted. The parents' refusal to condone their eldest daughter's decision to wed a divorced man, and Mrs. Price's subsequent refusal to recognize the Marlborough marriage, had caused an enduring rupture in the relationship, and neither mother nor daughter could surmount what had at the time seemed to each of them such devastating acts of personal betrayal. Mrs. Price never visited her daughter in England, and Lily's flying trips to the United States allowed little time for more than perfunctory reunions. It was perhaps Lord William who made the most concerted effort to repair the breach. Although he never ventured to the United States and never met his mother-in-law, he felt, according to his biographer, that it "would be a pleasure to her, and his duty to write regularly giving account of his wife and son's doings . . . ending in a sincere attachment on both sides."[10] Mrs. Price left $10,000 in her will to the English grandson she had never met.

The last decade of Lily's life in England had brought her into the Edwardian era that for her, as for most of her class, was experienced as little more than a comfortable shift from the reign of one sovereign to that of a designated heir. Those living at society's pinnacle during what has been called the "long garden party" or "golden afternoon" of Edward's VII's reign were not immediately aware that their world was about to disappear forever. Despite the shock provided by the Liberal Party victory of 1906, they neither interpreted it as "a public gesture of dismissal" nor doubted their presumed right to rule. The First World War made manifest what had until then seemed no more than a blip in the established order. Without the war, noted historian Samuel Hynes, it was likely that "the old ruling class ideas would simply have withered away in a slower if no more seemly fashion."[11]

Although Lily died oblivious to the turmoil facing the aristocratic world she had conquered, her stepson, the ninth Duke of Marlborough, experienced the transition step by agonizing step. Separated from his wife, Consuelo, in 1906, divorced in 1921, and disastrously remarried and again divorced, Sunny did not adjust gracefully to changed circumstances. Portrayed as "a character of almost Proustian pitifulness,"[12] he found solace in his love and nurturance of Blenheim and in conversion to Catholicism. He never had a kind word to say for his father, never forgave him for selling estate assets, and was to a large degree successful in convincing the world that he had single-handedly resuscitated the "wreck" of a palace he inherited.[13] Despite "successive crashes of taxation," wrote Winston Churchill shortly after his cousin's 1934 death, the ninth Duke of Marlborough succeeded in preserving and embellishing his family domain and "Blenheim passes from his care in a finer state than ever."[14]

Some seventy-nine country mansions in England, Scotland, and Wales disappeared between 1870 and 1919 as owners gave up costly assets that generated no revenue,[15] and Lily's beloved Deepdene vanished along with the class for whose members it had been built. In 1920 the house and 50 acres of the estate were sold for conversion into a hotel; 2,200 more acres were sold the following year to be developed as housing lots.[16]

Shane Leslie, the Beresford cousin who so fondly remembered the Deepdene of his boyhood, had occasion to visit the Deepdene Hotel in the mid-1930s. "I know no passage in literature," he wrote, "describing the curious ghost-like feeling which exudes from an old and Stately Home of England after it has gone down in the world." A town bypass, one of the first in the country, had been cut through the hillside in front of the house, ruining Deepdene's famous gardens, and nothing was as Leslie remembered. How strange he found it to visit "a home unseen for so many years. . . . Who remembers now the Beresfords and all their wild humours? Who ever spent such Christmases as we did? I began to feel the painless agonies of a ghost: the recapture of hours when the soul had no pangs and the young body no pains."[17]

Deepdene entered a third life during the Second World War as the wartime headquarters of the Southern Railway Company, and the underground chambers that had once secreted nude marble statues were transformed into a bombproof bunker to house the railway's nerve center. British Rail left Deepdene in the mid-1960s, and in 1969 the great house was demolished and replaced by a modern office block.[18]

One of young William's two guardians, the Marquess of Waterford, died in 1911 at the age of thirty-six in a drowning accident in the Clodagh River that ran through the Curraghmore estate. As his wife was left with six young children of her own to care for, it was felt to be asking too much for her to mother William as well, and the boy was turned over to his other guardian, his uncle Marcus, and his wife, Louisa, who lovingly raised him to adulthood. William died in 1919 shortly before his twenty-second birthday. He was, noted the *Dorking Advertiser*, "delicate throughout his life," and "was debarred from sharing in the illustrious and strenuous life of his father and uncles."[19] William's adult height was reported to be over six feet, but his specific health problems were never recorded; it is likely that he was a victim of the influenza pandemic that killed nearly 200,000 residents of England and Wales in 1918–19. He left a will disposing of his estate, valued at the astonishing sum of £432,553. Sums of £2,500 each were allotted to his former nurse and tutor, and an annuity of £1,000 was left to his uncle Admiral Lord Charles Beresford. The rest of his inheritance was placed in trust for the benefit of his uncle Marcus, and after him for Marcus's wife, Louisa.[20] When his surrogate parents passed away, Louisa in 1920 and Marcus in 1922, William's estate was divided among his cousins: the children of the sixth Marquess of Waterford, "other than such cousin as may be the present Marquess."[21]

Lily's possessions began showing up at auction in 1911, when five of her finest pieces of jewelry sold for high prices: among them a "very fine pearl necklace of forty-six pearls" that went for £16,100.[22] Other bits of her property, including artwork acquired during her marriage to the Duke of Marlborough, were gradually sold off. A last flurry of commercial activity in connection with her belongings came in 1923, some fourteen years after her death, when the contents of Lily's home in Hove were sold after the death of Lord Marcus. Two London sales and a three-day premises sale disgorged Lily's remaining possessions, many of which had been originally purchased for her London property. Most of them, including several pieces of important Louis XV and XVI case furniture displaying a taste for marquetry and ormolu mounts, had no personal connotations. Here and there, however, were to be found tangible mementos of Lily's life after she moved beyond her Troy, New York, childhood. Among these were an eighteenth century engraving of a duke and duchess of Marlborough and their family, and a pair of hoofs, mounted in silver to form an ashtray and cigar lighter and inscribed with the name of Lord William Beresford's favorite racehorse, *Myall King*, winner of India's Viceroy's Cup in 1887, 1888, and 1890.[23]

Lily had shown herself to be a woman of remarkable resilience, and her self-reliance and optimistic confidence in coping with changing circumstances proved what was considered to be the American penchant for adaptability. Her tact in settling financial boundaries for two husbands without demeaning them, and her interest in and aptitude for learning directly, for absorbing indirectly, and for applying her accumulated knowledge and skills creatively were tributes to her intelligence and capability. Lily would not have thought of herself as a feminist, but she deserves respect for the way in which she took control of her own destiny and, with little fanfare, created a distinctive life in warm-hearted, gracious, and generous style. She traveled a long way from her roots, and proved herself an admirable woman in a fascinating era.

Appendix

Table I. Value of Ten Pounds Over Time; 1880 as Base	
1880	£10
1890	£9-1s
1900	£9-4s
1910	£9-2s
1920	£24-7s
1930	£15-7s
2010	£738

Table II. Value of Ten Dollars Over Time; 1880 as Base	
1880	$10
1890	$8.90
1900	$8.21
1910	$9.29
1920	$20.20
1930	$16.90
2010	$220.00

The above tables are rough compendiums of pound and dollar values by decade between 1880 and 1930 based on consumer prices. As they show, the thirty-year period between 1880 and 1910 was a stable, somewhat deflationary, era. Inflation began to increase with World War I.

The exchange rate between dollars and pounds fluctuated narrowly in the 1880–1910 period, with £1 equal to approximately $4.85. The rate has moved frequently since then; as of May 2011, £1 equaled $1.62.

NOTES

ABBREVIATIONS USED:

CHAR   Chartwell Trust Papers
FDM   Frances, Duchess of
        Marlborough
JRC   Jennie Randolph Churchill
        (Jennie adopted these initials
        for herself shortly after the
        death of Lord Randolph
        Churchill)
JSC   John (Jack) Spencer Churchill
LDM   Lily, Duchess of Marlborough
LRC   Lord Randolph Churchill
LWB   Lord William Beresford
NYSSC/LCH
        New York State Surrogate's
        Court, New York County,
        Proving of the Last Will
        and Testament of Louis C.
        Hamersley
NYSSC/HER
        New York State Surrogate's
        Court, New York County,
        Louis C. Hamersley Estate
        Records and Accounting
WSC   Winston Spencer Churchill

PROLOGUE
Pages 1–4

1. *New York Herald*, 24 Nov 1887.

2. Wagner-Martin, *Telling Women's Lives*,
121.

CHAPTER 1: FAMILY BACKGROUND, CHILDHOOD, AND YOUTH
Pages 5–22

1. Lancaster Woman's Club, *Patches of
Garrard County*, 198–99; Buchanan,
DuVals of Kentucky, 241; and notes and
papers of Forrest Calico, Garrard
County Public Library, Lancaster, KY.

2. Ibid.

3. Schroeder, *Shaping a Maritime Empire*,
3–7, 16, 188–89.

4. *Troy Times*, 26 Nov 1888.

5. *Washington Post*, 27 Nov 1888.

6. Rezneck, *Profiles Out of the Past of Troy*,
3, 5.

7. Sylvester, *History of Rensselaer County*,
passim; and Weise, *Troy's One Hundred
Years*, passim.

8. Ibid.

9. Townsend, *Washington, Outside and Inside*,
616–17.

10. Todd, *Story of Washington*, 370.

11. Tayloe, *Tayloes of Virginia*, 25; and
Wilson, *Washington*, 232.

12. Wilson, *Washington*, 232–33.

13. Tayloe, *Tayloes of Virginia*, 25.

14. Clay-Clopton and Sterling, *Belle of the
Fifties*, 29–30.

15. Trollope, *North America*, 305, 315.

16. Watson, *In Memoriam: Tayloe*, 79.

17. Clay-Clopton and Sterling, *Belle of the
Fifties*, 119.

18. Stephen E. Warren to his brother, 17
Mar 1852, Warren Family Papers,
New York State Library, Albany.

19. Mrs. Nathan Warren to Stephen E.
Warren, 21 Mar 1853, Warren Family
Papers, New York State Library,
Albany.

20. Stephen E. Warren to Mrs. Nathan
Warren, 11 Mar 1855, Warren Family
Papers, New York State Library,
Albany.

21. United States Federal Census data,
1860 and 1870. Based on the
consumer price index, the Prices'
1860 worth was $1,570,000 in
2010 dollars; in 1870, after inflation
attributable to the Civil War, it was
$1,380,000.

22. *New York Times*, 31 Mar 1862.

23. *Troy Times*, 26 Nov 1888.

24. Lomax, *Leaves from an Old Washington
Diary*, 204.

25. Jacob, *Capital Elites*, 44.

26. Clay-Clopton and Sterling, *Belle of the
Fifties*, 120.

27. Whyte, *Uncivil War*, 17.

28. Hopkins, "When I Was a Little Girl," 27.

29. Clay-Clopton and Sterling, *Belle of the Fifties*, 120.

30. Stock, *Better Than Rubies*, 186.

31. Green, *Washington: Village and Capital*, 214.

32. Dix, "The Education of Women," 26–28.

33. Sage, *Emma Willard and Her Pupils*, 120, 217.

34. Scott, "The Ever Widening Circle," 3–5, 8.

35. Troy Female Seminary, 1867 *Catalog*, 7–13.

36. Undated news clipping from *Troy Times* (Nov 1892), Troy Scrapbook 24, Troy Public Library.

37. Kenneth L. Brock to Alice Kenney, 28 Feb 1983, Emma Willard School Archives, Troy.

38. Undated news clipping, Troy Scrapbook 24, Troy Public Library.

39. *Troy Times*, 26 Nov 1888.

40. *Philadelphia Inquirer*, 25 Jul 1897.

41. Whyte, *Uncivil War*, 181.

42. Twain and Warner, *Gilded Age*, 295–96, 312.

43. Whyte, *Uncivil War*, 182.

44. Jacob, *Capital Elites*, 202–03.

45. Watson, *In Memoriam: Tayloe*, 45.

46. *Washington Post*, 2 May 1885.

47. *Troy Times*, 26 Nov 1888; *Troy Press*, 26 Nov 1888; and *Troy Observer*, 25 Nov 1888.

48. *Troy Budget*, 30 Oct 1910.

49. *Dallas News*, 30 Aug 1891.

50. Butler, *From Home-spun to Calico*, 45.

51. Elm Hill School Records; and Trent, *Inventing the Feeble Mind*, 89.

52. Tyor and Bell, *Caring for the Retarded in America*, 16.

53. Elm Hill School Records.

54. Trent, *Inventing the Feeble Mind*, 70.

55. Elm Hill School Records, Resident Register, 1851–1889, 65.

56. Butler, *From Home-spun to Calico*, 32.

57. *Washington Post*, 2 May 1885.

58. *New York Times*, 5 Nov 1899.

59. *Washington Star*, 4 Jan 1872.

60. *Washington Star*, 11 Jan 1872, and 5 Mar 1873.

61. Undated news clipping, Troy Scrapbook 24, Troy Public Library.

62. NYSSC/LCH, 421; and *New York Times*, 8 Nov 1876.

CHAPTER 2:
LOUIS CARRÉ HAMERSLEY
Pages 23–29

1. *Memorial History of the City of New York*, 158–60.

2. *National Cyclopedia of American Biography*, vol. 7, 298.

3. *Memorial History of the City of New York*, 161.

4. Ibid.

5. Chemical Bank, *History of the Chemical Bank*, 14, 79–84.

6. *Fifth Avenue*, 60; and *New York Times*, 18 Apr 1915.

7. Ibid.

8. NYSSC/LCH, 659.

9. Jones, "Autobiography."

10. Ibid.

11. NYSSC/LCH, 223, 809.

12. Ibid., 658.

13. *New York Times*, 30 Jun 1888.

14. *New York Tribune*, 5 May 1883.

15. Cited in NYSSC/LCH, 743.

16. Ibid., 743, 671, 94–95, 226.

17. Wharton, "The Long Run," 327.

18. McAllister, *Society as I Have Found It*, 158.

19. Lee, *Edith Wharton*, 29.

20. *Brooklyn Eagle*, 25 May 1884; and NYSSC/LCH, 118.

21. NYSSC/LCH, 672, 754, 603–04, 779, 736, 721–22.

CHAPTER 3:
COURTSHIP AND MARRIAGE I
Pages 30–47

1. NYSSC/LCH, 421.
2. Coo, "White Sulphur Springs," 356.
3. *New York Times*, 12 Jan 1909.
4. Bouligny, *Tribute to W. W. Corcoran*, 18.
5. *Town Topics*, 9 May 1889.
6. Deacon, *Elsie Clews Parsons*, 5.
7. Jones, "Autobiography."
8. *Washington Post*, 15 Aug 1880.
9. *Fifth Avenue*, 9–10.
10. *New York Times*, 1 Nov 1870.
11. NYSSC/LCH, passim.
12. Fleming, *Lady Colin Campbell*, 37.
13. Jones, "Autobiography."
14. Ibid.
15. *Town* (New York), 29 Apr 1882, and 19 Nov 1881.
16. *New York Times*, 18 Apr 1879.
17. *New York Times*, 8 Feb 1881, 11 Feb 1881, and 15 Feb 1881.
18. Wharton, *Age of Innocence*, 5, 13.
19. *New York Times*, 5 Feb 1881.
20. Patterson, *First Four Hundred*, 57.
21. *New York Tribune*, 24 Mar 1888.
22. McAllister, *Society as I Have Found It*, 212–13.
23. *New York Times*, 21 Dec 1880.
24. *New York Times*, 21 Feb 1882.
25. Jaher, "Style and Status," 263, 279.
26. Daniel Huntington, Notebook, National Academy Museum Archives, New York, 25.
27. Rives, *Coaching Club*, 65–66.
28. Decies, *"King Lehr" and the Gilded Age*, 25–27.
29. NYSSC/LCH, 646.
30. Ibid., 578.
31. Ibid., 604–05.
32. Ibid., 801, 566, 212.

33. *Washington Post*, 21 Nov 1886.
34. *New York Times*, 3 Apr 1880.
35. Ibid.
36. *New York Times*, 28 Mar 1882.
37. Kolodin, *Metropolitan Opera*, 5.
38. NYSSC/LCH, 700.
39. Ibid., 711–17.
40. *Season*, 110.
41. NYSSC/LCH, 754, 749.
42. Ibid., 750, 364.
43. *New York Times*, 27 May 1884.
44. NYSSC/LCH, 138.
45. Bourget, *Outre-Mer*, 96.
46. NYSSC/LCH, 701–05, 726.
47. Ibid., 762, 752–53.
48. *New York Times*, 19 Jun 1883.
49. NYSSC/LCH, 559.
50. Ibid., 242–43.

CHAPTER 4:
THE HAMERSLEY WILL CASE
Pages 48–60

1. NYSSC/HER.
2. NYSSC/LCH, 98–100.
3. Ibid., 99–101.
4. Ibid., 102–05.
5. Ibid., 3–4.
6. Ibid., 596.
7. Jaher, "Style and Status," 277.
8. NYSSC/LCH, 14–15.
9. New York State Surrogate's Court, New York County, *Petition of J. Hooker Hamersley*, 4–5.
10. NYSSC/LCH, 715, 443, 168.
11. Ibid., 89–90, 565, 672, 712, 721.
12. *New York World*, 3 Jan 1897.
13. Deacon, *Elsie Clews Parsons*, 59.
14. NYSSC/LCH, 566, 55.
15. *New York World*, 1 May 1884; and *New York Herald*, 1 May 1884.
16. Jones, "Autobiography."

17. *New York World*, 1 May 1884.

18. NYSSC/LCH, 402–03.

19. Ibid., 179.

20. Ibid., 198.

21. Ibid., 217.

22. *New York Times*, 20 May 1884.

23. *New York Times*, 5 Mar 1885.

24. Unidentified news clipping, Saratoga County Historical Society, Ballston Spa, NY.

25. Unidentified news clipping, Saratoga County Historical Society, Ballston Spa, NY; and *New York Times*, 27 May 1884.

26. Unidentified news clipping, Saratoga County Historical Society, Ballston Spa, NY.

27. *New York Times*, 31 Mar 1885.

28. NYSSC/LCH, 817, 814.

29. Ibid., 815.

30. *New York World*, 7 Jan 1886.

31. NYSSC/HER.

32. *New York Times*, 4 Jun 1913.

33. De Witt, Lockman and De Witt Records.

Chapter 5: New York Widow
Pages 61–71

1. Longstreet, *Social Etiquette*, 203.

2. Ibid., 206.

3. *Brooklyn Eagle*, 13 May 1888.

4. Morris, *Makers of New York*, 207; and *Brooklyn Eagle*, 4 Feb 1899.

5. *Brooklyn Eagle*, 6 May 1888.

6. *Chicago Tribune*, 30 May 1886.

7. Ibid.

8. Unidentified news clippings, Saratoga County Historical Society, Ballston Spa, NY; and *New York Times*, 20 Jul 1892.

9. Unidentified news clipping, Saratoga County Historical Society, Ballston Spa, NY.

10. Ibid.

11. Ibid.

12. *Washington Post*, 9 Nov 1884.

13. *Catalogue, Tayloe Collection in the Corcoran Gallery of Art* (Washington, DC: Gibson Bros., 1895).

14. Will of Phebe Tayloe. Copy at Rensselaer County Historical Society, Troy.

15. Personal communication to author from Marisa Bourgoin, Archivist, Corcoran Gallery of Art, Oct 2006.

16. *New York Times*, 28 Mar 1886, 9 Jan 1879, and 12 Dec 1888.

17. *New York World*, 28 Mar 1886.

18. Patterson, *First Four Hundred*, 20–21.

19. *Town Topics*, 30 Mar 1890.

20. Montgomery, *Displaying Women*, 141–44.

21. Longstreet, *Social Etiquette*, 181.

22. Homberger, *Mrs. Astor's New York*, xii.

23. Logan, *Man Who Robbed the Robber Barons*, 130.

24. Montgomery, *Displaying Women*, 141–44.

25. "Anglo-Saxon Society Woman," 58.

26. Armstrong, "Society Journalism," 309.

27. "Anglo-Saxon Society Woman," 57.

28. *New York World*, 7 Nov 1886.

29. *New York Herald*, 24 Nov 1887.

30. *New York Times*, 14 Nov 1886.

31. *New York Graphic*, 13 Nov 1886.

32. *New York Telegram*, 13 Nov 1886; *New York Times*, 14 Nov 1886; and *New York World*, 9 Nov 1886.

33. *Washington Post*, 21 Nov 1886.

34. *Washington Post*, 6 Mar 1897; and *New York Times*, 1 May 1887, 5 Jun 1887, and 26 Jun 1887.

35. *Town Topics*, 11 Aug 1887.

36. 1887 Deed Book, Warren County Clerk's Office, Lake George, NY, 277; and *Glens Falls (NY) Messenger*, 5 Aug 1887.

37. *Glens Falls (NY) Messenger*, 30 Sep 1887.

CHAPTER 6:
THE DUKE OF MARLBOROUGH
Pages 72–86

1. *Town Topics,* 28 Apr 1888.

2. Churchill and Mitchell, *Jennie,* 13.

3. Trollope, *An Autobiography,* 252.

4. Martin, *Jennie,* vol. I, 100; and Montgomery-Massingberd, *Blenheim Revisited,* 98.

5. Rowse, *Later Churchills,* 217–28, 244.

6. Cannadine, *Aspects of Aristocracy,* 134.

7. Cited in Menzies, *Recollections and Reflections,* 79.

8. Citing Daisy Warwick in Leslie, *Marlborough House Set,* 168.

9. Escott, *Society in London,* 114.

10. Escott, *Platform, Press, Politics and Play,* 370.

11. *Truth,* 31 Jan 1895, 277.

12. Frewen, *Melton Mowbray,* 231.

13. "Wicked" was often used by contemporary journalists in referring to Marlborough (as in a 6 Feb 1887 *New York World* article about "Randolph's wicked brother"), and has been popular with Churchill family biographers.

14. Rowse, *Later Churchills,* 270.

15. Escott, *King Edward VII and His Court,* 50.

16. Leslie, *Marlborough House Set,* 2–5.

17. Ibid.

18. Kehoe, *Titled Americans,* 87.

19. *Illustrated American,* 26 Nov 1892, 517.

20. Marquess of Blandford to LRC, 25 Aug 1873, in Churchill, *Winston S. Churchill,* comp. vol. I, part I, 11.

21. *Chicago Tribune,* 3 Mar 1877.

22. Cited in Saint Aubyn, *Edward VII Prince and King,* 172.

23. Cited in Montgomery-Massingberd, *Blenheim Revisited,* 105.

24. Leslie, *Marlborough House Set,* 65.

25. It is unknown what became of the son born to Blandford and Edith Aylesford. According to the eleventh Earl of Aylesford (1918–2008), Guy Spencer was reared in France by foster parents and died while serving in the French army on the Western Front during World War I. (Lee Olson, *Marmalade & Whiskey: British Remittance Men in the West,* 67). On the other hand, a member of the Churchill family reported seeing him in London sometime after World War II. (Henrietta Spencer-Churchill, *Blenheim and the Churchill Family,* 151).

26. Balsan, *Glitter and the Gold,* 45.

27. Stone, *Road to Divorce,* 289, 369, 376, 383, 388–89, 435.

28. Brinsley-Richards, *Seven Years at Eton,* 372–73.

29. Escott, *Society in London,* 114.

30. Fleming, *Lady Colin Campbell,* 8; and Jordan, *Love Well the Hour,* 9–13, 164.

31. *New York Times,* 1 Jan 1887.

32. Cited in Green, *Blenheim Palace,* 32.

33. Cited in Montgomery-Massingberd, *Blenheim Revisited,* 97.

34. Thompson, *English Landed Society,* 310.

35. Cannadine, *Decline and Fall,* 27.

36. Ibid., 112.

37. Mitchell, *Daily Life in Victorian England,* 34.

38. Cited in Green, *Blenheim Palace,* 286.

39. *Chicago Tribune,* 15 Jul 1888; and *New York World,* 3 Nov 1895.

40. Collier, *England and the English,* 325.

41. Cited in Thompson, *English Landed Society,* 319.

42. *New York Times,* 26 Dec 1884.

43. *New York World,* 6 Feb 1887.

CHAPTER 7: MARLBOROUGH IN AMERICA, 1887
Pages 87–92

1. *New York Times,* 29 Aug 1887.

2. *Town Topics,* 25 Aug 1887.

3. *New York Times,* 11 Sep 1887.

4. *Town Topics*, 28 Nov 1889; and *New York Times*, 4 Apr 1895.

5. *Town Topics*, 8 Sep 1887.

6. *Town Topics*, 15 Sep 1887.

7. *New York Times*, 11 Sep 1887.

8. *New York World*, 21 Oct 1887.

9. Ibid.

10. Tate, *Edison's Open Door*, 134.

11. *New York World*, 10 Oct 1887; and *Town Talk* (London), 2 Jun 1888.

12. *New York Herald*, 11 Nov 1887.

13. *New York World*, 1 Dec 1887.

14. Ibid.

CHAPTER 8:
COURTSHIP AND MARRIAGE II
Pages 93–106

1. *New York World*, 30 Jun 1888.

2. *New York World*, 19 Apr 1888.

3. *New York World*, 27 Mar 1888.

4. Ibid.

5. *Town Topics*, 26 Apr 1888.

6. *New York World*, 17 Oct 1887.

7. *New York World*, 28 Feb 1888.

8. *Town Topics*, 5 Jul 1888.

9. *New York World*, 6 May 1888.

10. Montgomery, *"Gilded Prostitution,"* 90.

11. *New York World*, 12 Feb 1888, 19 Feb 1888, and 26 Feb 1888.

12. *New York Times*, 4 Mar 1888; and *New York World*, 18 Mar 1888.

13. *Brooklyn Eagle*, 6 May 1888.

14. *New York World*, 29 Oct 1890, and 3 Dec 1890.

15. *New York World*, 17 Jun 1888; and Marlborough, "Electric Lighting," 296–304.

16. *New York World*, 7 May 1888.

17. *New York World*, 1 Jul 1888.

18. *Vanity Fair*, 14 Jul 1888, 33.

19. *Troy Budget*, 1 Jul 1888.

20. *New York Telegram*, 12 May 1888.

21. *New York World*, 30 Jun 1888.

22. Cited in Leslie, *Lady Randolph Churchill*, 158.

23. *Town Topics*, 10 Dec 1903.

24. *New York Telegram*, 27 Jun 1888.

25. *New York Telegram*, 30 Jun 1888.

26. NYSSC/HER.

27. *New York Times*, 28 Jun 1888.

28. *Albany (NY) Argus*, 29 Jun 1888.

29. For the story of Louisa Caton, see Jehanne Wake, *Sisters of Fortune: Marianne, Bess, Louisa, and Emily Caton, 1788–1874* (London: Chatto and Windus, 2010).

30. *Brooklyn Eagle*, 29 Jun 1888.

31. *New York World*, 1 Jul 1888.

32. *Leeds Mercury*, 3 Jul 1888.

33. *Troy Budget*, 1 Jul 1888.

34. *New York World*, 30 Jun 1888; *Albany (NY) Times*, 30 Jun 1888; *Chicago Tribune*, 30 Jun 1888; and *New York Graphic*, 14 Jul 1888.

35. *New York Tribune*, 30 Jun 1888; and *New York Times*, 30 Jun 1888.

36. *New York Times*, 30 Jun 1888.

37. Ibid.

38. *Chicago Tribune*, 30 Jun 1888; and *New York World*, 1 Jul 1888.

39. *Brooklyn Eagle*, 30 Jun 1888.

40. *New York World*, 1 Jul 1888.

41. *New York Times*, 1 Jul 1888; *New York Sun*, 1 Jul 1888; and *New York Tribune*, 1 Jul 1888.

42. *New York Tribune*, 1 Jul 1888.

43. *Albany (NY) Argus*, 8 Jul 1888.

44. *New York Times*, 30 Jun 1888.

CHAPTER 9: TITLES AND HEIRESSES
Pages 107–114

1. *Titled Americans*, 9–10.

2. Ibid., 13–15.

3. Ibid., 16–19, 22.

4. Ibid., 20–21, 24–26.

5. Ibid., 156–93.

6. Everett, "Titles of Honor," 61, 64.

7. Martin, *Things I Remember*, 209.

8. Leslie, *End of a Chapter*, 113.

9. Cited in Martin, *Jennie*, vol. 1, 93.

10. Ibid., 91–93.

11. *Truth*, 15 Nov 1888, 863.

12. *New York World*, 19 Dec 1886.

13. Smalley, *London Letters*, vol. 2, 104–05.

14. Muirhead, *America the Land of Contrasts*, 48.

15. Smalley, *London Letters*, vol. 2, 10.

16. Billington, "Woman of America," 86.

17. *New York Journal*, 13 Oct 1895.

18. *Titled Americans*, 253–58.

19. *Chicago Tribune*, 1 Dec 1888.

20. Montgomery, *"Gilded Prostitution,"* 49.

21. Ibid., 111.

22. Ibid., 53, 85, 100.

23. Cannadine, *Decline and Fall*, 347.

CHAPTER 10:
SPECULATIVE MARRIAGE
Pages 115–132

1. *Vanity Fair*, 14 Jul 1888, 33.

2. *Western Mail* (Cardiff), 12 Jul 1888.

3. *Vanity Fair*, 14 Jul 1888, 33.

4. *Chicago Tribune*, 18 Jul 1888; and *Northern Echo* (Darlington), 23 Jul 1888.

5. *Washington Post*, 16 Jul 1888.

6. *Northern Echo* (Darlington), 23 Jul 1888.

7. *New York Times*, 21 Aug 1888.

8. *Chicago Tribune*, 9 Jul 1888.

9. *New York Times*, 21 Aug 1888.

10. *New York World*, 13 Nov 1887.

11. Ibid.

12. *Chicago Tribune*, 25 Nov 1888; and *Oxfordshire News*, 1 Aug 1888.

13. *New York Herald*, Paris ed., 7 Dec 1888.

14. *New York Herald*, Paris ed., 7 Dec 1888; and *Washington Post*, 4 Jan 1889.

15. *New York Herald*, Paris ed., 7 Dec 1888.

16. Cited in Martin, *Jennie*, vol. 1, 251.

17. Greville, *Gentlewoman in Society*, 161.

18. Cited in Churchill and Mitchell, *Jennie*, 147.

19. St. Helier, *Memories*, 223.

20. Escott, *Society in the New Reign*, 30; *London Times*, 6 Aug 1904, 23 Oct 1929, and 25 Oct 1929; and *Town Topics*, 7 June 1888, 20 Apr 1899, and 12 Nov 1903.

21. *Hearth and Home*, 7 Feb 1895, 457.

22. Cannadine, *Aspects of Aristocracy*, 130.

23. Badeau, *Aristocracy in England*, 148–53.

24. Dunraven, *Past Times*, vol. 1, 193; and [Field], *Things I Shouldn't Tell*, 74.

25. Bush, *English Aristocracy*, 75.

26. Crockett, *When James Gordon Bennett*, 116.

27. *Chicago Tribune*, 22 Nov 1887.

28. Escott, *Randolph*, 64–66.

29. *New York Times*, 29 Jun 1888.

30. Bapasola, *Finest View in England*, 133.

31. *Truth*, 26 Jul 1888, 144.

32. *New York Times*, 16 Dec 1888; and Escott, *London Society*, 33.

33. Leslie, *Lady Randolph*, 101; and Rowse, *Later Churchills*, 272.

34. *London Times*, 17 Sep 1885, and 12 Dec 1883.

35. *London Times*, 12 Dec 1883.

36. *Chicago Tribune*, 23 Oct 1888.

37. Jordan, *Love Well the Hour*, 106; and Atherton, *Adventures*, 284–85.

38. *Town Topics*, 13 Dec 1888.

39. Fowler, *In a Gilded Cage*, 106.

40. *San José (CA) News*, copying *London World*, 24 Jan 1889.

41. FDM to LRC, [Feb 1889], CHAR 28/109.

42. *Freeman's Journal* (Dublin), 5 Jul 1889.

43. *New York World*, 1 Jul 1888.

44. *Freeman's Journal* (Dublin), 11 Jul 1888.

45. Banner, *American Beauty*, 106, 11–13, 130–31.

46. O'Rell, *Jonathan and His Continent*, 18.

47. Stearns, *Fat History*, 8, 11.

48. *Philadelphia Inquirer*, 24 Aug 1890.

49. *Boston Globe*, 20 Apr 1890.

50. *Washington Post*, 13 Jul 1890.

51. *Town Topics*, 3 Jan 1889.

52. *Town Topics*, 24 Oct 1889.

53. *Town Topics*, 2 Aug 1888, 26 Jul 1888, and 19 Jul 1888.

54. Courtwright, *Dark Paradise*, 36–51.

55. O'Connor, *I Myself*, 133–35, 146.

56. *London-American*, 12 Apr 1901.

57. Courtwright, *Dark Paradise*, 51.

58. *Art Amateur* 20 (Dec 1888): 2.

59. *New York Times*, 2 Nov 1888.

60. *Art Amateur* 20 (Dec 1888): 2.

61. Personal communication to author from John Pennino, Archivist, Metropolitan Opera, 19 Oct 2007.

62. *Brooklyn Eagle*, 13 May 1889.

63. Doane, William Croswell, "Notes for Autobiography," Papers.

64. Will of Cicero Price. Copy on file at Surrogate's Court, Rensselaer County Courthouse, Troy.

CHAPTER II:
CHATELAINE OF BLENHEIM
Pages 133–143

1. *Country Gentleman*, 24 Nov 1888.

2. *Leeds Mercury*, 10 Dec 1888; and Pelham-Clinton, "Blenheim the Famous," 323.

3. *Jackson's Oxford Journal*, 27 Oct 1888; *Leeds Mercury*, 10 Dec 1888; and *Oxfordshire News*, 16 Nov 1892.

4. *Aberdeen Journal*, 11 Nov 1892.

5. Balsan, *Glitter and the Gold*, 60.

6. *Glasgow Herald*, 8 Sep 1888.

7. Pelham-Clinton, "Blenheim the Famous," 319.

8. Jackson, *Recollections*, 192.

9. O'Connor, *I Myself*, 255. The "brocade" reference was specifically to a torn fragment of damask "of a brilliant peculiar shade with a gleaming copper sheen on its surface" found by the duke on a Blenheim chair that he had reproduced as wall and drapery fabric for a drawing room in the Marlboroughs' London home. (*New York Sun*, 19 Jul 1891, copying *The Queen*, London.)

10. *New York Sun*, 19 Jul 1891, copying *The Queen*, London.

11. *Oxfordshire News*, 16 Nov 1892.

12. Wharton, *Buccaneers*, 442.

13. Pelham-Clinton, "Blenheim the Famous," 324.

14. NYSSC/HER.

15. Mandler, *Fall and the Rise of the Stately Home*, 206–09.

16. Blenheim's opening and closing dates and days and hours of public access were published annually in the advertising columns of *Jackson's Oxford Journal*.

17. Banks. "Home of the Duchess of Marlborough," 611.

18. Hill, *Women in English Life*, vol. 2, 112.

19. Horn, *Rise and Fall of the Victorian Servant*, 21–22.

20. Balis, *Rights, Duties, and Relations (Legal and Social) of Domestic Servants*, 43–44.

21. *Oxfordshire News*, 9 Jan 1889.

22. Ibid.

23. *Oxfordshire News*, 8 Jan 1890.

24. Cited in Montgomery, "*Gilded Prostitution*," 63.

25. Northrop, "Mrs. George Cornwallis-West," 511.

26. *London Daily News*, article on Woodstock, 14 Sep 1891.

27. Thompson, *English Landed Society*, 17.

28. *Aberdeen Journal*, 8 Jan 1889.

29. *Jackson's Oxford Journal*, 31 Oct 1891, and 11 Jan 1890.

30. *Glasgow Herald*, 10 Nov 1892.

31. *Oxfordshire News*, 2 Nov 1892.

32. *Jackson's Oxford Journal,* 1 Dec 1888, and passim.

33. *Jackson's Oxford Journal,* 7 Jan 1893, and 21 Jan 1893.

34. *Jackson's Oxford Journal,* 24 May 1890.

35. *Oxford Chronicle,* 25 May 1889.

36. *Jackson's Oxford Journal,* 30 May 1891, and 25 Mar 1893.

37. *Oxford Chronicle,* 25 May 1889.

38. Charlton, *Shire Horse Society,* 44, 38; and *Jackson's Oxford Journal,* 31 Mar 1888.

39. *Live Stock Journal,* 11 Nov 1892, 506.

40. *Oxford Chronicle,* 14 Sep 1889.

41. The traits of Marlborough Blenheims were discussed in the short-lived journal *Toy Dogs* (1902–03) on 26 Dec 1902, 347–48, and 6 Feb 1903, 451–52.

42. *Illustrated American,* 23 Feb 1895, 238.

43. *Oxford Chronicle,* 25 May 1889; and *Oxfordshire News,* 29 May 1889.

44. *Oxford Chronicle,* 25 May 1889; and *Oxfordshire News,* 22 May 1889, and 29 May 1889.

45. *Truth,* 30 May 1889, 1009.

CHAPTER 12:
THE LONDON CHALLENGE
Pages 144–156

1. O'Connor, *I Myself,* 255.

2. Bott, *Our Mothers,* 12.

3. Evans, *Party That Lasted 100 Days,* 7–8.

4. Escott, *Society in London,* 19.

5. Cited in Decies, *Turn of the World,* 252.

6. Tuchman, *Proud Tower,* 18.

7. *Modern Society,* 19 Nov 1892, 9.

8. Escott, *Society in London,* 18.

9. Escott, *Society in the New Reign,* 30.

10. *Modern Society,* 6 Apr 1889, 468.

11. Escott, *Society in London,* 32.

12. *San Francisco Call,* 15 May 1904.

13. Jeune, "'London Society,'" 458.

14. *Town Topics,* 7 Mar 1889.

15. Hamilton, *Days before Yesterday,* 335.

16. *Modern Society,* 20 Mar 1889, 442–43.

17. *Modern Society,* 16 Feb 1889, 297.

18. *Ladies' Gazette,* 23 Feb 1895, 15.

19. *Town Topics,* 7 Mar 1889.

20. *Truth,* 7 Mar 1889, 417.

21. *Social Etiquette,* 48–49; and Badeau, *Aristocracy in England,* 23.

22. Badeau, *Aristocracy in England,* 23.

23. Ibid., 26–27.

24. *Truth,* 9 May 1889, 849, 876.

25. *New York Times,* 4 Jun 1889.

26. *Truth,* 9 May 1889, 849.

27. *Reynold's Newspaper* (London), 12 May 1889.

28. *Town Topics,* 9 May 1889.

29. *Modern Society,* 11 May 1889, 583.

30. *Town Topics,* 9 May 1889.

31. *Truth,* 9 May 1889, 849, 876.

32. *Modern Society,* 11 May 1889, 583.

33. *Chicago Tribune,* 5 May 1889.

34. Reynolds, *Aristocratic Women,* 111–17.

35. Greville, *Gentlewoman in Society,* 48.

36. Reynolds, *Aristocratic Women,* 116.

37. *Reynold's Newspaper* (London), 17 Mar 1889; and *Glasgow Herald,* 31 May 1889.

38. *Lady's Pictorial,* 28 Jul 1889, 96.

39. *Oxford Chronicle,* 13 Jul 1889.

40. Escott, *Randolph,* 61.

41. *Vanity Fair,* 3 May 1890, 385.

42. *New York Herald,* Paris ed., 31 Mar 1890.

43. *Lady's Pictorial,* 28 Jun 1890, 1042.

44. "Anglo-Saxon Society Woman," 54.

CHAPTER 13: HOMECOMINGS
Pages 157–167

1. *New York World,* 29 Mar 1890.

2. *Town Topics,* 13 Mar 1890.

3. *New York Times,* 29 Mar 1890; and *New York World,* 29 Mar 1890.

4. *New York Mail and Express*, 28 Mar 1890; and *Town Topics*, 3 Apr 1890.

5. *New York Mail and Express*, 11 Apr 1890.

6. Juergens, *Joseph Pulitzer*, 227, 33, 155, 138–39.

7. Nelson, "The Duchess Interviewed," *New York World*, 30 Mar 1890.

8. Ibid.

9. Ibid.

10. Ibid.

11. Ibid.

12. *Town Topics*, 17 Apr 1890.

13. *New York Sun*, 6 Apr 1890.

14. *Boston Globe*, 20 Apr 1890.

15. *New York Times*, 13 Apr 1890.

16. *Town Topics*, 3 Apr 1890.

17. *New York Mail and Express*, 9 Apr 1890.

18. *New York Mail and Express*, 11 Apr 1890.

19. *New York World*, 20 Apr 1890.

20. *New York World*, 6 Apr 1890.

21. *New York World*, 4 Apr 1890.

22. *Philadelphia Inquirer*, 9 Oct 1890.

23. *New York World*, 7 Nov 1890; and *New York Times*, 9 Nov 1890.

24. *New York World*, 7 Nov 1890.

25. *New York Times*, 1 Jan 1891.

26. 24 May 1901 entry in diary of Eva Purdy Thomson, Joseph Downs Collection of Manuscripts and Printed Ephemera, Winterthur Library, document 1541, p. 282. LDM's note to Purdy dated 13 Oct 1890.

27. *New York World*, 19 Oct 1890.

28. *New York World*, 29 Oct 1890.

29. Tate, *Edison's Open Door*, 135.

30. *New York World*, 29 Oct 1890.

31. Nevins, *Abram S. Hewitt*, 558.

32. See bibliography for publication details.

33. *Town Topics*, 16 Apr 1891.

34. Marlborough, "Farms and Trotting Horses," 264–65.

35. *New York Times*, 8 Mar 1891.

36. *Lexington (KY) Leader*, 14 Nov 1890.

37. Cobb, *Kentucky*, 23.

38. Marlborough, "Virginia Mines and American Rails," 783.

39. Kincaid, *Wilderness Road*, 313–17; and *Manufacturers Record*, 1 Feb 1890.

40. Roberts, "The Building of Middlesborough," 30.

41. *New York World*, 21 Nov 1890.

42. Marlborough, "Virginia Mines and American Rails," 788.

43. Tompkins, *Rockbridge County*, 154.

44. Marlborough, "Virginia Mines and American Rails," 789.

45. Tompkins, *Rockbridge County*, 154–55.

46. Kincaid, *Wilderness Road*, 334.

47. Tompkins, *Rockbridge County*, 155–56.

48. *Washington Post*, 28 Nov 1890.

49. *Town Topics*, 18 Dec 1890.

50. *Lexington (KY) Leader*, 11 Dec 1890.

51. *Oxfordshire News*, 21 Jan 1891.

52. JRC to LRC, 24 Dec [1890], CHAR 28/101/20–22.

CHAPTER 14: AUTHENTIC MARRIAGE
Pages 168–179

1. Rowse, *Later Churchills*, 270.

2. *Chicago Tribune*, 10 Nov 1892.

3. O'Connor, *I Myself*, 150.

4. Atherton, *American Wives*, 144, 217.

5. *New York Sun*, 19 Jul 1891, copying *The Queen*, London.

6. Marlborough, "Merry England," 37, 45.

7. NYSSC/HER.

8. De Witt, Lockman and De Witt Records.

9. Livermore, *Trustees' Handbook*, 32.

10. NYSSC/HER.

11. *Washington Post*, 5 Mar 1891; and *Brooklyn Eagle*, 30 Mar 1891. Gerry had appeared as a character witness on Louis Hamersley's behalf at the 1884 will hearing.

12. NYSSC/HER.

13. Livermore, *Trustees' Handbook*, 19; and Loring, *Trustee's Handbook*, 18.

14. NYSSC/HER.

15. NYSSC/HER.

16. Livermore, *Trustees' Handbook*, 50.

17. De Witt, Lockman and De Witt Records.

18. *Jackson's Oxford Journal*, 28 May 1892; and *Pall Mall Gazette*, 24 Feb 1892.

19. *Pall Mall Gazette*, 24 Feb 1892.

20. *Vanity Fair*, 12 Sep 1891, 213.

21. *Chicago Tribune*, 22 Jun 1891.

22. *Belfast News-Letter*, 14 Nov 1892; and *New York Times*, 22 Jan 1893.

23. *Town Topics*, 2 Jun 1898.

24. LRC to JRC, 7 Nov 1891, CHAR 28/11/42–43.

25. *Vanity Fair*, 21 Nov 1891, 401, and 7 Nov 1891, 364.

26. *Vanity Fair*, 21 Nov 1891, 405; *Truth*, 26 Nov 1891, 1126; and *London World*, 2 Dec 1891.

27. *Country Gentleman*, 28 Nov 1891, 1630.

28. *London World*, 25 Nov 1891, and 2 Dec 1891; and *Jackson's Oxford Journal*, 28 Nov 1891.

29. *London World*, 26 Oct 1892; and Pless, *What I Left Unsaid*, 28.

30. *Aberdeen Journal*, 11 Nov 1892; and *Gentlewoman*, 8 Jun 1895, 737.

31. *Jackson's Oxford Journal*, 31 Jan 1891.

32. Pelham-Clinton, "Blenheim the Famous," 324.

33. *Modern Society*, 21 Jun 1890, 968.

34. Marbury, *My Crystal Ball*, 96–97.

35. Briggs, *Victorian Things*, 388.

36. Briggs, *Victorian Things*, 389; Marlborough, "Telephone and the Post Office," 320–31; and *London Times*, 29 Aug 1891, 5 Sep 1891, 23 Sep 1891, 23 Aug 1892, and 6 Sep 1892.

37. *Truth*, 17 Nov 1892, 1050.

38. *Vanity Fair*, 19 Nov 1892, 327; and *London Times*, 2 Oct 1891.

39. *Musical Times and Singing Class Circular*, 1 Jun 1891, 344.

40. *Fishing Gazette*, 19 Nov 1892, 411.

41. *Truth*, 30 Jul 1891, 215, and 16 Jun 1892, 1292.

42. *Jackson's Oxford Journal*, 27 Aug 1892, 10 Sep 1892, and 24 Sep 1892.

43. *Oxfordshire News*, 28 Sep 1892; and *Jackson's Oxford Journal*, 24 Sep 1892.

44. McMullen, *Victorian Outsider*, 247.

45. Marlborough, "The Salon and the Royal Academy," 54; Pennell, *Whistler Journal*, 11; and McMullen, *Victorian Outsider*, 249.

46. Pennell, *Whistler Journal*, 10–11. For preliminary sketch of the duke in dress robes, see Margaret F. MacDonald, *James McNeill Whistler: Drawings, Pastels, and Watercolours: A Catalogue Raisonné* (New Haven, CT: Yale University Press, 1994).

CHAPTER 15: DEATH OF THE DUKE OF MARLBOROUGH
Pages 180–190

1. *London Times*, 10 Nov 1892; *Brighton Argus*, 11 Nov 1892; *Pall Mall Budget*, 17 Nov 1892, 1703; and *Troy Times*, 11 Nov 1892.

2. Ibid.

3. *New York Times*, 12 Nov 1892.

4. *New York Times*, 10 Nov 1892.

5. LRC to JRC, 10 Nov 1892, CHAR 28/12/30–32.

6. Ibid.

7. Lord Lansdowne to Queen Victoria, 12 Nov 1892, [RA/VIC/N 48/153], Royal Archives, Windsor.

8. LRC to JRC, 10 Nov 1892, CHAR 28/12/30–32.

9. Ibid.

10. Marlborough's will was published in the *Oxford Chronicle* on 11 Feb 1893.

11. Forster, *Churchill's Grandmama*, 186.

12. *Oxfordshire News*, 16 Nov 1892; *Vanity Fair*, 19 Nov 1892, 327; *Jackson's Oxford Journal*, 19 Nov 1892; and *New York Times*, 15 Nov 1892.

13. *Chicago Tribune*, 28 Nov 1892.

14. *Vanity Fair*, 19 Nov 1892, 354.

15. Ibid., 327.

16. Lord Lansdowne to Queen Victoria, 12 Nov 1892 [RA/VIC/N 48/153], Royal Archives, Windsor.

17. *London Times*, 10 Nov 1892.

18. *Truth*, 17 Nov 1892, 1069.

19. *Vanity Fair*, 12 Nov 1892, 310.

20. *London Illustrated News*, 19 Nov 1892, 638.

21. *Oxfordshire News*, 16 Nov 1892.

22. *Vanity Fair*, 12 Nov 1892, 314. This quotation is from the second of two obituaries of the duke in this issue.

23. *Oxfordshire News*, 16 Nov 1892.

24. *Jackson's Oxford Journal*, 25 Mar 1893.

25. *Truth*, 24 Nov 1892, 1129; and *Aberdeen Journal*, 11 Nov 1892.

26. [Field], *Things I Shouldn't Tell*, 75.

27. *Vanity Fair*, 19 Nov 1892, 327; 3 Dec 1892, 354; and 14 Jan 1893, 20.

28. *Oxfordshire News*, 23 Nov 1892.

29. Jordan, *Love Well the Hour*, 163.

30. LRC to JRC, 10 Nov 1892, CHAR 28/12/30–32.

31. John F. Gallagher, introduction to Harris, *My Life and Loves*, xv.

32. Harris, *My Life and Loves*, 339.

33. Ibid., 340.

34. Ibid., 486–87.

35. Cited in Martin, *Jennie*, vol. I, 291.

36. Harris, *My Life and Loves*, 488n.

37. *Jackson's Oxford Journal*, 25 Mar 1893.

38. LDM to Frank Harris, 21 Nov 1892, Frank Harris Collection, Harry Ransom Center, University of Texas, Austin.

39. Fowler, *In a Gilded Cage*, 104, 116–17.

40. Weintraub, "Shaw's Goddess," 241–42.

41. Wyndham, *Mayfair Calendar*, 47.

CHAPTER 16: ALONE AGAIN
Pages 191–208

1. *Modern Society*, 19 Nov 1892, 9.

2. *Troy News*, 14 Nov 1892.

3. *Town Topics*, 8 Mar 1894.

4. *Brooklyn Eagle*, 20 Feb 1894.

5. O'Rell, *Her Royal Highness*, 128, 154.

6. *New York Times*, 11 Nov 1892.

7. *New York Times*, 27 Oct 1895.

8. *Town Topics*, 9 Jul 1896.

9. Escott, *Society in the New Reign*, 33.

10. *Vanity Fair*, 3 Dec 1892, 354.

11. *New York Times*, 22 Jan 1893.

12. *Vanity Fair*, 17 Dec 1892, 388.

13. *London World*, 16 Nov 1892.

14. *Belfast News-Letter*, 21 Nov 1892.

15. *Oxfordshire News*, 21 Dec 1892.

16. Richards, "Land Agent," 440–43, 454.

17. *Vanity Fair*, 7 Jan 1893, 2.

18. *Jackson's Oxford Journal*, 31 Dec 1892, and 7 Jan 1893.

19. *Birmingham Post*, 11 Jan 1893.

20. *Oxford Chronicle*, 25 Feb 1893.

21. Banks, "Home of the Duchess of Marlborough," 606.

22. *Jackson's Oxford Journal*, 15 Apr 1893.

23. *London Times*, 20 Dec 1892.

24. *Truth*, 16 Mar 1893, 562; and *Oxford Chronicle*, 11 Mar 1893.

25. Fox and Gooday, *Physics in Oxford*, 163–64.

26. *Ladies' Home*, 9 Jul 1898, 332, and 2 Jul 1898, 248.

27. *Jackson's Oxford Journal*, 16 Jan 1909.

28. Gilbert, *Churchill*, 35.

29. WSC to LRC, 6 Jan [Feb] 1893, in Churchill, *Winston S. Churchill*, comp. vol. I, part I, 362.

30. LDM to LRC, 9 Feb 1893, in Churchill, *Winston S. Churchill*, comp. vol. I, part I, 365.

31. WSC to JRC, 2 Apr 1893, CHAR 28/19/4.

32. LDM to LRC, 5 Apr 1893, in Churchill, *Winston S. Churchill*, comp. vol. I, part I, 373.

33. Cited in Gilbert, *Churchill*, 36.

34. Cannadine, *Aspects of Aristocracy*, 131.

35. LDM to WSC, 3 Aug 1893, CHAR 1/9/39.

36. Gilbert, *Churchill*, 22.

37. LRC to WSC, 9 Aug 1893, CHAR 1/2/66–68.

38. Cited in Leslie, *Lady Randolph*, 185.

39. LDM to WSC, 3 Aug 1893, CHAR 1/9/39.

40. WSC to JRC, 11 Jan [1894], in Churchill, *Winston S. Churchill*, comp. vol. I, part I, 433–34.

41. LDM to WSC, 20 Aug 1893, CHAR 1/9/42.

42. WSC to JRC, 15 Mar [1895], in Churchill, *Winston S. Churchill*, comp. vol. I, part I, 570.

43. WSC to JRC, 2 Mar 1895, in Churchill, *Winston S. Churchill*, comp. vol. I, part I, 560.

44. Cannadine, *Aspects of Aristocracy*, 131.

45. LRC to FDM, 3 Sep 1893, in Churchill, *Winston S. Churchill*, comp. vol. I, part I, 404.

46. LRC to FDM, 28 Oct 1893, in Churchill, *Winston S. Churchill*, comp. vol. I, part I, 424.

47. WSC to LRC, 20 Nov [1893], in Churchill, *Winston S. Churchill*, comp. vol. I, part I, 426.

48. WSC to JRC, 20 Nov 1893, CHAR 28/20/2.

49. Stuart, *Consuelo and Alva Vanderbilt*, 74–75, 122; and Stasz, *Vanderbilt Women*, 63, 97–103.

50. Stuart, *Consuelo and Alva Vanderbilt*, 83; and Stasz, *Vanderbilt Women*, 99.

51. *Town Topics*, 27 Jul 1893, 9 Aug 1894, and 26 Sep 1895.

52. *Town Topics*, 27 Jul 1893.

53. *Hampshire Telegraph*, 4 May 1895.

54. *Cable*, 5 Dec 1896, 360.

55. *Surrey Advertiser*, 13 Jan 1894; and Addis, "Deepdene," 388.

56. *Dorking Advertiser*, 14 Jun 1894.

57. *Lady's Pictorial*, 22 Jun 1895, 957.

58. FDM to LRC, 11 Sep 1894, CHAR 28/109/10–11.

59. Ibid.

60. FDM to LRC, 30 Nov 1894, CHAR 28/109/5.

61. WSC to JRC, 17 Dec [1894], CHAR 20/28/55–56.

62. JSC to LRC, 21 Dec 1894, CHAR 28/30/122–123.

63. Cited in Martin, *Jennie*, vol. I, 317.

64. Martin, *Jennie*, vol. 2, 11.

CHAPTER 17:
LORD WILLIAM BERESFORD
Pages 209–215

1. *Vanity Fair*, 22 Nov 1894, 346.

2. *Chicago Tribune*, 30 Apr 1895.

3. Winchester, *Statesmen*, 93.

4. Smalley, *London Letters*, vol. 2, 83–84.

5. Langtry, *Days I Knew*, 72.

6. Cited in Leslie, *Film of Memory*, 74.

7. Smalley, *London Letters*, vol. 2, 84.

8. *Washington Star*, 14 Nov 1874; and *New York Times*, 18 Dec 1910.

9. Beresford, *Book of the Beresfords*, 121.

10. *New York Times*, 18 Dec 1910.

11. *Kennebec (ME) Journal*, 26 Apr 1902.

12. Menzies, *Lord William Beresford*, 6; and *Kennebec (ME) Journal*, 26 Apr 1902.

13. *Bow Bells* (London), 19 Apr 1893, 396.

14. Charles Beresford, *Memoirs*, 160.

15. *London Times*, 31 Dec 1900.

16. *Illustrated Sporting and Dramatic News*, 5 Jan 1901, 708.

17. Cannadine, *Aspects of Aristocracy*, 84.

18. Hamilton, *Days before Yesterday*, 311.

19. *London Times*, 31 Dec 1900.

20. Menzies, *Lord William Beresford*, 125–26.

21. *London Times*, 31 Dec 1900.

22. Buckland, *Sketches of Social Life*, 10.

23. *Illustrated Sporting and Dramatic News*, 5 Jan 1901, 709.

24. *Vanity Fair*, 26 Apr 1890, 361.

25. Menzies, *Lord William Beresford*, 254.

26. Whyte-Melville, *Satanella*, 189.

27. Crawford, *Mr. Isaacs*, 77–78.

28. Kipling, "A Germ-Destroyer," 126–27.

29. Bennett, *"Charlie B." A Biography*, 172.

30. Edwardes, *Bound to Exile*, 173.

31. *Kennebec (ME) Journal*, 26 Apr 1902.

32. Menzies, *Lord William Beresford*, 75.

33. *Modern Society*, 5 Jan 1901, 266.

34. Cited in Menzies, *Lord William Beresford*, 266.

CHAPTER 18:
COURTSHIP AND MARRIAGE III
Pages 216–233

1. *Illustrated London News*, 16 Nov 1897, 623.

2. *Vanity Fair*, 17 May 1894, 305.

3. Badeau, *Aristocracy*, 39.

4. "Marriage Settlement executed by The Most Noble Lily Warren Duchess of Marlborough on her Marriage with The Honorable William Leslie de la Poer Beresford, London, 29 Apr 1895." Copy on file at Riverhead County Center, Riverhead, NY.

5. *Vanity Fair*, 11 Apr 1895, 228.

6. *Harper's Weekly*, 27 Apr 1895, 391.

7. *New York Times*, 21 Apr 1895.

8. *Brooklyn Eagle*, 30 Apr 1895.

9. *Ladies Gazette*, 27 Apr 1895, 142.

10. *Brooklyn Eagle*, 30 Apr 1895.

11. *Ladies' Home*, 16 Jul 1898, 332.

12. WSC to JRC, 2 May [1895], CHAR 28/21/31–33.

13. *Brooklyn Eagle*, 30 Apr 1895.

14. *Town Topics*, 16 May 1895.

15. WSC to JRC, 2 May [1895], CHAR 28/21/31–33.

16. *Glasgow Herald*, 10 May 1895; and *Surrey Mirror*, 3 May 1895, and 17 May 1895.

17. Cited in Urquhart, *Ladies of Londonderry*, 78.

18. *Modern Society*, 9 Nov 1889, 1383.

19. *New York Times*, 23 Jun 1895.

20. *Life*, 29 Aug 1895, 661.

21. *Vanity Fair*, 8 Aug 1895, 92.

22. *Irish Times*, 27 Sep 1895.

23. Addis, "Deepdene," 388.

24. Leslie, *Film of Memory*, 78.

25. Churchill, *My Early Life*, 136, 105–06.

26. Ibid., 106.

27. Leslie, *Long Shadows*, 30–31.

28. Anson, *Book*, 260–61.

29. Warren, "Entertaining Their Majesties," 38.

30. *Modern Society*, 19 Oct 1895, 1545.

31. Warren, "Entertaining Their Majesties," 38–39.

32. *Illustrated Sporting and Dramatic News*, 5 Oct 1895, 152. Among other journals that published illustrations of Deepdene in connection with the royal weekend were *Lloyd's Weekly Newspaper*, the *Pall Mall Budget*, and the *Illustrated London News*.

33. Benson, *Mother*, 110, 114; and Edward King, *Personal Letters*, 50–51.

34. *Modern Society*, 5 Oct 1895, 1482.

35. Churchill, *My Early Life*, 107–08.

36. Ibid.

37. *New York World*, 15 Apr 1888.

38. *Truth*, 25 Jan 1894, 196.

39. *Belfast News-Letter*, 4 Oct 1895.

40. *Modern Society*, 12 Oct 1895, 1516.

41. *Western Mail* (Cardiff), 16 Oct 1895.

42. Albert Edward, Prince of Wales to
Alfred Montgomery, 10 Oct 1895,
[RA/VIC/ADD A 5/463], Royal
Archives, Windsor Castle.

43. *Dorking Advertiser*, 8 Oct 1896.

44. *Dorking Advertiser*, 30 Jan 1896, and 6
Feb 1896.

45. *Dorking Advertiser*, 23 Jul 1896, and 22
Jul 1899.

46. *Hampshire Telegraph and Sussex Chronicle*, 4
May 1895.

47. Stuart, *Consuelo and Alva Vanderbilt*, 103.

48. FDM to JRC, 19 Jul 1894, CHAR
28/42/23.

49. *Fun* (London), 19 Nov 1895.

50. Stuart, *Consuelo and Alva Vanderbilt*, 106.

51. Balsan, *Glitter and the Gold*, 41.

52. *New York Times*, 24 Nov 1895.

53. *London Times*, 6 Jan 1896.

54. Churchill, "Charles, IXth Duke of
Marlborough," 9.

55. WSC to JRC, 8 Dec [1896], CHAR
28/22/34–35.

56. *Pall Mall Gazette*, 11 Jun 1897.

57. *Vanity Fair*, 22 Jul 1897, 59.

CHAPTER 19: NEW ROLES FOR LILY
Pages 234–252

1. Albert Edward, Prince of Wales
to JRC, 24 Aug [1896], CHAR
28/48/47–48.

2. *Town Topics*, 5 Nov 1896.

3. Lewis, "'Tis a Misfortune to be a
Great Ladie,'" 27–28, 47.

4. *New York World*, 3 Jan 1897.

5. Menzies, *Lord William Beresford*, 295–96;
Dorking Advertiser, 31 Dec 1896;
Brooklyn Eagle, 31 Dec 1896; and *New
York World*, 3 Jan 1897.

6. *Derby Mercury*, 6 Jan 1897.

7. *Horse and Hound*, 23 Jan 1897, 56.

8. Allinson, *Book for Married Women*, 24–26.

9. JRC to WSC, 29 Jan 1897, in
Churchill, *Winston S. Churchill*, comp.
vol. I, part 2, 728.

10. *New York World*, 3 Jan 1897.

11. JSC to JRC, [14 May 1897], CHAR
28/31/63–64.

12. Leslie, *Film of Memory*, 79.

13. *Philadelphia Inquirer*, 21 Feb 1897.

14. *Town Topics*, 9 Jun 1898.

15. *Town Topics*, 28 Oct 1897.

16. *Chicago Tribune*, 30 Apr 1895.

17. *Town Topics*, 30 Jul 1896.

18. Vosburgh, *Career of Mr. Pierre Lorillard*,
147–48.

19. *Town Topics*, 3 Sep 1896.

20. *New York Times*, 14 Dec 1898.

21. Lambton, *Men and Horses*, 240.

22. Vamplew, *Turf*, 50.

23. *Brooklyn Eagle*, 30 Sep 1899.

24. WSC to JRC, 18 Nov [1896], CHAR
28/22/26–27.

25. Thompson, *Newmarket*, 265, 330.

26. *Lady's Realm*, Feb 1899, 381–82.

27. *Onlooker*, 27 Oct 1900.

28. *Lady's Realm*, Feb 1889, 382; and
Onlooker, 20 Oct 1900.

29. *Onlooker*, 3 Nov 1900.

30. *Era*, 2 Dec 1899.

31. JRC to WSC, 23 Sep [1896] in
Churchill, *Winston S. Churchill*, comp.
vol. I, part 2, 685.

32. WSC to JRC, 14 Oct [1896], CHAR
28/22/11–13.

33. WSC to JSC, 9 Mar 1897, CHAR
28/152A/99–106.

34. WSC to LWB, 2 Nov 1897, CHAR
28/23/69–70.

35. WSC to JRC, 22 Dec [1897], CHAR
28/23/90–92.

36. WSC to JRC, 23 Dec 1896; and WSC
to JRC, 1 Jan 1897, in Churchill,
Winston S. Churchill, comp. vol. I, part
2, 716.

37. Churchill, *My Early Life*, 136.

38. WSC to LWB, 2 Nov [1897], CHAR
28/23/69–70.

39. JSC to JRC, [1898], CHAR
28/31/93.

40. Langdon, unpublished family history, 61.

41. Ibid., 62–63.

42. Ibid.

43. Leslie, *Film of Memory*, 78–79.

44. *Lady's Pictorial*, 6 Jul 1889, 8.

45. *Cable*, 5 Dec 1896, 360.

46. *Lady's Pictorial*, 6 Jul 1889, 8.

47. *Cable*, 5 Dec 1896, 360; *Country Gentleman*, 27 May 1899; and *Jackson's Oxford Journal*, 20 May 1899.

48. Cited in Menzies, *Lord William Beresford*, 291, 298; and *Chicago Tribune*, 3 Jan 1897.

49. *Garden* (London), 19 May 1900, 367; "Deepdene, Dorking," *Country Life*, 62–68; and Addis, "Deepdene," 389.

50. *Lady's Realm*, Sep 1897, 540.

51. *Liverpool Mercury*, 28 Jan 1897.

52. Price, *Dame Fashion*, 158–59.

53. *Los Angeles Times*, 24 Nov 1895.

54. Escott, *Social Transformations*, 420.

55. *New York Times*, 26 Jul 1908.

56. *New York Times*, 26 Mar 1899; and *Lady's Realm*, Sep 1900, 556.

57. *Lady's Realm*, Sep 1900, 556.

58. Hawkin, *Chart Park*, 7–13.

59. *Dorking Advertiser*, 21 Nov 1925.

60. Menzies, *Lord William Beresford*, 297.

61. Rossmore, *Things I Can Tell*, 92.

62. Menzies, *Lord William Beresford*, 316.

63. *Aberdeen Journal*, 28 Jun 1899.

64. Marlborough, "Some Reminiscences of My Uncle"; and *Vanity Fair*, 1 Apr 1897, 217.

65. *London Times*, 4 Dec 1900.

66. *London Times*, 11 Dec 1900.

67. *New York Times*, 28 Oct 1900.

68. *Town Topics*, 3 Jan 1901, and 2 Jun 1898.

69. Balsan, *Glitter and the Gold*, 53.

70. Curzon, *Lady Curzon's India*, 90.

71. Balsan, *Glitter and the Gold*, 133.

72. *Lady's Pictorial*, 27 Oct 1900, 714.

73. Undated news clipping from *Sheffield Telegraph* in scrapbook recording August 1901 Unionist demonstration at Blenheim Palace, in Charles Richard John Spencer-Churchill, (ninth) Duke of Marlborough, Papers.

CHAPTER 20: 1901 AND BEYOND
Pages 253–267

1. Menzies, *Lord William Beresford*, 315.

2. Leslie, *Film of Memory*, 80.

3. Charles Beresford, *Memoirs*, vol. 1, 161.

4. *London Times*, 16 Jan 1901.

5. *Country Gentleman*, 1 Dec 1900.

6. *Truth*, 17 Jan 1901, 146.

7. Lambton, *Men and Horses*, 245–46.

8. *Truth*, 17 Jan 1901, 146.

9. *Brooklyn Eagle*, 9 Feb 1901.

10. Hirsch, *William D. Whitney*, 585.

11. WSC to JRC, 9 Jan 1901, CHAR 28/26/83–86.

12. *Town Topics*, 3 Jan 1901.

13. *Town Topics*, 17 Jan 1901.

14. *Anglo-American*, 29 Mar 1902.

15. Cited in Martin, *Jennie*, vol. 2, 116.

16. *London Times*, 8 Mar 1904.

17. *New York World*, 18 Sep 1904.

18. *Lady's Pictorial*, 22 Feb 1902, 264.

19. *Dorking Parish Magazine*, 1906; and *Dorking Advertiser*, 30 Apr 1904, and 2 Jul 1904.

20. *Dorking Advertiser*, 9 Jul 1904.

21. *Dorking Advertiser*, 6 Feb 1904.

22. *Dorking Advertiser*, 2 Jan 1904, and 16 Jan 1909.

23. *Boston Globe*, 3 Apr 1904.

24. Mitford, *Pursuit of Love*, 85.

25. *Boston Globe*, 3 Apr 1904.

26. *Lady's Realm*, Jan 1904, 296.

27. Ward, Lock, *Pictorial Guide to Brighton*, 16, 38; and Walton, *English Seaside Resort*, 70.

28. Ward, Lock, *Pictorial Guide to Brighton*, 46; and Walton, *English Seaside Resort*, 81.

29. Ward, Lock, *Pictorial Guide to Brighton*, 19, 30.

30. *New York Times*, 17 Jan 1909.

31. *Lady's Realm*, Dec 1906, 295.

32. *Sketch*, 18 May 1904, 162.

33. *Era*, 21 Jan 1899.

34. *Sketch*, 18 May 1904, 162.

35. *London Times*, 24 Feb 1908; and *Dorking Advertiser*, 16 Jan 1909.

36. *New York Tribune*, 8 Apr 1904.

37. *Washington Post*, 28 Jan 1895.

38. *Dorking Advertiser*, 16 Jan 1909.

39. *Long-Islander*, 15 Jan 1909; and *Town and Country*, 30 Sep 1905, and 25 Aug 1906.

40. *Town Topics*, 28 Sep 1905.

41. *Bystander*, 24 Jan 1906; and Willoughby, "Lily Duchess of Marlborough," 3.

42. Mallet, *Life with Queen Victoria*, 203; and Cannadine, *Aspects of Aristocracy*, 143.

43. *San Francisco Call*, 19 Jun 1905.

44. *Dorking Advertiser*, 16 Jan 1909.

45. LDM to WSC, 29 Aug 1908, CHAR 1/74/19; and *London Times*, 11 Sep 1908.

46. *Dorking Advertiser*, 16 Jan 1909.

47. Jalland, *Death in the Victorian Family*, 209.

48. *Dorking Advertiser*, 16 Jan 1909.

49. *Dorking Advertiser*, 16 Jan 1909; and *Irish Times*, 18 Jan 1909.

50. Anson, *Book*, 259.

51. Lawrence Timpson was the husband of Katharine Livingston, whose mother, Katharine Hamersley Livingston, was a daughter of Louis's uncle John W. Hamersley and a sister of his cousin Hooker. Born in 1850, the elder Katharine died in 1873 days after giving birth to her namesake. The younger Katharine married Timpson, born in 1865, in 1900.

52. *Dorking Advertiser*, 23 Jan 1909; and Anson, *Book*, 259–60.

53. *Dorking Advertiser*, 23 Jan 1909.

54. *London Telegraph*, 12 Jan 1909.

CHAPTER 21: AFTER LILY
Pages 268–274

1. Wills of Lily Warren Beresford, Duchess of Marlborough. Copy of English will on file at Warren County Municipal Center, Lake George, NY; copy of American will on file at Riverhead County Center, Riverhead, NY.

2. Typical annual wages for servants in 1906 were: butler: £55–90; lady's maid, £25–40; head gardener, £70–120; under-gardener, £40–45; coachman, £70–90. A butler and lady's maid would have received room and board in addition to their salary. From Horn, *Rise and Fall of the Victorian Servant*, 129–30.

3. Lily Warren Beresford, English will.

4. De Witt, Lockman and De Witt Records; and *New York Times*, 1 May 1910.

5. *New York Times*, 4 Jun 1913.

6. *New York Times*, 27 Apr 1910.

7. *New York Times*, 4 Jun 1913.

8. *New York Times*, 3 Jun 1942.

9. Will of Elizabeth Price. Copy on file at Warren County Municipal Center, Lake George, NY.

10. Menzies, *Lord William Beresford*, 319.

11. Hynes, *Edwardian Turn of Mind*, 4, 10–11, 13.

12. Cannadine, *Aspects of Aristocracy*, 137.

13. "Wreck" was the word Shane Leslie used in reference to the state of Blenheim as inherited by his cousin the ninth Duke of Marlborough in recording notes of a conversation with the duke after a visit to Blenheim on 24 Jul 1932. Shane Leslie Papers, GTM, Gamms 163, Box No. 43, Folder No. 6, Georgetown University Library.

14. Churchill, "Charles, IXth Duke of Marlborough," 8.

15. Cannadine, *Decline and Fall*, 119.

16. *London Times*, 20 Mar 1920; and Worsley, *England's Lost Houses*, 165.

17. Leslie, *Film of Memory*, 80–81.

18. www.railwayclocks.net/SR_10816_ Info_Page.htm, accessed 6 Apr 2008; and Worsley, *England's Lost Houses*, 165.

19. *Dorking Advertiser*, 8 Feb 1919.

20. *London Times*, 5 Jun 1919.

21. Ibid.

22. Christie, Manson and Woods, *Magnificent Jewels*, 12 Jul 1911, items 53 through 57; prices reported in *London Times*, 13 Jul 1911. The necklace of large pearls worn by Lily in the image that appears on page 128 may be the one referred to.

23. Knight Frank and Rutley, *Catalogue of Old French Furniture, Pictures, Porcelain, Silver, Bronze, etc.*, 6 Jul 1923, 14, 4.

BIBLIOGRAPHY

MANUSCRIPTS AND MANUSCRIPT COLLECTIONS

Chartwell Trust Papers, 1874–1945. Churchill College Archives. Cambridge, UK.

De Witt, Lockman and De Witt. Records, 1800–1906. MS164. New-York Historical Society. New York.

Doane, William Croswell. Papers. New York State Library. Albany.

Elm Hill Private School and Home for the Education of Feeble-Minded Youth. Records, 1842–1951. Library of the College of Physicians of Philadelphia. Philadelphia.

Langdon, Dorothy. Unpublished family history. Dorking Museum and Heritage Centre. Dorking, UK.

Leslie, Sir Shane. Papers. Georgetown University Library Special Collections Research Center. Washington, DC.

New York State Surrogate's Court (New York County). Hamersley, Louis C., Estate Records and Accounting. New York.

Spencer-Churchill, Charles Richard John, ninth Duke of Marlborough. Papers. Manuscript Division, Library of Congress. Washington, DC.

Warren Family. Papers, 1813–1896. New York State Library. Albany.

BOOKS AND ARTICLES

Addis, M. E. Leicester. "Deepdene." *Frank Leslie's Popular Monthly*, October 1895, 385–90.

Allinson, Dr. T. R. *A Book for Married Women*, London: F. Pitman, 1894.

"The Anglo-Saxon Society Woman." *Blackwood's Edinburgh Magazine*, January 1902, 54–66.

Anson, Clodagh. *Book: Discreet Memoirs*. London: G. Bateman Blackshaw, 1931.

Armstrong, Lucie H. "Society Journalism." *Woman's World*, April 1890, 309–11.

Atherton, Gertrude. *Adventures of a Novelist*. New York: Liveright [1932].

_____. *American Wives and English Husbands*. New York: International Association of Newspapers and Authors, 1901.

Badeau, Adam. *Aristocracy in England*. New York: Harper and Brothers, 1885.

Balis, Thomas Henry. *The Rights, Duties, and Relations (Legal and Social) of Domestic Servants and Their Masters and Mistresses*. London: Sampson Low, Marston, 1896.

Balsan, Consuelo Vanderbilt. *The Glitter and the Gold*. 1953. Reprint, Maidstone, UK: George Mann, 1973.

Banks, Elizabeth L. "The Home of the Duchess of Marlborough." *Ainslees*, December 1899, 606–14.

Banner, Lois W. *American Beauty*. New York: Alfred A. Knopf, 1983.

Bapasola, Jeri. *The Finest View in England: The Landscape and Gardens at Blenheim Palace*. Woodstock, UK: Blenheim Palace, 2009.

Bennett, Geoffrey Martin. *"Charlie B." A Biography of Admiral Lord Beresford*. London: Dawnay, 1968.

Benson, E. F. *Mother*. New York: George H. Doran, [1925].

Beresford, Charles. *The Memoirs of Admiral Lord Charles Beresford*. Vol. 1. Boston: Little, Brown, 1914.

Beresford, Hugh de la Poer. *The Book of the Beresfords*. Chichester, UK: Phillimore, 1977.

Billington, Mary Frances. "The Woman of America." *Woman's World*, December 1889, 84–87.

Bott, Alan. *Our Mothers*, London: Victor Gollancz, 1932.

Bouligny, M. E. P. *Tribute to W. W. Corcoran of Washington City*. Philadelphia: Porter and Coates, 1874.

Bourget, Paul. *Outre-Mer: Impressions of America*. New York: Charles Scribner's Sons, 1895.

Briggs, Asa. *Victorian Things*. Chicago: University of Chicago Press, 1989.

Brinsley-Richards, James. *Seven Years at Eton, 1857–1864*. London: R. Bentley, 1883.

Buchanan, Margaret Gwin. *DuVals of Kentucky from Virginia, 1794–1936: Descendants and Allied Families*. Lynchburg, VA: J. P. Bell, [1937].

Buckland, C. T. *Sketches of Social Life in India*. London: W. H. Allen, 1884.

Bush, M. L. *The English Aristocracy*. Manchester, UK: Manchester University Press, 1984.

Butler. B. C. *From Home-spun to Calico: A Centennial Address Delivered at Luzerne, July 4, 1876*. Albany, NY: Weed, Parsons, 1877.

Cannadine, David. *Aspects of Aristocracy: Grandeur and Decline in Modern Britain*. New Haven: CT: Yale University Press, 1994.

_____. *Decline and Fall of the British Aristocracy*. New Haven, CT: Yale University Press, 1990.

Charlton, A. B. *Shire Horse Society, 1878–1928*. London: Printed for the Society by William Clowes and Sons, 1929.

Chemical Bank and Trust Company (New York). *History of the Chemical Bank, 1823–1913*. [Garden City, NY: Country Life Press], 1913.

Churchill, Perregrine, and Julian Mitchell, *Jennie, Lady Randolph Churchill: A Portrait with Letters*. New York: St. Martin's Press, 1974.

Churchill, Randolph S. *Winston. S. Churchill*, Vol. 1, *Youth, 1874–1900*. Boston: Houghton Mifflin, 1966 (and companion volumes).

_____. *Winston. S. Churchill*, Vol. 2, *Young Statesman*, 1901–1914. Boston, Houghton Mifflin, 1967 (and companion volume).

Churchill, Winston S. "Charles, IXth Duke of Marlborough, K. G." In *Charles, IXth Duke of Marlborough, K. G. Tributes*, by Winston Churchill and C. C. Martindale, 5–11. London: Burns, Oates and Washbourne, 1934.

_____. *My Early Life: A Roving Commission*. London: Thornton Butterworth, 1930.

Clay-Clopton, Virginia, and Ada Sterling. *A Belle of the Fifties: Memoirs of Mrs. Clay, of Alabama, Covering Social and Political Life in Washington and the South, 1853–1866*. New York: Doubleday, Page, 1905.

Cobb, Irwin S. *Kentucky*. New York: George H. Doran, 1924.

Collier, Price. *England and the English from an American Point of View*. New York: Charles Scribner's Sons, 1912.

Coo, John Esten. "The White Sulphur Springs." *Harper's New Monthly Magazine*, August 1878, 337–56.

Courtwright, David T. *Dark Paradise: A History of Opiate Addiction in America*. Cambridge, MA: Harvard University Press, 2001.

Crawford, F. Marion. *Mr. Isaacs: A Tale of Modern India*. New York: Macmillan, 1883.

Crockett, Albert Stevens. *When James Gordon Bennett Was Caliph of Baghdad*. New York: Funk and Wagnalls, 1926.

Curzon, Mary. *Lady Curzon's India: Letters of a Vicereine*. Edited by John Bradley. New York: Beaufort Books, 1986.

Deacon, Desley. *Elsie Clews Parsons: Inventing Modern Life*. Chicago: University of Chicago Press, 1997.

Decies, Elizabeth Wharton Drexel Beresford. *"King Lehr" and the Gilded Age*. Philadelphia: J. P. Lippincott, 1935.

_____. *Turn of the World*. Philadelphia: J. B. Lippincott, 1937.

"Deepdene, Dorking, the Seat of Lord William Beresford." *Country Life*, 20 May 1899, 624–28.

Dix, Morgan, Rev. "The Education of Women." In *The Season: An Annual Record of Society in New York, Brooklyn, and Vicinity*, 26–28. Edited by Charles H. Crandall. New York: White, Stokes, and Allen, 1883.

Dunraven, Wyndham Thomas, fourth Earl of. *Past Times and Pastimes*. 2 vols. London: Hodder and Stoughton, [1922].

Edward, King of Great Britain. *Personal Letters of King Edward VII.* Edited by J. P. C. Sewell. London: Hutchinson, 1931.

Edwardes, Michael. *Bound to Exile: The Victorians in India.* New York: Praeger, 1969.

Escott, T. H. S. *King Edward VII and His Court.* Philadelphia: George W. Jacobs, 1903.

_____. *Platform, Press, Politics and Play.* Bristol, UK: J. W. Arrowsmith, [1895].

_____. *Randolph Spencer-Churchill as a Product of His Age.* London: Hutchinson, 1895.

_____. *Social Transformations of the Victorian Age: A Survey of Court and Country.* 1897. Reprint, Folcroft, PA: Folcroft Library Editions, 1973.

_____. *Society in London by a Foreign Resident.* London: Chatto and Windus, 1885.

_____. *Society in the New Reign.* London: T. F. Unwin, 1904.

Evans, Hilary, and Mary Evans. *The Party That Lasted 100 Days: The Late Victorian Season: A Social Study.* London: Macdonald and Jane's, 1976.

Everett, William. "Titles of Honor." *New England Magazine,* September 1895, 60–65.

[Field, Julian Osgood]. *Things I Shouldn't Tell.* Philadelphia: J. B. Lippincott, 1925.

Fifth Avenue: Glances at the Vicissitudes and Romance of a World-Renowned Thoroughfare, Together with Many Rare Illustrations That Bring Back an Interesting Past. New York: Printed for the Bank of New York, 1915.

Fleming, G. H. *Lady Colin Campbell: Victorian Sex Goddess.* Adlestrop, UK: Windrush Press, 1989.

Forster, Margaret Elizabeth. *Churchill's Grandmama.* Stroud, UK: History Press, 2010.

Fowler, Marian. *In a Gilded Cage: American Heiresses Who Married British Aristocrats.* New York: St. Martin's Press, 1993.

Fox, Robert, and Graeme Gooday. *Physics in Oxford, 1839–1939: Laboratories, Learning and Daily Life.* Oxford: Oxford University Press, 2005.

Frewen, Moreton. *Melton Mowbray and Other Memories.* London: Herbert Jenkins, 1924.

Gilbert, Martin. *Churchill: A Life.* New York: Henry Holt, 1991.

Green, Constance McLaughlin. *Washington: Village and Capital, 1800–1878.* Princeton, NJ: Princeton University Press, 1962.

Green, David. *Blenheim Palace, Oxfordshire.* Blenheim: Blenheim Estate Office, 1950.

Greville, Violet. *The Gentlewoman in Society.* London: Henry, 1892.

Hamilton, Frederic Spencer. *The Days before Yesterday,* London: Hodder and Stoughton, 1920.

Harris, Frank. *My Life and Loves.* 1922–1927. Reprint, edited by John F. Gallagher. New York: Grove Press, 1963.

Hawkin, J. B. *Chart Park, 1897 to 1997: Centenary History of Dorking Golf Club.* (Copy at Dorking Museum and Heritage Centre, UK.)

Hill, Georgiana. *Women in English Life.* 2 vols. London: Richard Bentley and Son, 1896.

Hirsch, Mark D. *William C. Whitney: Modern Warwick.* New York: Dodd Mead, 1948.

Homberger, Eric. *Mrs. Astor's New York.* New Haven, CT: Yale University Press, 2002.

Hopkins, Mrs. Archibald, as told to Mary Lawton. "When I Was a Little Girl." *Good Housekeeping,* 19 July 1933, 26–27+.

Horn, Pamela. *The Rise and Fall of the Victorian Servant.* New York: St. Martin's Press, 1975.

Hynes, Samuel Lynn. *The Edwardian Turn of Mind.* Princeton, NJ: Princeton University Press, 1968.

Jackson, Thomas Graham. *Recollections: The Life and Travels of a Victorian Architect.* Edited by Nicholas Jackson. London: Unicorn Press, 2003.

Jacob, Kathryn Allamong. *Capital Elites: High Society in Washington. D. C., after the Civil War.* Washington, DC: Smithsonian Institution Press, 1995.

Jaher, Frederic Cople. "Style and Status: High Society in Late Nineteenth Century New York." In *The Rich, the Well Born, and the Powerful: Elites and Upper Classes in History,* edited by Frederic Cople Jaher, 258–84. Urbana: University of Illinois Press, 1973.

Jalland, Pat. *Death in the Victorian Family.* Oxford: Oxford University Press, 1996.

Jeune, Mary (later St. Helier). "'London Society' and Its Critics." *North American Review* 155 (October 1892): 456–65.

Jones, Rebecca. "The Autobiography of 'Silent Becky.'" Edited by Field Horne. *The Gristmill: Quarterly Journal of the Saratoga County Museum* 15 (Winter 1981) and (Spring 1981).

Jordan, Anne. *Love Well the Hour: The Life of Lady Colin Campbell (1857–1911).* Leicester, UK: Troubador Publishing, 2010.

Juergens, George. *Joseph Pulitzer and the New York World.* Princeton, NJ: Princeton University Press, 1966.

Kehoe, Elisabeth. *The Titled Americans: Three American Sisters and the British Aristocratic World into Which They Married.* New York: Atlantic Monthly Press, 2004.

Kincaid, Robert L. *The Wilderness Road.* Harrowgate, TN: Lincoln Memorial University Press, 1955.

Kipling, Rudyard. "A Germ-Destroyer." 1888, in *Plain Tales from the Hills.* Reprint, Garden City, NY: Doubleday, Doran, 1928.

Kolodin, Irving. *The Metropolitan Opera, 1883–1966: A Candid History.* New York. Alfred A. Knopf, 1966.

Lambton, George. *Men and Horses I Have Known.* London: Thornton Butterworth, [1924].

Lancaster Woman's Club. *Patches of Garrard County.* Lancaster, KY: Lancaster Woman's Club, 1974.

Langtry, Lillie. *The Days I Knew.* New York: George H. Doran, 1925.

Lee, Hermione. *Edith Wharton.* New York: Alfred A. Knopf, 2007.

Leslie, Anita. *Lady Randolph Churchill: The Story of Jennie Jerome.* New York: Charles Scribner's Sons, [1969].

_____. *Marlborough House Set.* Garden City, NY: Doubleday, 1973.

Leslie, Shane, *The End of a Chapter.* New York: Charles Scribner's Sons, 1916.

_____. *Film of Memory.* London: Michael Joseph, 1938.

_____. *Long Shadows,* London: John Murray, 1966.

Lewis, Judith. "'Tis a Misfortune to be a Great Ladie': Maternal Mortality in the British Aristocracy, 1558–1959." *Journal of British Studies* 37 (January 1988): 26–53.

Livermore, Rufus P. *Livermore's Trustees' Handbook.* New York: L. K. Strouse, 1885.

Logan, Andy. *The Man Who Robbed the Robber Barons.* 1965. Reprint, Pleasantville, NY: Akadine Press, 2001.

Lomax, Elizabeth Lindsay. *Leaves from an Old Washington Diary, 1854–1863.* Edited by Lindsay Lomax Wood. N.p.: Books, Inc., 1943.

Longstreet, Abby Buchanan. *Social Etiquette of New York.* New York: D. Appleton, 1883.

Loring, Augustus Peabody. *A Trustee's Handbook.* Boston: Little, Brown, 1907.

Mallet, Victor, ed. *Life with Queen Victoria: Marie Mallet's Letters from Court, 1887–1901.* Boston: Houghton Mifflin, 1968.

Mandler, Peter. *The Fall and Rise of the Stately Home.* New Haven, CT: Yale University Press, 1997.

Marbury, Elisabeth. *My Crystal Ball.* New York: Boni and Liveright, 1923.

Marlborough, eighth Duke of. "Electric Lighting." *New Review* 1 (1889): 296–304.

_____. "Farms and Trotting Horses of Kentucky." *Fortnightly Review* 55 (1891): 259–66.

_____. "Merry England." *New Review* 6 (January 1892): 31–47.

_____. "The Salon and the Royal Academy." *New Review* 3 (July 1890): 45–54.

_____. "The Telephone and the Post-Office," *New Review* 6 (March 1892): 320–31.

_____. "Virginia Mines and American Rails." *Fortnightly Review* 55 (1891): 570–83 and 780–97.

Marlborough, ninth Duke of. "Some Reminiscences of My Uncle, Lord Randolph Churchill." *Primrose League Gazette,* 1 Jan 1898, 6–7.

Martin, Frederick Townsend. *Things I Remember.* New York: John Lane, 1913.

Martin, Ralph G. *Jennie: The Life of Lady Randolph Churchill.* Vol. 1, *The Romantic Years, 1854–1895.* Toronto, Canada: New American Library, 1970.

_____. *Jennie: The Life of Lady Randolph Churchill.* Vol. 2, *The Dramatic Years, 1895–1921.* Garden City, NY: International Collectors Library, 1971.

McAllister, S. Ward. *Society as I Have Found It.* 1890. Reprint, New York: Arno Press, 1975.

McMullen, Roy. *Victorian Outsider: A Biography of J. A. M. Whistler.* New York: E. P. Dutton, 1973.

The Memorial History of the City of New York: Biographical. New York: New-York History, [1895?].

Menzies, Amy Charlotte. *Recollections and Reflections,* New York: George H. Doran, 1922.

Menzies, Mrs. Stewart (Amy Charlotte). *Lord William Beresford, V. C.: Some Memories of a Famous Sportsman, Soldier and Wit.* London: Herbert Jenkins, 1917.

Mitchell, Sally. *Daily Life in Victorian England.* Westport, CT: Greenwood Press, 1996.

Mitford, Nancy. *Pursuit of Love.* London: Hamish Hamilton, 1945.

Montgomery, Maureen E. *Displaying Women: Spectacles of Leisure in Edith Wharton's New York.* New York: Routledge, 1998.

_____. *"Gilded Prostitution": Status, Money, and Transatlantic Marriages, 1870–1914.* London: Routledge, 1989.

Montgomery-Massingberd, Hugh. *Blenheim Revisited: The Spencer-Churchills and Their Palace.* New York: Beaufort Books, 1985.

Morris, Charles. *Makers of New York: An Historical Work, Giving Portraits and Sketches of the Most Eminent Citizens of New York.* Philadelphia: R. Hamersley, 1895.

Muirhead, James Fullarton. *America the Land of Contrasts: A Briton's View of His American Kin.* London: J. Lane, 1902.

The National Cyclopedia of American Biography. Vol. 7. New York: James T. White, 1897.

Nevins, Allan. *Abram S. Hewitt: With Some Account of Peter Cooper.* New York: Harper and Brothers, 1935.

New York State Surrogate's Court. New York County. *In the Matter of the Petition of J. Hooker Hamersley to Intervene in the Proceedings for the Probate.* New York: D. Taylor, 1884.

_____. *Proving of the Last Will and Testament of Louis C. Hamersley, Deceased, before Hon. Daniel C. Rollins, Surrogate.* New York: n.p., 1885.

Northrop, W. B. "Mrs. George Cornwallis-West: An Interview." *Madame,* 13 September 1902, 511–12.

O'Connor, Elizabeth. *I Myself.* London: Methuen, [1910].

O'Rell, Max [Paul Blouet]. *Her Royal Highness, Woman, and His Majesty—Cupid.* New York: Abbey Press, [1901].

_____. *Jonathan and His Continent.* New York: Cassell, 1889.

Patterson, Jerry E. *The First Four Hundred.* New York: Rizzoli International, 2000.

Pelham-Clinton, Charles S. "Blenheim the Famous." *Cosmopolitan,* January 1890, 317–24.

Pennell, E. R., and J. Pennell. *Whistler Journal.* Philadelphia: J. B. Lippincott, 1921.

Pless, Daisy Fürstin von. *What I Left Unsaid.* New York: E. P. Dutton, 1936.

Price, Julius. *Dame Fashion.* London: Sampson, Low, Marston, [1912].

Reynolds, K. D. *Aristocratic Women and Political Society in Victorian Britain.* Oxford: Clarendon Press, 1998.

Rezneck, Samuel. *Profiles Out of the Past of Troy, New York, since 1789.* Troy: Greater Troy Chamber of Commerce, 1970.

Richards, Eric. "The Land Agent." In Mingay, G. E., ed. *The Victorian Countryside.* Vol. 2. London: Routledge and Kegan Paul, 1981.

Rives, Reginald William. *The Coaching Club: Its History, Records and Activities.* New York: Privately printed, 1935.

Roberts, Charles Blanton. "The Building of Middlesborough—A Notable Epoch in Eastern Kentucky History." *Filson Historical Quarterly* 7 (January 1933): 18–33.

Rossmore, Derrick Warner William Westenra, fifth Baron Rossmore. *Things I Can Tell*. New York: George H. Doran, 1912.

Rowse, A. L. *The Early Churchills: An English Family*. 1956. Reprint, Westport, CT: Greenwood Press, 1974.

_____. *The Later Churchills*. London: Macmillan, 1958.

Sage, Margaret Olivia Slocum. *Emma Willard and Her Pupils or Fifty Years of Troy Female Seminary: 1822–1872*. Edited by Mrs. A. W. Fairbanks. N.p.: n.p., 1898.

Saint Aubyn, Giles. *Edward VII Prince and King*. New York: Atheneum, 1979.

St. Helier, Mary (earlier Jeune). *Memories of Fifty Years*. London: Edward Arnold, 1909.

Schroeder, John H. *Shaping a Maritime Empire: The Commercial and Diplomatic Role of the American Navy, 1829–1861*. Westport, CT: Greenwood Press, 1985.

Scott, Anne Firor. "The Ever Widening Circle: The Diffusion of Feminist Values from the Troy Female Seminary 1822–1872." *History of Education Quarterly* 19 (Spring 1979): 3–25.

The Season: An Annual Record of Society in New York, Brooklyn, and Vicinity. Edited by Charles H. Crandall. New York: White, Stokes, and Allen, 1883.

Sloan, James Forman. *Tod Sloan, by Himself*. Edited by A. Dick Luckman. New York: Brentano's, 1915.

Smalley, George W. *London Letters and Some Others*. 2 vols. New York: Harper and Brothers, 1891.

Social Etiquette and Home Culture. New York: Harper and Brothers, 1881.

Stasz, Clarice. *The Vanderbilt Women: Dynasty of Wealth, Glamour, and Tragedy*. New York: St. Martin's Press, 1991.

Stearns, Peter N. *Fat History: Bodies and Beauty in the Modern West*. New York: New York University Press, 1997.

Stock, Phyllis. *Better Than Rubies: A History of Women's Education*. New York: Putnam, 1978.

Stone, Lawrence. *Road to Divorce: England, 1530–1987*. Oxford: Oxford University Press, 1990.

Stuart, Amanda Mackenzie. *Consuelo and Alva Vanderbilt: The Story of a Daughter and a Mother in the Gilded Age*. New York: HarperCollins, 2005.

Sylvester, Nathaniel Bartlett. *History of Rensselaer County, New York, with Illustrations and Biographical Sketches of Its Prominent Men and Pioneers*. Philadelphia: Everts and Peck, 1880.

Tate, Alfred O. *Edison's Open Door: The Life Story of Thomas A. Edison, a Great Individualist*. New York: E. P. Dutton, 1938.

Tayloe, W. Randolph. *Tayloes of Virginia and Allied Families*. Berryville, VA: By the Author, 1963.

Thompson, F. M. L. *English Landed Society in the Nineteenth Century*. London: Routledge and Kegan Paul, 1963.

Thompson, Laura. *Newmarket*. London: Virgin, 2000.

Titled Americans: A List of American Ladies Who Have Married Foreigners of Rank. New York: Street and Smith, 1890.

Todd, Charles Burr. *The Story of Washington, the National Capital*. New York: G. P. Putnam's Sons, 1893.

Tompkins, Edmund Pendleton. *Rockbridge County, Virginia: An Informal History*. Richmond, VA: Whittet and Shepperson, 1952.

Townsend, George Alfred. *Washington, Outside and Inside*. Hartford, CT: J. Betts, 1873.

Trent, James W. *Inventing the Feeble Mind: A History of Mental Retardation in the United States*. Berkeley: University of California Press, 1994.

Trollope, Anthony. *An Autobiography*. 1883. Reprint, New York: Dodd, Mead, 1935.

_____. *North America*. 1862. Reprint, edited by Donald Smalley and Bradford Allen Booth. New York: Alfred A. Knopf, 1951.

Tuchman, Barbara W. *Proud Tower: A Portrait of the World before the War, 1890–1914*. New York: Macmillan, 1966.

Twain, Mark, and Charles Dudley Warner. *The Gilded Age*. 1873. Reprint, New York: Oxford University Press, 1996.

Tyor, Peter L., and Leland V. Bell. *Caring for the Retarded in America: A History*. Westport, CT: Greenwood Press, 1984.

Urquhart, Diane. *The Ladies of Londonderry: Women and Political Patronage*. London: I. B. Tauris, 2007.

Vamplew, Wray. *The Turf: A Social and Economic History of Horse Racing*. London: Allen Lane, 1976.

Voigt, Charles Adolph. *Famous Gentleman Riders at Home and Abroad*. London: Hutchinson, [1925].

Vosburgh, W. S. *The Career of Mr. Pierre Lorillard on the Turf*. [New York]: Printed for P. Lorillard, 1916.

Wagner-Martin, Linda. *Telling Women's Lives*. New Brunswick, NJ: Rutgers University Press, 1994.

Walton, John K. *The English Seaside Resort: A Social History, 1750–1914*. New York: St. Martin's Press, 1983.

Ward, Lock and Company. *A Pictorial Guide to Brighton, Hove, the South Downs, Shoreham. Bramber, Lewes, Newhave, Seaford, etc*. London: Ward, Lock, 1906.

Warren, Mary Spencer. "Entertaining Their Majesties." *Lady's Realm*, November 1904, 38–46.

Watson, Winslow Marston, comp. *In Memoriam: Benjamin Ogle Tayloe*. Washington, DC: Privately printed, 1872.

Weintraub, Stanley. "Shaw's Goddess: Lady Colin Campbell." *SHAW The Annual of Bernard Shaw Studies* 25 (2005): 241–56.

Weise, Arthur James. *Troy's One Hundred Years, 1789–1889*. Troy: W. H. Young, 1891.

Wharton, Edith. *The Age of Innocence*. 1920. Reprint, New York: Charles Scribner's Sons, 1968.

_____. *The Buccaneers*. 1938. Reprint (with *Fast and Loose*), edited by Viola Hopkins Winner. Charlottesville: University of Virginia Press, 1993.

_____. "The Long Run." 1916. Reprinted in *The New York Stories of Edith Wharton*. New York: New York Review Books, 2007.

Whyte, James H. *The Uncivil War: Washington during the Reconstruction, 1865–1878*. New York: Twayne Publishers, 1958.

Whyte-Melville, G. J. *Satanella: A Story of Punchestown*. London: W. Thacker, 1899.

Willoughby, Leonard. "Lily Duchess of Marlborough at Deepdene, Dorking." *Tatler Sporting and Country House Supplement*, 22 April 1908, 3–4.

Wilson, Rufus Rockwell. *Washington: The Capital City, and Its Part in the History of the Nation*. Philadelphia: J. P. Lippincott, 1901.

Winchester, Henry William. *Statesmen, Financiers and Felons*. Abbeville: [H. M. W. Paillart], 1935.

Worsley, Giles. *England's Lost Houses*. London: Aurum Press, 2002.

Wyndham, Horace. *The Mayfair Calendar*. London: Hutchinson, [1925?].

Index